Luminos is the Open Access monograph publishing program from UC Press. Luminos provides a framework for preserving and reinvigorating monograph publishing for the future and increases the reach and visibility of important scholarly work. Titles published in the UC Press Luminos model are published with the same high standards for selection, peer review, production, and marketing as those in our traditional program. www.luminosoa.org

Indefensible Spaces

Indefensible Spaces

Policing and the Struggle for Housing

Rahim Kurwa

UNIVERSITY OF CALIFORNIA PRESS

University of California Press
Oakland, California

Suggested citation: Kurwa, R. *Indefensible Spaces: Policing and the Struggle for Housing*. Oakland: University of California Press, 2025. DOI: https://doi.org/10.1525/luminos.235

Library of Congress Cataloging-in-Publication Data

Names: Kurwa, Rahim, author.
Title: Indefensible spaces : policing and the struggle for housing /
    Rahim Kurwa.
Description: Oakland, California : University of California Press, [2025] |
    Includes bibliographical references and index. | This work is licensed
    under a Creative Commons (CC BY-NC-ND) license.
Identifiers: LCCN 2025001871 (print) | LCCN 2025001872 (ebook) |
    ISBN 9780520421486 (cloth) | ISBN 9780520401754 (paperback) |
    ISBN 9780520401778 (ebook)
Subjects: LCSH: Discrimination in housing—California—Antelope
    Valley—21st century. | African Americans—California—Antelope
    Valley—Social conditions—21st century.
Classification: LCC HD7288.76.U52 L67 2025 (print) | LCC HD7288.76.U52
    (ebook) | DDC 363.5/10979494—dc23/eng/20250208

LC record available at https://lccn.loc.gov/2025001871
LC ebook record available at https://lccn.loc.gov/2025001872

Manufactured in the United States of America

GPSR Authorized Representative: Easy Access System Europe,
Mustamäe tee 50, 10621 Tallinn, Estonia, gpsr.requests@easproject.com

34 33 32 31 30 29 28 27 26 25
10 9 8 7 6 5 4 3 2 1

To the tenants

CONTENTS

Preface — ix
Chronology — xv

Introduction — 1

1. Sun Village — 22

2. Redeeming the Right to Discriminate — 47

3. Apartheid's Afterlives — 75

4. Unmaking Home — 104

5. The Second Sun — 123

Conclusion — 147

Acknowledgments — 161
Methodological Appendix — 163
Notes — 167
References — 201
Index — 213

Preface

The Prismatic Periphery

Past the eastern edge of development in the Antelope Valley, far past where Los Angeles's vision of itself ends, lies Howard Arden Edwards's strange home. Built in 1928, it was a museum, nay, theater, of Native artifacts Edwards acquired in the valley. He purchased and traded for some items, but he also dug up burial sites and stole their contents. He fit these items into what he called the "Antelope Valley Indian Research Museum." His "research" involved placing the items he bought or stole into the stories he imagined about Native life in the Antelope Valley. He clumsily glued items, wrote on them, and mixed things from different places and peoples in service of his stories. Even the architecture reflected his bric-a-brac approach—built in the Tudor Revival style, the house resembles a Swiss chalet in the desert. He enlisted young people to help him paint symbols on the building and had them perform plays about Native life he invented from whole cloth. Edwards eventually sold the building to Grace Wilcox Oliver, who focused on turning it into a regional tourist destination.

Long after anyone could claim they didn't know better, the museum functioned as a site of production of a particular way of understanding Native life and settler presence in the valley. Today, the building is the Antelope Valley Indian Museum State Historic Park, having been purchased and revised by the California government. Edwards's artifacts were re-organized, and new, more accurate displays were created. But many of his exhibits were left as is, ostensibly due to their own "historical significance."[1] So Edwards's vision of Native life—the one that attracted tourists to pose in headdresses and grind their own corn—remains visible for us to examine. He thought of the people who lived in, around, or traveled through the Antelope Valley—Kitanemuk, Tataviam, Serrano, Nüwa (Kawaiisu), Paiute, Nüwü (Chemehuevi), and Vanyume—as fantastical in a way that set them apart

FIGURE 1. Antelope Valley Indian Museum, 2019. Source: Author.

from civilization.[2] The things he imagined them doing, thinking, and saying were rendered unfamiliar in a way that put distance between them and their spectators.

Edwards had a stake in the not-understanding of the place he lived. He had no meaningful right to the museum's land; he acquired it for free through a homesteading program.[3] Upon it he created a distorted understanding of the people who first lived there, delegitimizing their presence and asserting the legitimacy of his own through his role as its curator. Alongside life, settler colonialism is about land and understanding; Edwards stole both.

Edwards's outlandishness should not distract us from the fact that what he did was not unique. The distance he created between the Indigenous peoples of the region and the growing white society of the Antelope Valley—of which he was a part—played an important function in the valley. That distance is an important ingredient in attempts to kill, remove, repel, or replace people, not just at the national scale but locally.[4] His was the work of what Katherine McKittrick describes as "organiz[ing] human hierarchies in place and reify[ing] uneven geographies in familiar, seemingly natural ways."[5] Only upon such a canvas could the valley draw its compelling images of colonists building their lives. This negation of other people and ways of being has echoed throughout the valley as the region seeks to build itself from a question into a fact. But all around the valley are records of different ways of being. They make it known that the valley's present and its future are not written in stone.

At the northern edge of the valley, and perhaps at the margins of its memory, is a town called Rosamond. Charles Graves settled there in 1882, becoming one

FIGURE 2. Charles Graves. Source: "A Few Bits of Rosamond, CA, History," http://www.rosamondca.us/history.

of, if not the first, Black residents of the region. Graves was born into slavery in Kentucky in 1856. His father was killed in the Civil War, and after it ended, he decided to move west. Graves took the recently constructed Southern Pacific Railroad, eventually settling in Rosamond. At the time, the valley was enduring a years-long drought that collapsed several colonies. Graves stuck it out. He built a cattle ranch, became the city's postmaster, served as a ballot clerk in elections, and struck gold in the Tropico mines. His ensuing financial success allowed him to build Rosamond's first school in 1908, which he did with his wife, schoolteacher Cordia Anita Roberts. Graves died in Lancaster in 1938 after being struck by a car. Although sites in Rosamond—including a public school in the same location as his first one-room attempt—still bear his name, the public understanding of the valley frames Black presence as a recent and unwelcome phenomenon, rather than one predating much of white settlement.[6]

Shortly after Graves's arrival, from the early 1890s through the early 1910s, approximately eighty-five Japanese families, mostly farmers, moved to the valley. They helped develop agricultural techniques to make farming in the desert viable. Among these farmers were Yoshio and Kiyoko Ekimoto and their child Dennis. The family had arrived in the valley in 1910. Yoshio's father, Yohei, had purchased forty acres of farmland in 1912, just before passage of the state's Alien Land Law in 1913, which would have prohibited their property ownership.[7] For a time, life in Lancaster was good. The community grew large, and was clustered in the "Japanese Section," along Avenue D between 70th and 80th streets west in Lancaster.[3] There was a Japanese Farmers Association and a community hall that functioned as a school, church, and cultural center. But as the valley embraced World War II and the war economy, Lancaster turned on the Ekimotos. The family's land

FIGURE 3. The Desert Station of Southern Pacific Railroad at Palmdale, c. 1895. Source: California Historical Society and the University of Southern California Libraries.

and property were seized. In the trauma, Kiyoko miscarried. The family was incarcerated at Poston Internment Camp from 1942 to 1945. As the community was being dispossessed, white Lancaster residents vandalized it, destroying a memorial to deceased Japanese farmers in the valley.

As the wave of Japanese entry to the valley slowed, the socialists arrived. They settled in the southern edge of the valley, building a commune named Llano del Rio, whose story is famously told in Mike Davis's *City of Quartz*.[9] It bloomed in the 1910s as the project of Job Harriman, a socialist candidate for mayor of Los Angeles who narrowly fell short against the candidate of the city's business establishment. Nearly a thousand colonists flocked to the commune, building up housing, farming, and small industry through cooperative economics. Presaging the valley's aerospace future, the colonists even built a plane.[10] Today, the region is self-assured in its belief that the colony failed because a socialist mode of organizing life was a false promise. But records from the time suggest that it was access to water that, like everything in the valley, determined its viability.[11] Llano's water rights were already stretched thin, but when local agribusiness interests successfully lobbied the government to revoke them, their fate was sealed. They still might have failed with water, but without it no one could succeed. The Llano colonists were forced out.

FIGURE 4. Llano del Rio, 2019. Source: Author.

For what purpose did the valley drive out its colonists, conduct a pogrom against its farmers, racially segregate its land, and distort its history? All this served the aim of building the idyllic American suburb, a Levittown in the desert, superior to and economically independent of Los Angeles. The valley paved the desert, tore down the Joshua trees, and built in their place a massive aerospace industry. But it also helped create the idea that the valley was a white, capitalist place, without other histories of presence. This is the false but vitally necessary mantra required to frame the present-day continuity of demographic change as a unique threat.

Philosopher Charles Mills described this as "an ignorance that fights back."[12] How the valley's history is understood shapes how people think about and live in the valley today.[13] The valley's racial contract, in other words, must be asserted over a geography. And yet the valley's embrace of such a narrow range of possibility, constrained by commitments to capitalist, militarist development and anti-Black racism, has left it among the most policed[14] and most unequal places[15] in Los Angeles County, with one of the region's lowest life-expectancy rates.[16]

In this book, I zoom in to one of the many social struggles in the Antelope Valley, the Black community's fight for housing and home in the region. Through this case study, I examine the region's economy and its place in Los Angeles, as well as the shifting ways its commitment to racial capitalism has manifested. To see the Black struggle in the Antelope Valley is to glimpse a different path for each of these groups and the valley altogether, a path not so reliant on the denial of its past or on the narrow demands of racial capitalism to shape its future.

That story starts in 1939, a year after Charles Graves died, when Melvin Ray Grubbs began to sell the first parcels of land in the Antelope Valley to Black purchasers, building what he called "Sun Village" as a Black town independent from white dominion.[17]

FIGURE 5. A memorial to Japanese Americans, desecrated during World War II, is restored in 2008. Tom Shiokari (center), who had been sent to an internment camp during the war, was among the organizers of the restoration effort. Source: Photo by Michael Robinson Chavez/*Los Angeles Times* via Getty Images.

Meanwhile, communities forced out of the valley fought back as well. The Llano colonists relocated their utopian dream, founding New Llano in Vernon Parish, South Central Louisiana. It persisted as a communal enterprise through the Great Depression. New Llano's records show that poor people from around the country sought it out as a refuge in the 1930s.[18]

While in Poston, Yoshio Ekimoto became a plaintiff in Elmer Yamamoto's suit against the federal government over its internment program.[19] The case was merged into *Ochikubo v. Bonesteel*, filed while the Korematsu case was still being considered in the court system. The plaintiffs were represented by Saburo Kido of the Japanese American Citizens League, A.L. Wirin of the American Civil Liberties Union, Loren Miller of the NAACP and lawyer and author Carey McWilliams.[20] In 1984, at the age of seventy, Ekimoto gave testimony to the US Senate in which he recounted in detail the trauma of the internment period and called unequivocally for reparations.[21] More recently, descendants of Japanese farmers re-established the memorial in Lancaster.[22]

Howard Arden Edwards died in 1953. Fifteen years later, the Antelope Valley American Indian League was organizing regional powwows, asserting a present that his rendering of the past could not conceive.[23]

CHRONOLOGY

1882	Charles Graves arrives in Rosamond, northern Antelope Valley
1920	Prioleau family arrives at Bruce's Beach
1939	Melvin Ray Grubbs begins developing Sun Village
1941	Plans announced to transform Muroc Field into Edwards Air Force Base, inaugurating valley's aerospace era
1948	Proposition 14 (State Housing Agency) fails
1950	Pastor R. E. Edwards establishes First Missionary Baptist Church (now known as Living Stone Cathedral of Worship)
1954	Sun Village Women's Club Founded
1956	South Antelope Valley NAACP Chartered
1963	Rumford Fair Housing Act Passes
1964	Proposition 14 (Repealing Rumford Fair Housing Act) Passes
1965	Jackie Robinson Park officially dedicated
1966	*Gautreaux v. HUD* filed; the case would lead to the creation of housing vouchers
1990	Los Angeles County enters recession, valley endures wave of foreclosures
1996	Antelope Valley endures a second major economic and housing downturn
2007	Foreclosure crisis and Great Recession begin
2008	R. Rex Parris elected Mayor of Lancaster
2009	Significant expansion of anti-voucher policing partnership
2011	TCAL files suit against county and cities, county backs out of policing partnership
2012	Palmdale and Lancaster settle
2015	DOJ and LASD enter settlement

Introduction

Every Oasis Needs a Desert

In smoggy cities like Los Angeles, everything dissolves into the distance, and even stuff that's close-up seems far off.
—THOM ANDERSON, *LOS ANGELES PLAYS ITSELF*

The drive to the Antelope Valley can be a little heady. Coming from Los Angeles's westside, you go north up the 405, along with whoever else is driving north, perhaps to the San Fernando Valley or out of Los Angeles altogether. Just after the 405 turns into the 5—the concrete spine connecting northern and southern California—you exit to merge onto the 14.

I used to do this drive a lot during the summers in the 2010s, to conduct the interviews that would become the core of this book. Few people are driving to the Antelope Valley on weekday mornings, so traffic clears out and it's easy to find yourself speeding as the highway cuts through the Angeles National Forest. The route slopes up and down as it winds through the mountains and suddenly you find yourself amid the stunning Vasquez Rocks, full of jagged, reddish formations that dangerously draw the eye. In the 2010s, I knew I was getting to the valley when I began to see the billboards with PARRIS spelled out in large font. They were ads for the law firm founded by R. Rex Parris, who built a legal empire in the high desert region and eventually became the mayor of one of its two major cities, Lancaster. Seeing his billboards meant you were on his turf.

The Antelope Valley might be far from most of Los Angeles, but the two places are closely related. Los Angeles, as anyone briefly familiar with it can sense, doesn't add up. Housing is incredibly expensive, but the economy runs on underpaid and exploited workers in retail, service, garment, construction, food delivery, ride hailing, and so many other industries. Everywhere, people are being pushed out of the city as development for the rich and displacement for the poor churn through the neighborhoods. The violence of the process is palpable. You can see it on street placards detailing all the activities prohibited in urban areas as cities layer crime

FIGURE 6. Looking north at the Newhall Pass Interchange where the 5 and 14 highways merge. The 14 splits to the right, heading northeast towards the Antelope Valley. Source: trekandphoto, Adobe Stock.

legislation on top of crime legislation. You can see it on flyers beckoning "we buy homes for cash" that try to entice residents into making way for their replacements. You can see it in who you can't see anymore—the Black residents increasingly disappearing from Los Angeles. Among the many places they are going is the Antelope Valley. You can hear that in popular culture—rapper Afroman's *Palmdale* is the story of his family's move from the "slums of Los Angeles" to a two-story home in East Palmdale.

Whenever I made the drive, it was against traffic. In the morning, drivers poured down from the valley and into Los Angeles, commuting to service, technical, industrial, administrative, and other jobs throughout the metro area. In the evenings, when I'd finished my work and was driving down to Los Angeles, their headlights would shine back at me as they wound their way north, going home.

Today, the valley is seen as the least desirable, most economically depressed region of Los Angeles County. But people live in the Antelope Valley largely because of what happens in Los Angeles. What makes the expropriation, exploitation, and expulsion of Los Angeles possible is the presence of places like the Antelope Valley to absorb its consequences. If LA's math doesn't add up, here is the remainder.

Among the thousands of people who moved to this desert in recent decades was Michelle Ross. She was a participant in the Housing Choice Voucher program. Colloquially known as Section 8, it is the largest rental assistance program for

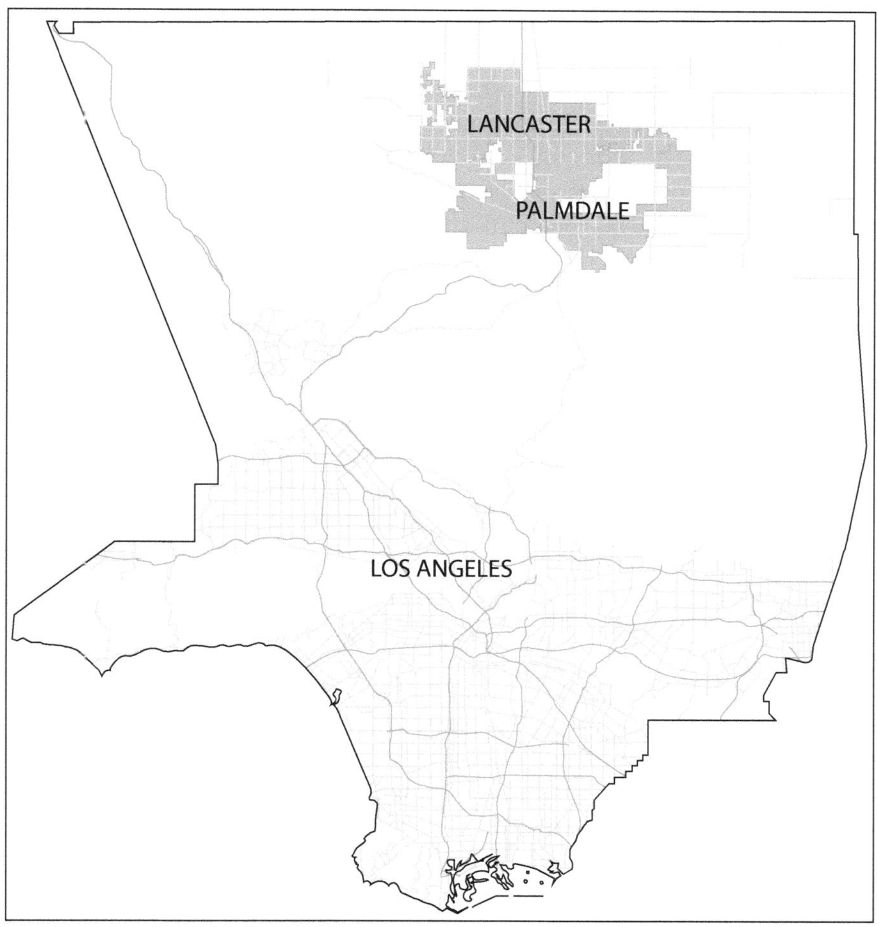

MAP 1. Map of highways connecting the Los Angeles metropolitan area to the Antelope Valley. Source: Author.

low-income families in the nation. In 2008, Ross used the voucher to move her family to the Antelope Valley, hoping that her children could have a nice home and attend good schools. Within three years she and her five children would be forced out of their home, contemplating leaving the valley altogether, and at the center of a federal lawsuit challenging the treatment of Black voucher tenants like herself.

This book is about the organized campaign to surveil, harass, police, and expel tenants like Michelle Ross from the Antelope Valley in the early 2000s and 2010s—how it emerged, what forms it took, what its effects were, and how people fought back. Its chapters will trace a century of Black place-making and white resistance to it in the valley, the evolution of the valley's reactionary politics and how they have congealed into the policing of housing, the effects of that policing on tenants, and the ways they have fought back. Crucially, this book will use the term "policing" to refer not just to the work of formal law enforcement and government agencies, but also to the practices of everyday people as they surveil and file complaints about their neighbors. In that vein, I use the policing of housing to refer to punitive regulation, police intervention, or policing practices applied to homes and their residents, regardless of the actor doing the policing. It is part of a broader process of "abandonment, exploitation, and stigmatization" that Tracy Rosenthal and Leonardo Vichlis describe as a "war on tenants."[1]

To contextualize these chapters, this introduction will examine three threads that come together in the policing of Michelle Ross's home. First, I describe the functional relationship between Los Angeles and the Antelope Valley, theorizing this periphery as the city's safety valve. Second, I trace how urban sociology and federal housing policy have voucherized public housing and increasingly shuffled tenants into places like the valley. And third, I show how the valley's punitive responses to their arrival reflect and extend broader trends of the policing of housing that have evolved to combat Black mobility and degrade Black homes, prefiguring new forms of resistance at the intersection of anti-policing and housing justice organizing.

MICHELLE'S STORY

About a year after Michelle Ross moved into her home in Palmdale, a city investigator named Gary Brody knocked on her door. He was accompanied by fifteen sheriff's deputies with their guns drawn. They searched her home for violations of her lease or other grounds upon which she might be evicted or punished. Appearing not to have found anything, they left. Investigators returned in November 2009 for a "compliance check," a home inspection program searching for grounds to evict tenants. This time they seemed interested in her children, but again nothing happened. The other shoe finally dropped in February 2010, when Ross was told that her lease was being terminated—in other words, she was being evicted—on the grounds that she had not informed the Housing Authority of her children's juvenile records.

It turned out, however, that the termination was not valid. Juvenile records are not permissible grounds to terminate a voucher contract, and the records never should have been made available to the Housing Authority in the first place. So the Ross family stayed in their home. But the compliance checks soon resumed, happening again in June and then November of 2010. Ross, like thousands of other tenants in the voucher program, had little recourse and virtually no opportunity to move elsewhere.

During the November 2010 search, Inspector Brody and twenty deputies visited the house when Ross was not home. When her son answered the door, "deputies ran into the home." Brody went into her garage to photograph two sport utility vehicles that she had allowed a friend to park there. One explanation for the search is that the investigators might have suspected that she was committing voucher fraud: if she could afford to own two SUVs, perhaps she was too well-off for the voucher program. Brody made her son call his mother and asked her about the vehicles. Ross believed that the Housing Authority subsequently confirmed that the vehicles belonged to her friend, not her.

The failed searches were accomplishing other punitive ends. The surprise inspections functioned as a source of intimidation, and an opportunity to assert power over and degrade voucher-renting families. And they signaled to Ross's neighbors that she was a voucher tenant, a suspicious other, a latent criminal. Having her voucher status exposed and herself defined in this manner by repeated public spectacles paved the way for her neighbors to begin harassing her even when the police, city, and Housing Authority did not. People stalked her home. Her name, address, and a photo of her home with the garage door open and the SUVs inside were published on an "I Hate Section 8" Facebook page. A commenter threatened to burn down her house. Her children were harassed at school, with language that laced anti-Black racism with anti-voucher sentiments. Not long after the Facebook post, her home was vandalized; a window was broken and "I hate Section 8 niggers" was spray-painted on the garage. As Norrinda Brown notes in her landmark study of the policing of voucher tenants in the Antelope Valley, the term "Section 8" had come to replace earlier race-based slurs.[2]

The continuities between how neighbors and government agencies policed tenants were striking. The sheriff's department, once so concerned about law-breaking at her address, provided no help when called, instead suggesting that her children had broken the window. Not long after, a group of young people drove by her house and threw "what appeared to be urine" at her children, while calling them "Section 8 niggers." Ross told the *Antelope Valley Press* she thought her children were in danger, saying, "You have no idea who's going to come out after you."[3] The paper reported that her sister had come to help "since she and her younger children were having trouble sleeping through the night as a result of the vandalism." Ross spoke of wanting to move, but not being able to afford it. Eventually, fearing for their safety, the family stopped sleeping at their home and searched for a new place to live close enough that her children would not have to change schools. In 2011 they moved to Lancaster, another Antelope Valley city just north of Palmdale.

The Ross family was by no means alone; what they were experiencing was the result of policies implemented widely across the valley. The myriad techniques the valley used to attack Black voucher tenants can be roughly placed into two categories. First, Lancaster and Palmdale entered a partnership with the Housing Authority of the County of Los Angeles, Los Angeles County Board of Supervisors, and Los Angeles County Sheriff's Department to share data and hire staff to target voucher tenants for inspections.[4] They encouraged the public to file complaints about voucher tenants through the Housing Authority's fraud hotline, and then aggressively pursued those complaints using the multi-agency powers described above. Second, the cities joined a nationwide trend by passing crime-free and nuisance housing ordinances that allowed neighbors to complain and ultimately evict their neighbors; once a property had enough complaints, the property owner would be fined until he or she evicted their tenants. Participation in policing allowed homeowners to empower themselves through the denigration of those they surveilled and reported to police, city, and Housing Authority regulators. In so doing, white homeowners and their allies redeemed their status in the valley one dispossession at a time, what Priscilla Ocen would come to describe as a new form of the racially restrictive covenant.[5]

The result was that, in 2008–2009, the cities of Lancaster and Palmdale, then home to 3,642 voucher households (about 11,000 people in total), received 434 calls to its fraud hotline complaining about tenants like Michelle Ross—more than the number of calls made about tenants in all the rest of Los Angeles County combined that year. As a result, the authority conducted 405 investigations and proposed lease terminations in 194 cases, again more than the number of terminations proposed in the rest of Los Angeles County. Tenants were spied on, had their homes invaded at all hours, and had their lives turned inside out by officials seeking to evict them from the valley. One in every twelve voucher tenants in Palmdale and one in every twenty-two in Lancaster had their leases terminated. The evictions primarily removed Black tenants from the once-majority-white valley, illustrating the usefulness of policing as a tool of racial segregation.

This policing-driven eviction scheme is at the center of this book, but to understand why it emerged and how people fought back against it, it's important to understand the social forces that produced it. My thesis is that the Antelope Valley acts like Los Angeles's safety valve, absorbing the people and economies displaced by its unequal systems of growth. This unequal and unsustainable condition is enforced in the valley through a system of policing that protects its internal inequalities and makes a genuine social transformation of the valley much harder. In what follows, I develop this theory of the Antelope Valley and peripheral places like it, arguing that they play a functional role in sustaining large metropolises. I then explore the intellectual and public policy trajectory that produced housing vouchers and sent the people who held them into peripheries like the valley. Finally, I trace policing's historical and contemporary role in the constraining of Black mobility. These three trajectories collided in the valley in the early 2000s, producing the widespread surveillance, policing, and eviction of voucher tenants from their homes.

TRAJECTORY 1: HOW THE ANTELOPE VALLEY BECAME LOS ANGELES'S SAFETY VALVE

Voucher tenants moving to the valley in the 2000s were part of a larger and longer trend of movement to the valley that has been central to its existence for over a century. This movement is understandable as an example of what David Harvey calls a spatial fix, a way for capital to resolve an imminent crisis of overproduction using space.[6] Ruth Wilson Gilmore shows how this has played out in the geography of California's prison construction boom, as the dilemmas caused by its four surpluses—land, capital, labor, and state capacity—were solved through the proliferation of prisons.[7] That too is the biography of the valley, but it is more than just the site of one spatial fix for Los Angeles. Rather, the valley is a site of serial spatial fixes for the metropolis. In that sense, it may be better to see it as Los Angeles's safety valve, to adapt Greg Grandin's metaphor for the role that territorial expansion played in cooling socio-political conflicts in American society.[8]

Though envisioned as a site of freedom, the valley is deeply dependent on state and external investment to sustain itself. This dependency has placed it on the other end of Neil Smith's "locational seesaw," experiencing bouts of development, abandonment, and re-development whenever doing so solves a problem for the urban core.[9] Its modern career is as a solution to Los Angeles's crises, but as it solves the metropolis's problems it only causes them to fester. In this sense, the Antelope Valley is both Los Angeles's consequence and its cause.[10]

Across the twentieth century and now into the start of the twenty-first, the Antelope Valley's economic fortunes have been dependent on solving imminent crises within the metropolitan core. By absorbing Los Angeles's surpluses of production and people, Lancaster and Palmdale have managed to persist even as their neighbors (for example, California City to the north and Lake Los Angeles to the east) have withered and declined. Between the start of the twentieth century, when it was a sparsely populated agricultural area, and the end of the century when it was a deindustrialized region in economic crisis, the valley was a glittering hub of aerospace testing and construction. It got that way through two spatial fixes—one in the aftermath of World War II and the other in the aftermath of the valley's de-development after the Cold War and successive economic downturns beginning in the late 1980s. The first spatial fix occurred when the valley absorbed Los Angeles's surplus military industrial production.

Threatened with the loss of military investment as the War Department sought to disperse construction across the western region, the county managed to capture that dispersal by offering the valley as an industrial base for aerospace testing and manufacturing.[11] The result was a firehose of federal dollars aimed at the valley, coming as lucrative defense contracts, subsidized housing construction and financing, and infrastructure investment. It created a white middle-class utopia—more perfectly racially segregated than Los Angeles itself. Service jobs were filled by Black workers forced to drive in from the city, who were barred from buying or renting in Lancaster and Palmdale. Thus, as Prentiss Dantzler notes, the spatial fix was not just an economic occurrence but also a racial one: the valley's prosperity was predicated in part upon the devaluation of Black workers and the valley's ability to economically exploit them.[12]

Those Black workers soon built their own town, Sun Village, on the outskirts of the valley. Sun Village became both the accomplishment of Black struggle and a platform for civil rights and fair housing organizing in the valley. The success of this organizing, particularly around fair housing, put the valley's white polity on the back foot, searching for decades for ways to reassert its old way of life. But when aerospace investment declined at the end of the Cold War, the valley was left neither rich nor segregated.

Rather than mark the end of the desert community, this moment precipitated a second spatial fix for Los Angeles. The economic collapse of the Antelope Valley once again turned it into a safety valve, absorbing people rendered surplus as Los Angeles restructured through recession, gentrification, and globalization. The valley is on the other side of what Ananya Roy calls racial banishment, the process of racialized dispossession characterized by the state's pushing people towards urban peripheries using processes of criminalization and punishment.[13] Between 1980 and 2020 the Black population in the Antelope Valley climbed from just 3 percent to roughly 15 percent, making it a key anchor of Black residency in the county. Today, one might see similar patterns of regional restructuring and peripheral displacement occurring in the Bay Area as well, as San Francisco's Black population, for example, has been halved over a decade, with Black residents pushed into peripheral cities like Antioch.[14]

Here, it is worth noting a word of caution about peripheralization. As Katherine McKittrick writes, "black geographies cannot be fully understood if they are primarily conceptualized through utterances such as 'invisible' or 'peripheral.'"[15] And indeed, one of the ways domination works is by "naturaliz[ing] both identity and place, repetitively spatializing where nondominant groups "naturally belong."[16] Thus while a first trajectory is about how the Antelope Valley came to be Los Angeles's safety valve, a second trajectory must be concerned with understanding who has been pushed into the valley and why, so as to resist the processes of naturalization that make the valley seem, in Thom Anderson's words, so "far off."

Indeed, many of those who are being pushed out of Los Angeles have found relief in the valley. Its affordable housing has made it an attractive destination. Many commute back to the metropolis for work. Among those who have come to the valley are the residents at the core of this book: tenants in the Housing Choice Voucher program.

The product of a bipartisan turning away from the New Deal, Housing Choice Vouchers replace public housing and embed rental assistance to poor families in the private market. Landlords get a reimbursement from the government in exchange for renting to a voucher tenant, but participation in the program is not mandatory. Because fair market rent was calculated over entire counties, landlords in struggling neighborhoods saw the fair market reimbursement rate as more than they would receive on the private market, while landlords in wealthier areas saw it as much less. In Los Angeles, these realities meant that vouchers have concentrated in the city's South Central corridor and in the county's economically lagging fringes, like the Antelope Valley. Between 2000 and 2010, the number of voucher tenants in the Antelope Valley more than tripled, from 5,101 to 15,853. In this manner the valley represented a solution to Los Angeles's crisis of gentrification and displacement, relieving the metropolitan core of tenants who could not afford its rising rents. This process is a microcosm of the larger transformation of Los Angeles as Black residents are pushed out of the city and into its peripheries. But it also illustrates that the transformation of much of the nation's rental support from public housing to vouchers has not been so much about giving tenants the power to move to better neighborhoods but may also be about making tenants mobile to better serve the spatial needs of capital.

TRAJECTORY 2: HOW HOUSING POLICY EVOLVED TO DISPERSE THE POOR

In the immediate aftermath of 1954's *Brown v. Board of Education*, the landmark civil rights case striking down segregated schooling, elected officials in Prince Edward County, Virginia, came up with a scheme to maintain segregated schooling in their county. Rather than integrate public schools, they defunded and then closed their public school system, while giving white students vouchers to help them enroll in newly created private schools, which came to be known as segregation academies for their exclusion of Black students.[17] Two years after the county's scheme was defeated, however, civil rights and fair housing advocates also turned to vouchers, thinking of them as a tool to combat racial segregation.

At the time, public housing tenants were organizing and protesting for improved conditions—for heat, elevator repairs, recreation space, the distribution of public housing across the city, and more.[18] Only one of their demands was lifted to prominence by fair housing advocates. The right to live anywhere in the city became an extension of the fight for fair housing in the private housing market, and legal advocates championed it through federal litigation.

Their case was 1966's *Gautreaux v. HUD*, which accused the Chicago Housing Authority of segregated siting of public housing, a practice that denied its tenants the right to fair housing. Among the remedies requested were vouchers for tenants to move across the city. How could a policy tool marshaled to reproduce racial segregation in education be relied upon to produce racial justice in housing? No answer appears in the reflections of Alexander Polikoff, lead lawyer in *Gautreaux v. HUD*.[19] But one might be obtained by searching the longer history of urban sociology and its influence on housing policy.

The ideas undergirding voucher policy extend back to the Chicago School of urban sociology. Robert Park and Ernest Burgess's vision of urban life became the template for sociological thinking about urban places and policy for most of the twentieth century. At work studying Chicago in the 1920s, they derived an ecological model of the city which recast human and political choices as natural, metabolic processes.[20] They saw the city as divided into concentric zones of destitution, opportunity, and prosperity, and understood mobility from inner zones outward as a natural and positive process of assimilation into the city's middle classes. Rather than acknowledge that their theory could not account for racial exclusion, the authors painted Black residents who did not fit their paradigm as themselves disordered and inferior.[21]

But the basic idea that mobility would solve inequality became the template for housing policy, embraced by liberal lawyers aiming to fight for civil rights in the context of housing, and approved by the Kerner Commission on Civil Unrest as a national strategy to defeat segregation and its consequences.[22] The commission called for expanding public housing, but explicitly advocated rent supplements, another term for vouchers, as a tool for Black mobility out of segregated and disinvested neighborhoods. By the 1970s, the *Gautreaux* remedies had begun to be implemented, including a guided voucher program to help public housing tenants move to whiter and more middle-class neighborhoods, and the Nixon administration, already curbing public housing funding and fair housing initiatives,[23] began the Experimental Housing Allowance Program (EHAP) to pilot vouchers at the federal level.[24]

From his vantage point studying the lives of tenants in the Pruitt-Igoe public housing project in St. Louis, Missouri, Lee Rainwater warned that movement-oriented federal policy reforms "have succeeded in moving people from one place to another, but they have provided very few with good housing."[25] But sociologists, liberal advocates, and policymakers doubled down on mobility as poverty's solution.

By the 1980s and 90s, scholars were turning their attention to the amorphous "underclass."[26] In highly influential work, William Julius Wilson pointed to the effects of disinvestment and deindustrialization on poor Black neighborhoods, and warned in addition that Black middle class residents, empowered by the advance of fair housing law, had been able to move out, leaving "the ghetto" bereft of internal and external modes of upliftment.[27]

These ideas, occasionally cited by HUD policymakers themselves, became part of the rationale for a wholesale shift in federal housing policy in the 1990s. The Reagan administration effectively picked up where Nixon left off, cutting public housing funding that virtually guaranteed that building conditions would suffer. The steep cuts to HUD's budget imposed by Nixon and Reagan set the stage for future demolition-focused policies in the 1990s.[28] A National Commission on Severely Distressed Public Housing and an Urban Revitalization Demonstration Program, created in 1989, were tasked with studying the conditions of public housing and determining the number of units considered "severely distressed." The commission assessed that 86,000 units, or 6 percent of the public housing stock, were severely distressed and should be rehabilitated.[29] As Edward Goetz notes, this suggested that 94 percent of housing stock was in good or acceptable condition and could be fixed without extreme measures.[30] This should have stood out as prima facie evidence of public housing's feasibility, but the report instead opened the door to a program of demolition and partial replacement, known as Housing Opportunities for People Everywhere (HOPE VI). It was, in Edward Goetz's words, a "discourse of disaster."[31] In total, HOPE VI led to the demolition of 220,000 public housing units in the 1990s and 2000s, potentially home to half a million people.[32] This scale of government-sponsored eviction and housing demolition rivaled urban renewal of the 1950s and 60s.[33] Among the partial replacements for demolished public housing were mixed-income redevelopments and vouchers.

In this way, vouchers have come to the fore of American housing policy through a form of what Derrick Bell called interest convergence theory, the idea that "the interest of blacks in achieving racial equality will be accommodated only when it converges with the interests of whites."[34] In vouchers, conservatives saw a strike against the New Deal and public housing, and for the broader subordination of public assistance to the private market. In vouchers, liberals saw an accomplishment of fair housing—the theoretical ability to move anywhere in a city. Their agreement set in motion a wholesale transformation of subsidized housing policy over the second half of the twentieth century.[35]

For academics, vouchers became a way to study neighborhood effects. Rather than consider the effects government policy can have on neighborhoods, neighborhood effects research studies the effects neighborhoods have on their residents. It's a framework designed to not understand reality. In absenting public policy it absolves those who make it and narrows prospects for change to the paltry solution of moving some people out of bad neighborhoods and into good ones (and saying nothing about those left behind).[36]

The Moving to Opportunity Demonstration Project became the nation's largest effort to assess these neighborhood effects, providing public housing tenants in five major cities with housing vouchers. Giving some tenants vouchers while not providing them to others allows researchers to see what effect moving has on people, relative to the baseline of not having moved.[37]

The demolition of public housing was sold as being in the best interests of tenants because it would empower them to move to places with more opportunity.[38] But evaluations of whether one can move to opportunity and whether doing so would improve one's economic and social well-being have proven disappointing on the researchers' own terms. For years, MTO evaluations have found that participants were not able to move very far, or to very different neighborhoods.[39] Moreover, movement had virtually no effects of on the incomes and employment rates of tenants, though there were positive effects on mental health, exposure to crime, and physical well-being.[40] It's important to note that this lack of effect was in comparison to doing nothing at all for tenants, the lowest bar possible. Because no government agency or philanthropy has funded such a study, it remains a thought experiment to consider how a control group that received improvements to public housing might have fared, including in comparison to voucher movers.

Meanwhile, the reality was that vouchers deprived tenants of rights while accomplishing little in the service of fair housing. Although tenants cannot be discriminated against based on race, landlords can discriminate based on voucher status.[41] While many jurisdictions have recently begun to ban that form of source of income discrimination, the bans are geographically uneven, often unenforced, and easily circumvented. While public housing tenants enjoyed a federally recognized right to organize as well as federal funds to support tenant councils, voucher tenants have neither.[42] And while vouchers technically give their holders the right to move anywhere in the city, the ability of landlords to selectively accept them and the short deadlines by which tenants must find housing mean that the most practical exercise of those rights is in the city's most depressed housing markets, if at all.[43] The result is that only about 60 percent of people with vouchers can actually use them before they expire.[44] And in many regions, voucher tenants have been forced into peripheries.[45] Those lucky enough to get a voucher and use it are subject to rules and constraints that make them more evictable than the average private market tenant—rules that affect who can live with or even visit them. Finally, emerging evidence suggests persistent shortcomings of the voucher approach. It is internally racially unequal, with white residents getting access to cheaper and higher-quality units than Black residents.[46] And it is comparatively less effective than other HUD subsidy programs, with voucher tenants spending more of their incomes on housing than public housing tenants,[47] and public housing tenants enjoying greater socio-economic advances per year of program participation than voucher tenants.[48]

The cost of gaining these paper-thin rights has been steep. Consider just the case of Chicago, where the Gautreaux case originated. Although vouchers have grown dramatically in the city, they have also given symbolic permission to policymakers to demolish nearly 20,000 units of public housing (what could be home to 50,000 people) and fail to build countless more. Much of the land where public housing once stood still lies fallow today, while the unhoused sleep in tents in parks and under overpasses.

TRAJECTORY 3:
HOW POLICING EVOLVED TO GREET THEM

Another way of thinking about vouchers is that their role is not so much about moving poor people to opportunity as it is to create an opportunity to move poor people. Making tenants mobile for capital has meant that the voucher program is structurally involved in the spatial fix—the process of resolving economic problems through a spatial solution. The bulldozers and wrecking balls dispatched for urban renewal in the '60s and public housing demolition in the '90s and 2000s are no longer needed. Tenants must move wherever the market takes them.

But if the voucher program is an opportunity to move tenants, we must also consider how American society has reacted to the mobility of poor people, and particularly of Black people. As Anne Bonds has argued, the politics of residential property are "fundamentally connected to practices of policing and the carceral management of urban space."[49] Here, society's carceral orientation to Black mobility has remained largely unchanged.

Consider the case of *Falloon v. Schilling*, litigated in 1882, the same year Charles Graves arrived in the Antelope Valley.[50] James Falloon sued his neighbor, Adam Schilling, for building an addition to his property with the intention of renting it to a Black family moving to Kansas (part of the exodus of Black families out of the Deep South in the early Jim Crow period). Falloon's claim was based in nuisance property law, casting Blackness itself as nuisance, and he and other "race nuisance" claimants sought the power to preempt Black residency in their neighborhoods, or evict Black tenants already there. Had he been successful, his claims would have been enforceable by police, just as restrictive covenants and municipal segregation ordinances were also, ultimately, backed by police enforcement. Falloon and his compatriots largely lost the race nuisance cases of the Jim Crow period, but the court decisions of that era did not foreclose the possibility of using nuisance law to racially segregate neighborhoods. Today, cities around the country have passed crime-free and nuisance housing laws that give their residents the powers Falloon once sought. Crime-free housing ordinances preempt renters with criminal convictions from obtaining leases, while nuisance ordinances allow neighbors to use complaint hotlines to evict neighbors. This book's chapters on how neighbors police voucher tenants illustrate the striking continuities between the race nuisance cases of the past and their successor policies in the present.

Yet Falloon represents only one instance in the history of policing as a mechanism for controlling Black mobility. Simone Browne documents how, in the colonial era, New York City employed "lantern laws" to regulate the after-dark public presence and movement of enslaved Black, mixed-race, and indigenous people.[51] During the slavery era, states like Oregon[52] and Illinois[53] enacted constitutional bans on Black migration, enforceable by police. Meanwhile, the Fugitive Slave Act empowered whites to act as vigilantes, capturing Black individuals in the North and accusing them of being fugitive slaves.[54] In the Jim Crow era, sundown towns across the country promised Black people that they would be killed should they remain in the town after dark.[55] And throughout the 1900s, police effectively endorsed violence, from vigilantism to riots, aimed at maintaining racial segregation.[56] In the early decades of the Aid to Families With Dependent Children (AFDC) Program, states tried to prevent poor families receiving AFDC support from migrating into their jurisdictions by stripping them of AFDC benefits once they entered the state.[57] And in direct response to the Great Migration, jurisdictions in the north increased police spending and incarceration.[58] Today, policing remains highly involved in the maintenance of racial segregation and the shaping of neighborhoods.[59]

Finally, the policing of where Black residents may live has extended to the policing of Black homes as well. In the 1950s, welfare agencies took it upon themselves to enter the homes of mothers on the AFDC program, welfare as we once knew it. The program was organized around the idea of the government as the substitute father—a nuclear family with a mother and father wouldn't need welfare because the father would work, but families lacking a father needed government assistance so that mothers could remain their children's primary caregivers rather than entering the workforce.[60] To ensure that aid was going only to mothers who were truly single, welfare offices had to have eyes into the private lives of poor women. States implemented man-in-the-house rules that allowed agents to enter women's homes in search of men, or evidence of a man's presence. Evidence of a man's presence substantiated welfare terminations. Enacted through midnight raids, the rules particularly affected AFDC recipients in public housing. Pruitt-Igoe tenant Jacqueline Williams described the rules as a condition of residency:

> Before we moved into Pruitt-Igoe, the welfare department came to our home, they talked with my mother about moving into the housing project, but the stipulation was that my father could not be with us. They would put us into the housing project only if he left the state. Mother and father discussed it and they decided that it was best for the twelve children for the father to leave the home, and that's how we got into the projects.[61]

This practice of family separation was playing out in the same years that Daniel Moynihan was formulating his critique of Black America as insufficiently committed to wedlock and family life. And it was enforced with brutal consequences. But families strove to be together and took great risks to do so. As sociologist Joyce Ladner described it,

> There was even a night staff of men who worked for the welfare department whose job was to go to the home of welfare recipients and they searched to find if there was a man in the home. Sometimes men came back at night to be with their families. Some were found in closets, hiding.[62]

The midnight raids were supposed to have ended with the 1968 *King v. Smith* Supreme Court ruling, which stipulated that the policies violated children's rights to aid.[63] But as this book will show, they have re-emerged through private actors who surveil voucher tenants and file complaints against them alleging that they have unauthorized guests. The practices have the same results, fifty years later. In this book, I extend the category of the home raid to illustrate how it has been a longstanding tactic of turning homes into mere housing—a place of shelter but not safety or belonging. The home raid is a central demarcator of what home is and who can have it.

That local residents have been empowered through law and policy to surveil and police their neighbors—to trigger home raids like those Michelle Ross experienced—is one of the more troubling observations this book offers. As the Antelope Valley's economic status declined through industrial loss and housing foreclosure, residents found themselves facing Angelenos priced out of the metropolis. They tried, in Mike Davis's words, to "raise the gangplanks" by finding ways to turn back this movement.[64] If the valley's heyday was marked by manufacturing and whiteness, and the valley's residents could not preserve manufacturing, they could at least preserve its whiteness. That they turned to policing Black neighbors, and particularly Black women in the voucher program, was partly about fighting to preserve a white place, and partly about preserving property values, but it was also about clawing back a social hierarchy threatened by a half-century of change. If white social status could not be raised through exclusion from the valley, it could be raised by subordinating others within the valley. Thus, by participating in policing, the valley's private market renters and homeowners have made themselves a superior form of citizenship, one which is inflated by wielding the power of law. From a Du Boisian perspective, there was a social and psychological wage of policing that offered something meaningful at a time when other more material elements of status were in freefall.[65] From the vantage of Cheryl Harris's work, we can identify characteristics of policing that, in the hands of everyday people, resemble property.[66]

Despite these structures, white supremacy in the valley has never held complete sway over its potential adherents. As this book will show, white defections from the system of white supremacy began with the family that partnered with Melvin Ray Grubbs to parcel the land that would become Sun Village, and would continue through the student anti-war and anti-racist mobilizations of the 1960s, the Skinheads Against Racial Prejudice (S.H.A.R.P.s) who fought the valley's Nazis in the 1980s, white opponents of the policing of housing who spoke up in public hearings in the 2010s, and some of the local residents I interviewed who bucked the moral panic over vouchers and abstained from participation in policing tenants. In turn, anti-Blackness has always been capacious—a Black mayor began some of the earliest opposition to voucher tenants, and among the mostly white local residents I interviewed, I contacted a handful of Latino respondents who also held anti-Black and anti-voucher views.

Ultimately, however, these three forces—the valley's role as Los Angeles's safety valve, the federal government's dispersal of poor tenants into depressed and peripheral housing markets, and the evolution of policing to constrain Black mobility, target Black homes, and substantiate non-Black citizenship—collided in the Antelope Valley in the early 2000s, producing the regional effort to police and evict Black tenants out of the valley.

A DIFFERENT VISION FOR URBAN SOCIOLOGY AND HOUSING POLICY

Since the early 2000s, scholars have returned to the concept of racial capitalism to understand the conjoined development of racism and capitalism, both in specific national case studies,[67] and as a broader, global process.[68] At both scales, however, the scholarship agrees that capitalism's growth occurs in part through racism, and that racism's persistence occurs in part through capitalism.[69] Applying this perspective can help develop a vision of urban sociology distinct from Park and Burgess's ecological template.

Indeed, new attention has been paid to how racial capitalism applies to urban sociology, and here is where a contrasting vision of urban sociology might emerge. As Prentiss Dantzler notes, the urban is both a site and a process—it is the geography upon which racial capitalism plays out.[70]

One example of how such an analysis of race and capitalism might contribute to a new understanding of urban processes is in the work of W. E. B. Du Bois.[71] While the mobility-oriented framework that helped produce the crisis in the Antelope Valley emerged from Park and Burgess, their era was also the era of Du Bois's urban sociology, which sought to understand the roles of racism and capitalism in the distribution of people across space.

Consider for example, his reflections on East St. Louis, site of a white riot against Black workers in 1917 that prefaced the nationwide white supremacist violence of Red Summer two years later.[72] When Du Bois traveled to East St. Louis to understand the causes of the riot, he chronicled a place and process whose traces remain present in American society, including the Antelope Valley, today. A "miserable town of liquor and lust," East St. Louis was the product of St. Louis, its "just and austere king." St. Louis had been growing rapidly, due in part to wartime industrial expansion. Du Bois noted that alongside its development came resistance to its terms; "the forces of evil have had some curbing from those who have seen the vision and panted for life." Yet this prompted the city's industries to relocate rather than reform. Their solution was to find new places for unfettered growth. In shifting the rail industry to East St. Louis, corporations created "a paradise for high and frequent dividends and for the piling up of wealth to be spent in St. Louis and Chicago and New York."[73]

Black workers leaving the South looked toward East St. Louis as a destination where they might find jobs and stability. But they arrived to find striking white rail workers who saw their presence as competition, undermining their strike. Whites in East St. Louis, Du Bois wrote, feared "not deprivation of the things they were used to and the shadow of poverty, but rather the definite death of their rising dreams." Turning their gaze from their employers to those who might otherwise have been their comrades, "they entered the Shadow of Hell, where suddenly from a fight for wage and protection against industrial oppression East St. Louis became the center of the oldest and nastiest form of human oppression—race hatred." So began the 1917 East St. Louis Riot, in which white workers turned upon their Black counterparts. When Du Bois arrived, he described the aftermath as he rode through the city, "past flame-swept walls and over gray ashes; in streets almost wet with blood and beside ruins, where the bones of dead men new-bleached peered out at me with sullen wonder."[74]

In his analysis of the trajectory of East St. Louis, Du Bois saw how a periphery became the site of a spatial fix for its metropolis, the role of capital in structuring place and worker antagonisms, and the way that racism cracked any basis for solidarity among people with shared interests. In so doing he refused the mechanistic, naturalized perspective that relied on concentric zones and mobility between them to explain the fates of residents.

Du Bois saw East St. Louis's riot as a harbinger, warning that the violence that swept the city had already been attempted in "Chicago, Indianapolis, Detroit, Cleveland, Pittsburg, Philadelphia, and New York." His warnings feel as true today in the valley as they did then. While the valley never endured a white riot in the style of 1917, its history is one of constant anti-Black violence, finally institutionalized through forms of policing that obviate the riot.

One way to heed Du Bois's warning about the conditions antecedent to the riot is to pay attention to the way capital exploits and extends racial hierarchy and how questions of wages can be turned to race-hatred—in other words, to grasp the mutually reinforcing relationship between racism and capitalism. If one accepts that a racial capitalism framework has something valuable to offer urban sociology, the next question is how and to what ends to apply it. To that end, summarizing a new wave of research on racial capitalism and urban sociology, Robert Vargas suggests that urban scholarship engaging racial capitalism can move from the ecological model of the city to a settler-colonial one, offer a longer historicization of the city that goes beyond the common 1960s starting point, attend to the academy's role in carcerality, and pair macro and theoretical work with microsociologies.[75]

This work will attempt to fulfill these mandates by offering the safety valve as a way of understanding the valley that moves past the ecological model. In addition to offering a longer history of the valley that accounts for its settler-colonial nature, the safety valve thesis is consonant with earlier urban sociological theories of internal colonialism. As the book transitions to a focus on the policing of tenants, it will attend to the role of academic institutions in legitimizing the policing of housing, and offer qualitative interviews that extend Du Bois's notion of the wages of whiteness to the case of participatory policing.

In so doing, I work from the premise that Los Angeles is a strong example of urban racial capitalism. The city did not develop as an entirely capitalist place—it imposed significant limits on economic activity in order to advance white supremacy, for example, by enforcing widespread racially restrictive covenants that barred Black renters and purchasers. But the city also did not develop entirely through racial exclusion. Rather that fully exclude them, it exploited Black residents as low-wage workers and took advantage of their weak market power to overcharge them for the city's worst housing stock. These forces help explain why some Black Angelenos went to the Antelope Valley, and especially to Sun Village. But the valley has also developed along the lines of racial capitalism. When Palmdale and Lancaster's strict walls of racial segregation fell in the 1960s, the region did not abandon racism in favor of more purely capitalist development. Instead, it evolved over decades to create a system of housing exploitation whereby landlords and the city's economy profited from Black voucher tenancy, while the tenants themselves remained policed and socially excluded. That these tenants were predominantly women suggests that this is a story of what Sarah Haley and Shauna Sweeney have discussed as gendered racial capitalism, the notion that capital exploited both racial and gendered difference.[76]

Returning to *Darkwater*, Du Bois wrote that he was left with two questions— "how to furnish goods and services for the wants of men and how equitably and sufficiently to satisfy these wants."[77] As Aldon Morris has documented, Park and Burgess overlooked Du Bois's urban sociological analysis as they worked on *The City*.[78] The mainstream of urban sociology would leave these questions unanswered as it investigated scholarly justifications for making poor people move rather than making their material conditions better.

From Du Bois's questions, we might recover an agenda for a way out of the degradation, dispersal, and policing of subsidized housing. This book will chronicle the efforts of tenants, activists, and lawyers in challenging the policing of housing. It is a continuation of the campaigns of public housing tenants resisting the policing of public housing, the regulation of gender and family within it, and the demolition of their homes. It extends the longer and broader struggle to define and demarcate the desert. And it drives new understandings of abolitionist practice and illustrates the co-constitutive aspects of housing justice and carceral abolitionism.[79] To end the policing of housing is to make home in the valley.[80]

OUTLINE OF THE BOOK

In the following chapters, I attempt to tell this story in full, anchoring it in a longer history of the valley and illustrating its implications for larger questions affecting the nation today: what is the role and future of places like the Antelope Valley, how should we understand the voucher program and its place in housing policy, how is the nature of policing changing and to what ends, and where do the struggles against policing and for housing justice meet?

In Chapter 1, I trace the first wave of Black movement to the Antelope Valley, which accompanied the valley's first assumption of the role of spatial fix for Los Angeles. The valley quickly became an aerospace construction and testing hub for the military during and after World War II. Black families being pushed out of Los Angeles as the city enforced racial segregation and blocked public housing found the valley a lifeline. The chapter focuses on Sun Village, one of several all-Black communities around the periphery of Los Angeles. Sun Village thrived in the 1950s and 60s, establishing the nation's first public park named in honor of Jackie

Robinson, and participating in local and national NAACP organizing. Sun Village was simultaneously a sanctuary from the racism of the valley and Los Angeles more broadly, and a foundation from which to build new organizing to overcome it, characteristics consonant with bell hooks's vision of home.[81]

To illustrate the sinews connecting Sun Village to Los Angeles, I anchor the chapter on the Prioleau family, tracing their civil rights organizing over two generations, from their establishment of the Bethel A.M.E. Church in Los Angeles to their struggle against eviction from Bruce's Beach, from their desegregation of the City of Los Angeles's swimming pools to their youngest daughter Lois Patton's role in founding the Sun Village NAACP and breaking the wall of residential segregation that had once defined the Antelope Valley. This chapter shows how both racial capitalism and militarism shaped Los Angeles's Black geography, including the relations between Black communities in the city's core and its periphery. It places Sun Village among the constellation of Black places on that periphery.

In Chapter 2, I turn to the valley's counter-revolution against fair housing. Despite overwhelming public backing, California's conservative establishment could not successfully prevent fair housing law from taking hold. How its constituents reacted to this failure to defend the valley's manufactured segregation is a critical question in urban and political history. In the valley, these events seemed to validate the outsider approach of the white power movement, spearheaded in Los Angeles by preacher Wesley Swift. Swift exerted a tremendous influence on white supremacist politics across the country by recording and disseminating taped lectures developing the ideas of what would come to be known as the Christian Identity Movement. His career served as a bridge between the American Nazism of the 1930s and the white power movement of the 1970s.

Although Swift was influential locally and nationally, neither he nor the valley at large could undo the growing Black presence in the '70s, '80s, and '90s. This chapter shows how policing became the mechanism by which white homeowners reinvigorated their property rights. It illustrates how the war on crime's extension into housing has created new powers for property owners through a thicket of civil, criminal, and administrative rules that turn the homes of poor renters into surveilled, quasi-carceral spaces. Through policies that allow governments and individuals to police housing and evict neighbors, property owners have regained the right to discriminate in housing.

Unable to defend their vision of the valley, its leaders have used policing to turn the homes of voucher tenants into indefensible spaces, permeable and precarious rather than private and protected. In Chapter 3, I focus on the city of Lancaster, where Mayor R. Rex Parris tried a variety of tactics to criminalize, remove, and prevent voucher renters from entering the city in the early 2000s (part of the second spatial fix). Seeing most of them fail, Parris and other city leaders settled on a participatory policing regime. In this system, private renters and homeowners are empowered to surveil their neighbors and file complaints against them to the city, Housing Authority, or police. Enough calls, regardless of merit, could result in a voucher tenant being evicted by their landlord, losing their voucher, or simply leaving in frustration.

The core of the chapter features anonymized interviews with forty-three private renters and homeowners engaged in surveilling and policing their neighbors. From my conversations with them, I theorize that the reasons people participate in policing go beyond attitudes of anti-Blackness or opposition to welfare programs. Participation in policing offers status and other benefits that are of value to participants. In this way, building from the work of Cheryl Harris, policing is cognizable as a form of property. Policing as property illustrates the stakes that private property owners and renters have in policing Black residents. To be able to police while others cannot, to degrade through policing, and to acquire a superior social status through policing—these are lucrative rewards not just in the Antelope Valley but in neighborhoods across the country.

Chapter 4 focuses on the targets of this policing, examining how the valley attacked tenants through degrading their homes, turning them into indefensible spaces. Forty anonymized interviews with tenants in the voucher program show the extent and wide-ranging consequences of the surveillance and policing being conducted by neighbors, the city, police, and housing officials. Casting social and family relationships as evidence that tenants were harboring "unauthorized tenants," neighbors and the local Housing Authority have brought broken-windows policing into the home. They launched roughly a thousand inspections of voucher tenants between 2007 and 2011, evicting hundreds each year. Paired with one-strike eviction policies based on drug and criminal charges, tenants faced a complex miasma of ways they could be evicted.

The most practical way to avoid this surveillance is to stay unknown and out of the public eye. Many voucher holders self-curtail a range of fully legal behaviors like inviting guests over, supporting family, and allowing children to play in the yard. In other words, the effect of the valley's policing regime was to turn family and social bonds into eviction liabilities. Tenants bear these conditions because the protection of housing is of highest importance, finding alternate housing through the voucher program is extremely difficult, and being evicted or pushed out would also be disruptive to the lives and education of their children. Not only does this reality illustrate the long life of welfare's "man in the house" rules and midnight raids, but it adds another case to the broad scholarship illustrating how social services have become venues of criminalization, surveillance, policing, and family separation. The result, I argue, is a devolution of home to mere shelter.

Finally, in chapter 5, I use interviews with local activists, public officials, civil rights attorneys, and tenants to review the ways that Black residents in the Antelope Valley overturned some of the region's worst policing practices. This mobilization represents a continuation of earlier struggles waged by Black residents of Sun Village in the 1960s. I focus on the activism of one local group, The Community

Action League (TCAL), which responded to a wave of reports about voucher evictions through mobilization on two registers: on one, they mobilized sustained community opposition to voucher policing, and on the other they filed litigation on behalf of evicted voucher tenants, helping to build the nation's first federal suit asserting that policing practices violated fair housing. I interview members of TCAL who worked on this campaign and lawyers who worked on the case about their strategies. I follow the case's settlement and examine how residents interpret its outcomes today. And I ask what implications this mobilization might have for similar cases in municipalities around the country.

In the book's conclusion, I explore what the Antelope Valley's case means for places like it around the nation. In the most narrow accounting, by eliminating policing programs that empowered white residents to police subsidized housing tenants, activists and their legal allies reduced the scope of policing in the Antelope Valley, as well as the powers afforded to private homeowners and renters. Beyond the fight against policing, it was a fight for civil rights, for tenant rights, against eviction, and for home, family, and community. And in the broadest sense, it was a fight against the unjust social and economic order that has made dispossession, dispersal, and domination part of the cost of securing housing for low-income households. In this way, it has something to offer our understanding of housing justice struggles in Los Angeles and across the country.

To suggest the Antelope Valley that could be, I explore the mutual stakes of efforts to reduce policing and punishment and efforts to secure housing justice. The two are conceptually linked: logics of punitiveness, retribution, and disposability echo across our systems of mass incarceration and mass eviction. If the policing of housing operates on the premise that some tenants deserve to be made homeless, its counter logic is the universal right to housing—homelessness is not an acceptable solution to any social problem. Tenants, including the ones whose stories are told in this book, do not have to be perfect to deserve housing.

From the valley's case study, practical directions emerge. Cutting down the thicket of HUD regulations that disempower tenants, weaken their privacy rights, and increase eviction risks would make voucher tenants' homes more private and stable as opposed to surveilled and precarious. And eliminating crime-free and nuisance housing ordinances would end their role as levers of eviction and segregation. More broadly, rather than policing scarce subsidized housing, we should expand public housing programs to meet their need, while supporting tenants' efforts to gain the power to determine the fate of their housing. Zooming out to the national level, I show that parts of this agenda are already well at work, and that the Antelope Valley's legacy can be seen in efforts to challenge the policing of housing in places all around the country.

1

Sun Village

The history of Sun Village is the history of the Antelope Valley and the history of America. . . . [It] should be sung throughout the valley.
—JAMES BROOKS

In 1962, Lois Patton and her family were the first Black residents to break the Antelope Valley's wall of segregation and move to a home in Palmdale. Lois and her husband Patrick founded the South Antelope Valley NAACP, participated in a dizzying number of community and religious organizations in Sun Village, and are remembered as among the most important figures in the Antelope Valley's history. But Lois Patton was not born in Sun Village; indeed, when she was born it did not exist. She was the youngest daughter of George and Ethel Prioleau, a military family who had come to Los Angeles to retire at Bruce's Beach, and who were subsequently evicted by its white supremacist society.

Tracing this family's story across two generations, from Los Angeles to the Antelope Valley, illustrates how Los Angeles's use of scarcity and segregation combined to contain its Black residents within a small geography or push them out of the city altogether. In turn, however, their generations of resistance illustrate the continuities of struggle from core to periphery and across major shifts in Los Angeles's economic geography.

This chapter, then, is about the first large wave of Black migration to the Antelope Valley in the aftermath of its first moment as a spatial fix for Los Angeles. Black movement to the valley occurred in the 1940s–1960s as families like the Pattons moved to the valley to take jobs in its booming aerospace military industry and evade Los Angeles's entrenched structures of racial segregation. Blocked from renting or purchasing property in the valley's main cities Lancaster and Palmdale, they built a town called Sun Village on its periphery. It would come to be one of roughly two hundred Black towns across the United States, formed as refuges, experiments, and visions of alternate futures.[1] Like many others, it quickly became a site of community building and civil rights organizing, culminating in its residents breaking the wall of residential segregation, the key fulcrum of anti-Blackness in the valley for decades.[2] And while it has had ebbs and flows of population, investment, and political power, the social and cultural institutions its founders created and its members have sustained, including the churches, park, and organizations described in this chapter, have endured throughout the valley's history.

The circumstances that necessitated Sun Village happened at both the state and local level, as California and Los Angeles developed their housing systems along the twin imperatives of segregation and scarcity. In California, this was represented by the battles over two statewide referenda, both named Proposition 14, that concretized scarcity and segregation in the state. The first was a 1948 effort to create and fund a statewide public housing development agency. Despite its backing by a broad coalition of unions and civil rights groups, it was defeated by the real estate industry's political mobilization. The second, in 1964, represented that industry's re-emergence as a statewide political force, as it used the referendum to reverse the state's landmark Rumford Fair Housing Law.

In Los Angeles, the same commitments to segregation and scarcity would come to produce Sun Village. After World War II, Los Angeles County used the Antelope Valley to capture military investment that was being marked for dispersal outside major coastal cities. Rather than losing these dollars, developing the valley allowed the county to continue to enjoy significant federal investment as well as the economic activity and taxes that flowed from it. Through this investment it provided white Angelenos good jobs and subsidized, segregated housing in the valley. While this process played out, Los Angeles was also forcing Black residents into a housing crisis. It enforced racially restrictive covenants that locked Black renters and purchasers out of wide swaths of available homes, while turning down federal dollars to build public housing in the city that might alleviate that crisis. These pressures forced Black residents to live within the crowded South Central area or consider moving to the city's peripheries, igniting the first wave of Black migration to the valley and the construction of Sun Village.[3]

Tracing this history expands an understanding of Black Los Angeles across a broader geography of settlement and struggle. It illuminates how deeply American militarism has shaped the geography of Black Los Angeles, both by confining the geography of public housing in the city and by drawing Black residents to places like the valley to work in defense production. It will also show how reliance on the military for economic stability or racial progress has repeatedly failed. The communities made through these processes, like Sun Village, have at times been places of community building, freedom from restrictive covenants, and sites of civil rights organizing and popular mobilization. Crucially, many Sun Village residents remained connected to the larger freedom struggles of Los Angeles's core. But Sun Village was not the only periphery of Los Angeles that became a site of

Black struggle, and its history can be productively linked to peripheries around the region that played such a role. Sun Village could be seen as part of an archipelago of Black places ringing the Los Angeles core, places such as Allensworth, San Bernardino, Lanfair Valley, Coachella, Victorville, Indio, Valle Verde, and Palm Springs.[4] The story of the Black desert, however, starts on a Black beach.

ENFORCING SEGREGATION IN LOS ANGELES

Lois Patton's parents, Major George Washington Prioleau and Ethel Prioleau, arrived in Los Angeles in 1920 following his retirement from military service, purchasing a home on 35th Place as well as a cottage at Bruce's Beach. Located in the all-white city of Manhattan Beach, just south of Santa Monica, Bruce's Beach became an important site of Black placemaking in the Los Angeles area. Willa and Charles Bruce had purchased the land to accommodate a seaside resort and residences for Black families. The resort included a cottage where visitors could purchase lunch, rent swimming clothes, and shower. It quickly became popular, attracting Black visitors, beachgoers, and vacationers, and even new residents, like the Prioleaus, who bought their own plots in the development.[5]

George Washington Prioleau was born to enslaved parents on May 15, 1856, in Charleston, South Carolina. As a young adult he attended Wilberforce University in Ohio, majoring in theology and beginning service as a pastor in an African Methodist Episcopal (A.M.E.) Church. Prioleau quickly rose to prominence. By 1889 he became a professor of theology at Wilberforce, and in 1895 President Grover Cleveland appointed him chaplain of the 9th Cavalry in the US Army, one of the segregated Black Army regiments that came to be known as the Buffalo Soldiers. Prioleau was disaffected by his experience in the military, having encountered severe racism during his army recruitment work in the American South. He wrote public letters and editorials challenging racial segregation and criticizing "the hypocrisy of fighting a war for liberation in Cuba" while denying it at home.[6] Prioleau was deeply affected by the experience of soldiers being denied seating at restaurants and being jeered at by whites. Eventually, "he concluded that patriotic duty and military service would not erase the color line in the minds of many whites."[7] He left the army in 1920, retiring as a major. At the time the Prioleaus arrived, Los Angeles County's Black population had just doubled, from just over 9,000 in 1910 to over 18,000 in 1920.[8]

After settling in Los Angeles, the Prioleaus thrived. They began to attend the First A.M.E. Church, founded by Biddy Mason in downtown Los Angeles, but soon came to believe that Black residents on the west side needed a church closer to them. To fill this need, they established the Bethel A.M.E. Church at 1511 West 36th Street in 1921. George devoted himself to the church, serving as pastor without taking a salary and working on improving the building. In June of 1924, the Prioleaus welcomed their last child, Lois Emma, to the world.

FIGURE 7. Major George W. and Ethel S. Prioleau and Family, 1920. Source: Anna L. Gonzales.

Yet Los Angeles remained committed to racial segregation. Its white population—represented by homeowners' associations, the Ku Klux Klan and other violent collectives, and the whites-only real estate association—steadily built legal and social barriers to Black residential integration to prevent the prosperity of the Prioleaus and others. They used restrictive covenants to prevent Black purchases, and when these were struck down by courts, re-wrote covenants to continue to forbid Black residents from occupying homes. Meanwhile, real estate agents refused to show properties in white neighborhoods to Black purchasers, and whites individually and communally used violence to maintain segregation. These forces worked to block Black residency outside the Central Avenue corridor, including Bruce's Beach, which lay outside this line to the far west.[9]

White residents of Manhattan Beach were determined to evict the families living in the Bruce's Beach area. As early as 1915, they complained to the City Council about colored families gathering at Bruce's Beach for picnics and leisure. White families complained to the city that the presence of Black families would decrease their property values. Led by real estate agent George Lindsey, who characterized Bruce's Beach as a "negro invasion," the city began to search for legal means to evict its residents.[10] By 1924 the city council had passed an ordinance seizing the land by eminent domain to build a park. The Bruces responded by suing the city for racial discrimination, but to no avail.

The coming years were unrelenting. The KKK began organizing openly in the area, holding a lecture on the "Ideals of Pure Americanism" in 1924.[11] Residents soon found themselves the target of arson and cross-burnings intended to drive them out of the area.[12] In 1927, while painting the church, George Prioleau fell from a ladder, sustaining internal injuries that eventually proved fatal. He died on July 15, 1927.[13] By 1929, all the Black property owners of the condemned lots had been forced to accept buyouts, knowing that violence would only escalate if they remained.[14] Ethel Prioleau had the cottage moved from Bruce's Beach to 25th Street and Bayview Drive, but restrictive covenants threatened much of the area, and the family remained at its 35th Place residence, near the Bethel A.M.E. Church it had established.

Meanwhile, Black activists and organizations across Los Angeles continuously fought against racial segregation throughout this period. The NAACP, Urban League, the *California Eagle* (led by activist and publisher Charlotta Bass), and others used collective action, political pressure, and legal challenges to steadily chip away at the city's segregation structures during the 1920s, '30s, and '40s. They challenged restrictive covenants, protected Black homes from attack, ensured collective awareness of social issues, and devised novel challenges to segregation.

The efforts extended to challenging segregated public accommodations as well, and it is here that the Prioleau family's legacy of struggle reappears. Los Angeles began to officially segregate its public swimming pools in 1925. Early efforts to challenge the policy had foundered, having been met with rulings that the city had reasonably provided separate but equal accommodations; the NAACP hesitated to try again for fear of a court setting a negative precedent. But Betty Hill, a founding member of the Los Angeles NAACP chapter, decided to press on with a campaign to desegregate public swimming pools, even if she lacked formal institutional support. She recruited her neighbor, Ethel Prioleau, to send her children to the Olympic Park pool on a "whites only" day.[15] Once turned away, Prioleau had grounds to sue, and Hill did so on her behalf. By 1931, Judge Walter S. Gates ruled in their favor, finding that the city's segregationist pool policy was unconstitutional and ordering it to be ended.[16] The victory was seen as a triumph with implications for civil rights struggles far beyond California, and Hill and Prioleau continued to work together in the years that followed, campaigning against segregation through the Women's Political Study Club.

ENFORCING SCARCITY IN THE HOUSING MARKET

During this time, the city's rising labor and civil rights groups also fought for the construction of public housing as a solution to the city's racialized housing shortage. The city grew from about half a million residents in 1920 to 2 million in 1950, and its Black population rose from 20,000 to 200,000 in that time. However, the city had not built enough housing to accommodate this wartime and Great Migration–driven growth. Tenants experienced overcrowding, lived in slum conditions, and built shantytowns. Patterns of poor housing quality coincided with the city's quickly entrenching patterns of racial segregation, reflecting national trends at the time.

Pressed into action, the Roosevelt administration assigned the Public Works Administration to clear slums and build housing, but the program was stymied by a court ruling that the government could not acquire land for public housing through eminent domain. Instead, the administration turned to federal legislation, passing the 1937 Housing Act to authorize the construction of public housing that would replace slum conditions with what it envisioned as decent, safe, and sanitary housing, authoring local public housing authorities to use eminent domain to acquire land and mobilize federal funds for construction.[17]

From the start, California's conservative political actors were hostile to public housing. Republican Governor Frank Merriam vetoed the state bill that would enable state and local agencies to make use of federal public housing funds three times.[18] But faced with enormous federal incentives and public pressure "from labor, civic organizations, religious groups, and mobilized groups within the city's racial and ethnic communities" to build housing, Los Angeles created a local housing authority. In 1940, the Housing Authority completed its first project, Ramona Gardens in Boyle Heights, and ten more projects in the following years.[19] Construction was accelerated by the need to accommodate war workers. By 1945, more than 53,000 residents were living in 12,275 units of public housing.[20] Following federal guidelines, their racial composition and distribution had been carefully calibrated to match existing patterns of segregation. Yet another 100,000 residents had applied for public housing but could not be accommodated.

The system of racial segregation coupled with insufficient production of public housing fueled a prolonged housing crisis. Organizations in Los Angeles responded with demands for both fair housing and public housing.[21] The city's young Housing Authority was poised to contribute to both goals until it was met with conservative and business opposition, which framed public housing as a dangerous step towards socialism. The anti-public housing campaign successfully managed to stifle the movement, leaving Los Angeles with a relatively small stock of public housing compared to cities like New York and Chicago. The public housing that was built largely matched emergent patterns of segregation and spatial disadvantage, with most projects located in South Central Los Angeles or East Los Angeles, or in predominantly Black neighborhoods like Venice's Oakwood.[22] Coupled with the practice of matching public housing residency patterns to existing patterns of racial segregation, public housing doubled down on racial segregation.

A wide public housing coalition of groups in Los Angeles turned to other levers of housing production as existing efforts failed to build enough public housing to solve the crisis. Civil rights groups like the NAACP and the National Negro Congress, labor groups like the Los Angeles Building Trades Council, the California State Federation of Labor, the California CIO Council, and political groups like the Progressive Citizens of America wrote a statewide proposition that would create a state housing authority authorized to use state finances to supplement local public housing construction. The measure—1948's Proposition 14—was supported by public housing tenant councils, the American Veterans Association, Americans for Democratic Action, and the American Jewish Congress. But it was opposed by the *Los Angeles Times*, big business, and real estate associations. That well-funded opposition, and the Red Scare tactics it tapped into, defeated Proposition 14 by a 2–1 margin in November 1948.[23] Two years later, voters in the state approved Proposition 10, a referendum to amend the state's constitution (adding Article 34) to create a new hurdle to the construction of public housing by mandating that no new public housing could be built without electoral approval of local voters.[24]

The 1937 Housing Act had not provided enough funds to build public housing in sufficient quantities, a problem that persisted until an update to the Housing Act was passed in 1950. The new funding was used in cities around the country, but in Los Angeles, the city's right wing had choked off the possibility of using those funds in a substantial way.[25] One of the few ways public housing was able to grow in the city was by piggybacking on the war effort. Authorized by the Lanham Act and administered federally by the Federal Public Housing Authority and locally by the City Housing Authority, the city built "five permanent and twenty-one temporary public war housing projects," aiming to house the enormous workforce the war industry required.[26] After the war, many of these projects were converted (or converted back) to public housing. In this manner, the war industry shaped the geography of Black Los Angeles.

Like the struggle against segregation, the campaign for public housing showed how difficult it was to achieve a measure of housing justice in Los Angeles. But this did not mean that the government would never pour resources into housing construction for Los Angeles families. Antelope Valley's coming boom would illustrate that if it served the needs of the white majority, there was no limit to the public investment that the government could muster.

THE VALLEY AS SAFETY VALVE

For a time, the Antelope Valley remained a stranger to these developments. Its lack of access to water kept it sparsely populated and stifled any major economic growth, save for gold mining, alfalfa farming, and other low-water activities. This slowly began to change as Japanese farmers arriving in the 1910s developed new farming techniques that made larger-scale production possible. In the 1930s, the valley's farmers developed new wells that could solve the region's irrigation problems. Now, the vast expanse of high desert could begin cultivating pears, apples, almonds, and livestock; soon it was marketing itself as Los Angeles's future bread basket.

As the valley itself developed, outside eyes also began to see its value. During the Great Depression, the Civilian Conservation Corps opened a camp in Valyermo, at the southern edge of the valley. Its weekly newspapers, published in 1935 and 1936, chronicle the lives of young men working, learning, and playing sports in the camp, as well as visiting Palmdale and Lancaster for social outings.[27] People sought out the valley for their health, hoping to benefit from its relatively clean air. Many went there for tuberculosis treatment and isolation, and some were forcibly removed to the valley for treatment by Los Angeles police.[28] But as its profile grew, it became clear that the Antelope Valley's existing links to Los Angeles were insufficient. The county quickly authorized new highway construction to remedy this problem.

Throughout the early 1900s, Los Angeles relied on convict labor to build some of its most important infrastructure. Arresting people en masse using the state's harsh anti-vagrancy law, the city put these convicts to work paving downtown's dirt streets and facilitating the rapid economic development of the area.[29] The same process unfolded in the effort to link the Antelope Valley to the urban core. Angeles Forest Highway construction started in 1932, and was carried out by convict labor.[30] A county detention camp began the preliminary work, after which additional county funds were provided and additional labor was sourced from prisons. By 1936, three prison camps were staffing the construction project through the completion of twenty to thirty miles of roadway into the valley.[31]

These infrastructure connections made it possible to envision more growth for the valley, namely military investment. Indeed, the valley would come to represent a cunning solution to a wartime crisis in Los Angeles. The region's advantage, available land, had made it a hub of aerospace and defense industry development, but war planners also grew concerned that the concentration of development in major cities left them vulnerable to attack. The resulting imperative to decentralize defense production threatened to deprive Los Angeles of critical economic activity by relocating investment to other cities in the Sunbelt. But the valley presented a spatial fix for Los Angeles—satisfying the federal dispersal imperative while still allowing the county to capture its economic rewards in the form of investment, jobs, and tax receipts.[32]

In 1941, the Civil Aeronautics Authority, Works Progress Administration, and U.S. Army selected Palmdale as the site for a major airport and aviation training school, setting it on the path of military development that would shape its next several decades. The initial federal investment of $315,000 was followed that decade by hundreds of millions of dollars to expand the small bombing range and landing strip known as Muroc Field into a major site of wartime training, an installation now known as Edwards Air Force Base.[33] To house these Air Force personnel, the region needed federal housing assistance. While the Red Scare had halted one form of public housing in the city, in the Antelope Valley the booming post-war aerospace economy saw a new boom of federal housing construction—but again for aerospace and military workers. The post-war movement of Black Angelenos to the valley would soon reveal that this suburban, militarized form of public housing was segregated too.

In February 1943, the *South Antelope Valley Press* reported that Lancaster would soon be getting its first federally built housing project, Lancaster Homes.[34] The project was "the first civilian family housing project in the United States to be authorized by the Defense Plant Corporation and the Army Air Force." It had twenty buildings of four apartments each for families, alongside two additional buildings—one for single men and one for single women. The housing was built by the Defense Plant Corporation and spearheaded by the Polaris Flight Academy, which needed to provide housing for flight instructors, mechanics, and other training base workers. That Los Angeles was fighting public housing in the city but building it in the valley speaks to the narrow and militarized conditions under which it would adopt elements of social democracy.

This process of the war industry locating more plants in the valley and then building more housing to accommodate their workers continued throughout the decade. Another major plant was announced in 1943 for B-25 bomber construction. By 1946, the press was talking of a building boom forecasted for the Palmdale area, spurred mainly by the Civilian Production Administration which was authorizing funds for the construction of one hundred private homes in the valley. The expansion of Edwards Air Force Base pushed the Federal Housing Administration to repurpose the Palmdale Air Base into another housing project for fifty families.[35] In 1946, Lockheed announced plans to relocate a flight assembly line from San Fernando Valley to fifty acres of land in Palmdale.[36]

The next year, World War II ace Chuck Yeager broke the sound barrier at Muroc Field. It was a breakthrough moment, marking the valley's ascendancy in military importance as well as its changing identity. Its old reputation as a hardscrabble place for gold mining and farming was giving way to a new reputation: aerospace valley. Pilots stationed at the Air Force base competed to outperform each other in flights as they pushed American air and space power forward. Off hours, they flocked to Pancho Barnes's nearby Happy Bottom Riding Club to drink and swap stories.[37] The space cowboys attracted the attention of Tom Wolfe, whose book *The Right Stuff* followed the pilots who trained for the U.S. space program's first human space flight, Project Mercury.[38] Wolfe's book was adapted into a movie of the same name, spreading the valley's lore farther into popular culture.

Development in the form of schools, additional housing, small businesses, dam construction, sewer lines, and trash collection grew in correlation to this investment, enabling Lockheed to invest again in the 1950s, this time $1.3 million to build a jet fighter plant.[39] In 1952, the Air Force announced plans for $50 million in future construction spending.[40] And the ongoing boom necessitated another round of federal housing creation, this time with the FHA permitting the construction of 1,200 homes. The homes were to be sold or rented under relaxed credit standards to defense workers and members of the armed forces including Army, Navy, and Air Force servicemembers, as well as employees of Lockheed, Northrup, Douglas, and other military contractors who were also building hangars and other infrastructure in the region.[41] Within a month, 12,500 people had applied for the homes.[42] The postwar boom grew Palmdale's population by 83 percent between 1950 and 1953,[43] when the city's population topped 5,000 people living in an estimated 1449 homes.[44] The next year, Lockheed was showcasing its XFV prototype (a plane built for the Navy that would take off and land vertically) while Corvair was announcing plans to build a $2.5 million facility for F-102 interceptor jets for the Air Force. The FHA stepped in again that year, using Title IX of the Housing Act (empowering the construction of housing in critical defense areas) to issue an additional 600 mortgages for the valley.[45]

Despite federal desegregation of the armed forces, Palmdale and Lancaster's whites-only nature remained rigidly intact through the military boom years of the '40s, '50s, and '60s.[46] And just as the valley's land was segregated, so too became its sky.

In 1961, President John F. Kennedy selected Ed Dwight to begin training to be the nation's first Black astronaut. Dwight grew up near an air field in Kansas City, watching pilots fly planes and mechanics repair them. He joined the Air Force in 1953, quickly rising to the top of his class, earning rave reviews from instructors and superiors. And so it was an unsurprising surprise that he was chosen for astronaut training—stunning that any Black man was selected, but logical that it would be Ed Dwight.

NASA training took place at Edwards Air Force Base, in the northern part of the Antelope Valley, meaning Dwight landed in a region defined by white

FIGURE 8. Ed Dwight poses with wife and children, April 1, 1963. Source: George Birch. Los Angeles Public Library Photo Collection/Los Angeles Public Library.

economic, political, and social power, perpetuated by what one of Sun Village's long-time pastors, Bishop Henry Hearns, described in an interview as "the same old Mississippi ideas." No one more powerfully symbolized the valley than Chuck Yeager, who had become flight school commandant by the time Dwight arrived. Yeager had made the Antelope Valley famous but was now being usurped by a Black man with national press attention like the valley had never seen—Dwight was invited to speaking engagements, given awards in the city, asked for photographs, and interviewed by magazines. And so Yeager, buttressed by the rumors that Dwight had been chosen for his race rather than his capabilities, determined not to let him succeed. In a 2019 interview with the *New York Times*, Dwight recalled learning that on the day he arrived, Yeager promised the base, "We can get him out of here in six months. We can break him." As training continued, Dwight recalled, "Every week, right on the dot, he'd call me into his office and say, 'Are you ready to quit? This is too much for you and you're going to kill yourself, boy.' Calling me a boy and I'm an officer in the Air Force."[47]

The story from there becomes murky. Even in a video interview half a century later, Dwight does not speak directly about his treatment, though the Air Force has obliquely apologized for it. But one thing is clear: Captain Ed Dwight couldn't get to the moon from the Antelope Valley. Though he graduated from the training, he knew he had somehow been stonewalled by Yeager and Edwards Air Force Base. So, he left the service in 1966, entering private life before becoming a world-renowned sculptor. It would take until 1983 for Lieutenant Colonel Guion Bluford, Jr., to become the first Black astronaut to reach space.

SUN VILLAGE

Whatever NASA leadership thought at the time, in the light of history it seems obvious that Ed Dwight was never going to be allowed to succeed in the Antelope Valley. It would take until 2024 for Dwight, then ninety years old, to reach space through the civilian Blue Origin program.[48] White supremacy was the dominant organizing principle of the valley from the very start of its military industrial boom. In some ways, the valley temporarily achieved a system of apartheid that was more complete than in Los Angeles itself. With few exceptions, Black workers whose labor was necessary to the region's white wealth were completely segregated within the valley—clustering just east of Palmdale in what was to become known as Sun Village. The process ensured that the white valley was more middle-class because its low-wage workers were simply not there.

While the postwar boom of desegregated defense industry jobs offered an alternative to the discriminatory hiring practices of Los Angeles proper, Black workers could only access employment on the lower rungs of the industry and they could not live in the cities where they were employed. Unable to purchase or rent homes in Palmdale and Lancaster, Black workers often had to find difficult workarounds. Peg Lee, a retired administrator of the Jackie Robinson Park in Sun Village, recounted that Black workers from Watts and Compton would commute to the Antelope Valley, or sometimes find temporary accommodations during the week before returning to the city on weekends. Daisy and Oscar Gibson exemplified the problem. Daisy was a comedian and actress, but her husband Oscar was the first Black employee of the Shopping Bag grocery store in Lancaster. He had to commute from Los Angeles, a trip that took two hours each way before better roads and highways were built.

This unsustainable dynamic found the beginnings of a solution in the late 1940s when Melvin Ray Grubbs partnered with the white owners of the Sun Village Land Corporation to sell a thousand acres of land five miles east of Palmdale, across the dry stream bed known as Little Rock Wash.[49] Born in Oklahoma in 1900, Grubbs was a Black lawyer who moved from Chicago to California to begin working in real estate.[50] Through his company, Sun Village Incorporated, he made the lots available for purchase by Black families.[51] Bishop Henry Hearns explained Grubbs's strategy to me as finding ways to thrive under conditions of segregation. "He had very choice words, 'Ain't no use trying to get so and so up off your back, because they don't want you. So why don't we build our own community right here?'" His approach was deeply political and pragmatic at once, and it found success quickly.

Sun Village would quickly establish its own institutions to provide for residents what they needed in a manner as independent of the valley as possible. Oscar and Daisy Gibson moved to Sun Village in 1959.

Newspapers covered Sun Village early on. A 1947 headline in the *South Antelope Valley Press* read: "Colored Sub-Division Being Promoted East of Palmdale."[52] Sun Village meant the chance to buy land and build a home outside of the structures of racially restrictive covenants. And even after 1948 *Shelley v. Kraemer* ruling invalidating the enforcement of such covenants, it continued to represent a place of relative and contingent housing freedom: free from the California Real Estate Association's discriminatory guidelines, free from HOLC's redlining, free from discrimination by white sellers and renters. Peg Lee explains, "They couldn't build their home in Watts, or Compton, remember, or even certain parts of Los Angeles. So, a lot of them did build homes there. But, a lot of them had wanted to move out. It was cheaper to move outside the city." Lee situated Sun Village as an escape or workaround to the restrictive covenant system, explaining that "it was the only place that they could stay outside of LA besides Valle Verde."[53]

Word about Sun Village got around. It was advertised on Hunter Hancock's radio show in Los Angeles and in *Los Angeles Times* classifieds, and soon Black Angelenos began moving up in greater numbers.[54] By 1954 the *Los Angeles Sentinel*, one of the region's most important Black newspapers, was reporting on the Antelope Valley as a "land of opportunity," citing its population boom (30 percent in 1953), its employment opportunities in the desegregated defense industry, and the $20 million in defense appropriations that were flowing into the valley for housing and other development.[55] Ads noted that living in Sun Village offered some level of self-sufficiency, including the ability to farm and raise animals, and many residents recall doing so.[56]

But insofar as the Antelope Valley was relatively underdeveloped in the 1940s and '50s, Sun Village was even more-so—it lacked gas, electricity, paved roads, and sewage services. Covering the region's history in a 2012 article for the *Los Angeles Times*, Ann Simmons described Virginia Joe Miller and her husband Jerry's first years in Sun Village: "Jerry's commute to his job driving a catering truck at Edwards Air Force Base was more than 30 miles away. The couple used a generator for indoor lighting. Houses were scattered through the settlement. Some nights, the streets were so dark that residents coming home late stayed with friends on the outskirts of town because they couldn't find their houses." Simmons wrote of another early resident, "Cecil J. Harris, 79, recalled that his mother, a domestic worker, bought an acre in 1945 and built a home out of used lumber. There was no gas. People kept propane tanks in their yard."[57]

Residents reflecting on Sun Village's history talked about how segregation was enforced during these early decades. Commenting to the *Los Angeles Times* in 1989, William Shaw explained, "Blacks couldn't live in Palmdale," and added that Palmdale residents "would tell you that directly to your face."[58] Bishop Henry

Hearns recounted moving to the Antelope Valley in 1965 to work at Edwards Air Force Base and coming face to face with the valley's strict segregation:

> There weren't that many people here, but Palmdale and Lancaster did not welcome African-Americans into the city. Not at all. So in the process of that, I started working out at Edwards and became the chief of the environmental office out there. Began to meet some of the white people who lived in Palmdale and Lancaster, some of the pastors who were white who pastored the churches in Palmdale and Lancaster and we became friends.
>
> So I was able to get in and out of those cities by the relationships I had with those people who were there. But the realtors would never send us to buy a house in Palmdale nor Lancaster because they knew you weren't welcome.

When asked how formal this system was, Hearns explained that realtors informally upholding white racism was sufficient to keep the region separate: "Well they knew what the conditions were in Palmdale and Lancaster. They just weren't going to send you there." But even if realtor steering appeared informal, Daniel Martinez HoSang notes that it was entrenched in the California Real Estate Association (CREA)'s Code of Ethics until 1951. The organizations' formal guidance to realtors in the state instructed realtors never to introduce to a neighborhood "a character of property or occupancy, members of any race or nationality, or any individual whose presence will clearly be detrimental to property values in the neighborhood."[59]

Another resident recalled her parents having to drive to and from Sun Village using back roads, because Black motorists would be shot at if seen driving on Highway 14. In a 1989 article about Sun Village, Sebastian Rotella described how dangerous it was for Black residents to drive through the white regions of the valley: "Another longtime resident, who worked at North American Aviation, the forerunner of Rockwell International, recalled an unpleasant ritual: County sheriff's deputies would stop and search his car regularly on Palmdale Boulevard as he headed for a midnight maintenance shift."[60] In another Sun Village retrospective, reporter Ann Simmons wrote, "Racial prejudice was rife in neighboring communities, where a black person could wait three hours to get served in a restaurant or store."[61]

In these conditions, Sun Village residents developed strong religious institutions, civic organizations, and civil rights mobilizations. These pathways wove together during the 1950s and 1960s. In 1950, Pastor R. E. Edwards opened the First Missionary Baptist Church in Sun Village, on 100th Street East. The church was known as "The Tent" as its first incarnation was as a wooden structure with a tent canopy. Edwards led the church until 1965 when Bishop Henry Hearns, the son of a Mississippi sharecropper, came to the valley to work at Edwards Air Force Base. Under Hearns, the church gained an educational building, and then in 1975 a new sanctuary on the site of the original church (with its cornerstone intact).

Today, with newer, larger buildings, it is known as the Living Stone Cathedral of Worship.

Bishop G. L. Talley, an early and longtime civic leader in Sun Village, was born in Texarkana, Arkansas, in 1918, moving to Los Angeles in 1939. After becoming a minister, he served in the war, and returned to become a barber. In 1951, he purchased land in Sun Village and moved there with his family. The *Antelope Valley Press* report on his life emphasized that Talley bought the land sight unseen, illustrating the distance involved in such a move, the difficulty of transit between the city and valley, and the risk that those moving were willing to take. Talley founded the Antelope Valley Church of God in Christ in 1952. It too operated from a home in its first years, before a church was built and opened in 1956. Talley later served as the first president of the Sun Village Chamber of Commerce. Also in 1956, Sun Village residents founded the African Methodist Episcopal Church (later called the St. John A.M.E. Church) in the home of Reverend and Mrs. X. C. Runyon.

Churches were not the only social institution to grow in the desert. In 1954, Sun Village residents, led by Bernyse Hunter, and including members such as Jesse Culver, founded the Sun Village Women's Club, both a social organization and a major force in building and improving Sun Village.[62] As a letter from the club to the California State Association of Colored Women's Clubs described, the group's early work was oriented around services and education for their children: "We were successful in getting some of our streets black-topped so that buses would come into our area to pick up our children. We were also successful in getting the first Negro teacher hired in the Keppel Union School District."[63]

This work securing resources and access for children was necessarily also the work of civil rights, another major focus of organizing in Sun Village. As Lee recalls, although Black students were allowed to enroll at Palmdale High School, children were not allowed to play there. So, the club turned to making its own park in Sun Village. Jessie Carroll, elected as president in 1957, led the effort to purchase several acres of land that would be given to the county for the construction of a public park, eventually completed in 1965.

THE JACKIE ROBINSON PARK

The Sun Village Women's Club focused on parks and public space as part of their broader efforts to secure educational access for children, resources such as paved roads and lighting for the area, and community building events for youth. Elected president of the Sun Village Women's Club in 1957, Jessie Carroll led an effort to acquire land and secure an agreement from the county to develop the land into a public park. The club held fundraisers, secured donations from Sun Village residents, and pooled together its own members' donations to acquire adjacent plots of land in the future park site. As it secured these parcels, it sold them to the county in coordination with County Supervisor Warren M. Dorn. In 1958, the county purchased four acres from the club and from Jessie and Bruce F. Carroll for a total of $4,025.[64] By 1960, they had expanded the site to nine acres, and with Dorn's support, the county had agreed to name the park after Jackie Robinson.[65] As the *Valley Times* reported,

> A nine-acre recreational site in the Sun Village area of Antelope Valley has been named Jackie Robinson Park in honor of the first Negro to break into major league baseball. The Board of Supervisors approved a motion made by Warren M. Dorn who said the name was suggested by the Sun Village Women's Club. 'It is fitting that Los Angeles County honor Jackie Robinson, who was born and educated here and who began his athletic career at Pasadena Junior College and UCLA,' Dorn said.[66]

This was to be the first park in the nation named in Robinson's honor, and it made for a sharp contrast with Robinson's own life history. In his autobiography, Robinson recalls white neighbors in his hometown of Pasadena calling the police on his family, signing petitions to attempt to remove them, and harassing him and his brother when they were outside their home.[67] In contrast to the park now planned in his honor, Robinson grew up with only limited access to public accommodations. Pasadena's Brookside Park had been gifted to the city by the family of Robert Owens, one of the most prominent Black landowners in the area during the 1800s. But the city segregated the park and limited Black residents to access its pool just one day a week, Wednesdays. Despite Betty Hill and Ethel Prioleau's pool desegregation victory in Los Angeles, Pasadena maintained its segregated pool until 1947.[68]

But just because the county had agreed to support a park in Sun Village did not mean it would be created. To force the issue, Jessie Carroll argued to the county supervisors that five hundred families and a total of one thousand children in Sun Village had no opportunities for organized recreation. Her persuasion led to the county approving $171,205 in construction funds in 1962. The groundbreaking took place on November 19, 1963, and construction lasted nearly two years.[69] The park, with community facilities, a children's playground designed with aerospace themes, open fields, and a baseball diamond, was completed and dedicated on June 16, 1965. The Los Angeles City Council voted unanimously to declare the day Jackie Robinson Day, and Robinson attended the dedication in Sun Village.

Soon, the park was in constant use. A schedule published in the *Antelope Valley Press* in 1966 shows time slots stretching from 9:00 a.m. on Monday to 7:00 p.m. on Sunday, filled with volleyball, table games, children's story hour, sewing and knitting classes, softball, archery, swimming trips, and arts and crafts.[70] Aerial photos taken in 1968 show the park as an oasis of greenery surrounded by tracts of desert dotted with Sun Village's homes.

In a 1970 retrospective, the Sun Village Women's Club's leaders wrote, "We are few in number to some of the clubs that belong to the National Association of

FIGURE 9. Sun Village Women's Club with Jackie Robinson and Supervisor Warren Dorn at the Jackie Robinson Park groundbreaking. Source: County of Los Angeles Department of Parks & Recreation.

Colored Women's Clubs, Inc. but with a president like Mrs. [Jessie] Carroll and with the determined few we have, we intend to live up to our motto, "Building as We Climb.'" The park they built in Sun Village remains a vital community institution today.

SUN VILLAGE'S CIVIL RIGHTS MOVEMENT

On June 27, 1956, the NAACP Board of Directors voted to charter the South Antelope Valley Branch of the NAACP, along with branches in Roselle, New Jersey, and Milton, West Virginia.[71] Of the twenty-four branches in Southern California, South Antelope Valley was the smallest. Records indicate that the branch had

FIGURE 10. Aerial View of Jackie Robinson Park, July 22, 1968. Source: County of Los Angeles Department of Parks & Recreation.

69 dues-paying members in its first year, then subsequently 73, 61, 22, 35, 135, and 112 in 1962. Its president was Lois Emma Prioleau Patton, the youngest child of Major George Washington and Ethel Prioleau.

As a child, she attended grade school in Los Angeles, and then started college at the University of Southern California in 1943, taking night classes so she could work as a clerk and typist during the day.[72] In 1947, she married Patrick N. Patton, a Lockheed employee working on aircraft assembly at its Burbank plant. But their story soon came to resemble that of Daisy and Oscar Gibson. When Patrick was transferred to Lockheed's Palmdale plant in 1954, the family attempted to move to Palmdale. Turned away, they purchased an acre in Sun Village.[73]

Following in her mother's footsteps, Lois applied for a teaching position at Keppel Union School in 1957 and became the second Black teacher ever hired there. While teaching at Keppel, she continued to finish her bachelor's degree, commuting to San Fernando Valley State College (now known as California State University Northridge), and eventually earning a master's degree from the University of La Verne. And she founded the South Antelope Valley chapter of the NAACP, serving as its president during much of the 1960s.

FIGURE 11. Lois Patton. Sources: Lancaster Museum of Art and History, Patton Family.

One of the first activities of the SAV-NAACP was to support NAACP organizing in Little Rock, Arkansas. Patton and Freedom Fund Drive chairwoman Mrs. Edward Turley helped the branch raise money for the NAACP's Freedom Fund. The chapter made the "Honor Roll of Branches Contributing to the Freedom Fund" in 1957 with a contribution of at least $100.[74] The branch also had a youth council with reports of roughly twenty or more participants during the late 1950s and early '60s. NAACP Field Secretary Althea T. L. Simmons visited the youth conference in late May, 1962.[75]

The *South Antelope Valley Press*, the main newspaper covering the region during these years, maintained a "news from" section with reports of activity from the area's smaller communities—places like Llano, Littlerock, Pearlblossom, and Quartz Hill. The reports covered the social and economic lives of residents of these areas, from the important to the mundane. By 1958, Sun Village residents had gotten their community included in the section, and for several years Sun Village's everyday happenings were included alongside that of other well-known and predominantly white areas of the valley. Maurice McGowan (also involved in the A.M.E. Church), wrote the first "News from Sun Village" columns, which were also written by Clifton L. Hightower, Mary Watkins, and Saleta Gibson. His earliest report in the paper covers a 1958 graduation ceremony organized by the Sun

Village Women's Club for the village's students who had graduated from Palmdale High School. The event was held in the First Missionary Baptist Church with Reverend Edwards as a speaker. Other reports in the column illustrated connections between Sun Village and Los Angeles, as residents traveled down to the city for church conventions, or invited speakers up to make presentations in Sun Village.

While many of the activities covered in the "News From Sun Village" section were implicitly political, the section soon began to include the town's much more explicit political work. The February 21, 1958, issue describes the Negro History Week organizing in progress, including a day of education and activities held at Reverend Edwards's First Missionary Baptist Church. The day centered around a talk by Professor Frank Whitley titled, "The History of Negro Advancement as a People." The next column on the page provides the first account of the South Antelope Valley (Sun Village) NAACP—congratulating the group on its 1957 fundraising for the NAACP Freedom Fund and conveying a thank-you from the chapter's president to community members who contributed. The next week's "News From Sun Village" feature told of the remainder of 1958's Negro History Week, including a program on the lives of singer Marian Anderson and diplomat Ralph Bunche, and the recitation of Paul Laurence Dunbar's poetry. In 1962, another Negro History Week report recounted a teach-in by South Antelope Valley NAACP leaders Walter Spiva and Patrick Patton at the Community Methodist Church in Lancaster. The paper reported that "topics of discussion were on national sit-ins, Freedom Riders, and the local problems of minority groups in the Antelope Valley."[76] These reports illustrated how Sun Village's community building was transforming into a struggle to desegregate the region, a struggle which brought the local NAACP into the larger Civil Rights Movement.

In the organization's 1960 appeal to the U.S. Commission on Civil Rights, Housing Chairman Patrick N. Patton described a three-part fulcrum of racial apartheid facing Black residents: education, employment, and housing segregation. He reported that Lancaster and Palmdale had been closed to Black residents, workers, and students.[77] First, his memo noted how realtors worked with lenders to exclude Black purchasers from the market, explaining, "The realtors have an agreement among themselves not to sell to Negroes, they are also in an agreement with the financial institutions that they are not to approve a Negroes credit." The memo noted that this forced some to move back to Los Angeles, but others who wanted to stay in the valley experienced racial steering, which also created segregated schooling. "Every realtor refers all Negroes to a place called Sun-Village. . . . This condition causes all of the elementary school age Negroes to report to two schools which are located in Littlerock, Calif." Finally, Patton noted that the system was ingrained by restrictive covenants, meaning it would persist indefinitely unless changed. "We also know that in the sales contract that there is a clause stating that they can not resell to Negroes." He added, "The intensity of this condition is becoming alarmingly worse."

FIGURE 12. Patrick N. Patton does flush riveting on a P-38 wing jig at Lockheed Aircraft Corporation in Burbank. Source: Housing Authority Collection/Los Angeles Public Library.

In response, the South Antelope Valley NAACP engaged in a decade-long fight to integrate education, secure fair employment practices, and end residential segregation, efforts that, while not fully successful, would transform the Antelope Valley.

The report's focus on education, employment, and housing was mirrored by the organization's work in the decade to follow. Starting with education, the South

Antelope Valley NAACP recognized that because effective racial segregation required both segregated housing and segregated schools, the work of segregating the Antelope Valley required the construction of schools within Black neighborhoods. This would preclude Black students from attending schools in farther-away white neighborhoods, and allow them to be given worse educations if the schools were disparately funded. The Keppel Union School Board, faced with a growing Black population within one part of its mostly white district, tried just such a tactic to ensure that Sun Village's children could not attend school in Palmdale and Lancaster. The proposal involved the use of a bond measure to fund the school's construction, but the bond required a public vote. The South Antelope Valley NAACP encouraged voters to reject the bond to prevent the advancement of segregated schooling. A report on their activities in 1963 described a first victory in this campaign: "A proposed bond issue to build a junior high school in Littlerock (Keppel Union School District) failed this week. NAACP branch officials have opposed the proposed location of the school on the grounds that it would result in a de facto segregated school."

The NAACP defeated the bond measure twice, and as a result, the board was pushed to respond to Sun Village residents who made clear that the plans would entrench segregation in the valley. As Althea Simmons noted in her 1963 West Coast Regional report:

> The Citizens Fact Finding Committee, organized after the second defeat of a bond issue which will be used to build a school that NAACP claims would be a de facto segregated one, submitted a report to the School Board stating that: ' . . . ultimately the district must choose between a system of segregated schools, or spending extra money for transportation or build more tiny 'half' (schools without cafeteria, library, multi-purpose room or sheltered play area) schools ringing the Negro area.'

The board chose segregation, attempting the bond again in 1964. This time it made the NAACP the villain of the campaign, and the tactic worked. The Superintendent of the Keppel Union School District published a 2-column 18-inch appeal in the local press urging citizens not to "let NAACP deprive your children of an education." That appeal had more sway than the NAACP's argument that the district's plan would result in the de facto segregation of the region's schooling. The NAACP lost the vote 653 to 254. The Board's assurances that it favored integration and that it could use busing to promote integration in the future if needed did little to assuage civil rights concerns.[78]

These concerns were well-founded, and they extended beyond education into struggles to achieve Black economic power in a series of employment battles in the valley. While the Antelope Valley's economy was growing through agriculture, aerospace, and defense contractor employment, the vibrant Los Angeles labor movement also took the opportunity to unionize workplaces across the valley. A 1952 report by the California Federal of Labor noted that "due to the increased building activity in the Antelope Valley area, the Council has established a branch office in the Palmdale-Lancaster area where many contracts have been signed, and the membership of the local unions has increased considerably by the organizing activities through the Lancaster office."[79]

By 1956, the federation reported that "95 per cent of the building in this valley at present is union," and reported the existence of Carpenters, Painters, Lathers and Teamsters Unions, as well as unionization campaigns by the Typographical Union, Butchers, Clerks, Barbers, Culinary Workers, Building Services, and Machinists (who were organizing at Lockheed, North American, Northrop and Convair).[80] By 1957, federation reports treated the region as a labor stronghold, writing that "Activities in the Antelope Valley area continue full scale, with organizing efforts by the several service trades as well as the building trades." After noting that union representatives had roles in highway planning for the valley, the federation concluded that, "This previously farm and ranch area is rapidly becoming an urban area, and is accepting the philosophy of organized labor readily. . . ."[81]

By the 1960s, however, the Antelope Valley remained a two-tiered economy that either excluded or subordinated Black workers. Organizing against this systematic economic segregation became an important part of the South Antelope Valley NAACP's work. Herbert Hill, national labor secretary of the NAACP, was invited to Palmdale to speak about civil rights on September 27, 1963.[82] He fell ill and was replaced by Max Mont, the representative for the West Coast Labor Committee of the NAACP and the West Coast Executive Director of the Jewish Labor Committee. Mont, on behalf of Hill, urged workers in the valley to report discrimination on the job to Hill and the NAACP's Los Angeles office.[83] This information-gathering was put to good use, as the South Antelope Valley NAACP was able to pressure aerospace companies to promote Black employees. Noting that "The President's Executive Order forbidding discrimination in hiring or upgrading by firms engaged in governmental contracts has not been implemented by effective enforcement procedures," Simmons reported that NAACP branches had to individually pressure firms to hire and promote Black workers. Through this strategy, Simmons wrote, South Antelope Valley NAACP had been able "to get eight Negroes upgraded to lead men on the B-70 program" whereas previously there had only been one, and secured promotions from B to A mechanics for 150 additional Black workers.[84] Every job counted—Simmons's reports to the national office sometimes included reports of single hires in important circumstances, such as a Black secretary being hired at a bank in Quartz Hill.

While the Pattons helped lead employment desegregation work through the SAV-NAACP, they, like the Prioleaus in the prior generation, made the work a family affair. One of the Pattons' children, David, recounted how his parents involved him in a campaign against employment segregation in the valley when he was a junior at Palmdale High School. One evening his parents told him to apply for a job at the local supermarket, Shopping Bag. Lois and Patrick had just come home from a Palmdale Chamber of Commerce meeting where the SAV-NAACP had issued a warning that they would organize a boycott of the local businesses unless they began employing more minorities. Shopping Bag's hiring manager had been in attendance, and the Pattons wanted to see if the warning swayed him; like most businesses in the valley, Shopping Bag had few if any Black workers. David got the job.

Over the next several decades, pressure on the valley's major industries to hire Black employees, promote and pay them fairly, and end workplace discrimination and harassment would continue. But these efforts would be exceeded by the larger fight against residential segregation that the South Antelope Valley NAACP fought through the 1960s. Their work included documenting their circumstances, attempting to break the color line in the Antelope Valley, and advocating for state and federal fair housing legislation, namely California's 1963 Rumford Fair Housing Act and the federal 1968 Fair Housing Act.

The Pattons became the first family to break the Antelope Valley's color line in 1962. Risking abuse and violence, and with the help of a Black realtor, the Pattons purchased a home in Palmdale in 1962. Although few written histories of Sun Village or the South Antelope Valley NAACP exist, this moment is consistently reported in them and cited as a moment that began to change the balance of power in the valley. Lois would continue to serve in the SAV-NAACP, teach at Keppel, and sing in the church choir with Patrick.

But the Pattons' individual success could not be scaled up in the face of broad structures of racial discrimination and economic inequality. The SAV-NAACP joined the statewide NAACP campaign to pass Byron Rumford's Fair Housing Bill. The "Letters for AB 1240" campaign engaged local branches in efforts to push the state assembly to pass the measure. While branches in the city were securing community organizations' endorsements and presenting at the UAW's statewide labor conference, SAV-NAACP organized letters from Sun Village. Simmons's 1963 report about branch activities praised the chapter's "commendable" role in the campaign.[85]

The fair housing campaign proved partly successful. Republicans gutted the bill through an amendment that exempted single-family homes; the final law applied mostly to large apartment buildings and public housing. But its passage on September 20, 1963, represented an important step along a trajectory of desegregation, strengthening past legislation and complementing efforts in other areas like employment. Immediately thereafter, in October 1963, Fred Carter, a consultant for the Fair Employment Practices Commission, visited the Antelope Valley to explain the Rumford Fair Housing Act and how it related to Black households in the area.

But opportunities to capitalize on the Rumford Act were short-lived. As the next chapter will describe, the law would be temporarily overturned by 1964's Proposition 14, and it would take until 1966 for Proposition 14 to be ruled unconstitutional, and 1968 for Congress to supersede Rumford with the stronger Fair Housing Act. Nevertheless, as the sixties progressed, Black residents increasingly dispersed through the Antelope Valley while continuing to press for social and economic advancement. These developments unsettled the valley's decades-long spatially organized power structure, and necessitated a period of re-organization.

Amidst all the records of organizing against Jim Crow in the desert, an update related to policing appeared in a February 1963 compendium of NAACP West Coast Regional Branch Reports. Ten incidents of police brutality had been reported to the NAACP in Los Angeles. And three had been reported in the Antelope Valley, with SAV-NAACP responding by requesting official investigations of the matters.[86] While the monthly reports do not convey details of the incidents or counter-organizing, they show that this mechanism of subordination, which would come to be the main fulcrum of inequality in the valley, had always been present. In the next chapter, I trace the valley's myriad efforts to preserve its social hierarchies, and to ensure that desegregation would not equate to desubordination. While not always successful, these efforts broadened conservative politics to touch on more spheres of life in the latter half of the twentieth century. Over time, these campaigns of violence and institutionalized discrimination would coalesce into policing. Policing would come to manage the valley's transformation from a hierarchy based on spatial exclusion to one based on subordination amid inclusion. Yet, as this book will trace, the institutions built by the SAV-NAACP and Sun Village Women's Club would remain vital and present in the struggles yet to come.

2

———

Redeeming the Right to Discriminate

Take a day and walk around
Watch the Nazis run your town
Then go home and check yourself
You think we're singing 'bout someone else?

—FRANK ZAPPA, "PLASTIC PEOPLE"

COVENANTS

In 1946, Pastor Wesley A. Swift endorsed the Ku Klux Klan in a speech to the American Legion in Big Bear Lake, a small resort town near the Antelope Valley, where a series of cross burnings had recently taken place and from which five Black residents had recently been "run out."[1] Swift was a political figure who bridged the right's pro-Nazi period in the 1940s and its Ku Klux Klan era in the 1960s, and whose ideas and disciples would shape the right's violent and separatist strains from the 1970s on. As a pastor, he established a church in the valley where he developed the gospel of Christian Identity, today recognizable as Christian Nationalism.

"'The Klan is here in Bear Valley to stay," Swift told the veterans' group. "We intend to form restrictive covenants, here and elsewhere, in order to hold the line of pure Americanism."[2] But the line of "pure Americanism"—a term he borrowed from the Klan—was breaking.[3] Restrictive covenants would soon be rendered unenforceable, the Fair Housing Act would pass, and the valley would find it harder and harder to exclude Black residents.

And yet sixty-five years after Swift's speech, legal scholar Priscilla Ocen would write that the Antelope Valley had invented a new form of the racially restrictive covenant, as Black tenants in the Housing Choice Voucher program were systematically ousted from their homes. V. Jesse Smith recounted this historical transition in a similar way: "In Sun Village they were blatant, they were open about it. It was quite explicit, we don't want you here. In Section 8, they tried to do it through legislation, and tried to use crime as a new form of segregation." As Ocen writes, the system worked through "police officers and public officials enforcing private citizens' discriminatory complaints," a system that functionally "excludes Black women and their children from publicly subsidized housing in traditionally white neighborhoods."[4]

My goal in this chapter is to explain how the valley traversed the path from the era of the old racially restrictive covenant to the era of the new. To do this, I focus on what happened after the Sun Village NAACP broke through the line of residential segregation that served as the basis for the valley's system of apartheid. Although their wealth was the product of massive but temporary military investment, the valley's white residents saw the prospect of racial integration as the biggest threat to their way of life. Civil rights and fair housing meant sharing the valley's economy: Black residents could not be relegated to the valley's worst jobs as easily as before, neighborhoods could not remain entirely white and reap property value gains based on that exclusion, and educational institutions could not rely on residential segregation to keep public schools segregated. When fair housing began to take hold, it did not just break the valley's system of residential segregation; it represented a devaluing of white property and an abrogation of white property rights.

The 1960s saw the valley's white polity win repeatedly in electoral efforts to oppose fair housing but suffer loss after loss as those votes were nullified by courts and, eventually, the 1968 Fair Housing Act. It is in this context that Wesley Swift proselytized an existential fight for white supremacy. His sermons assured listeners that they were right to oppose race mixing, and his embrace of violence offered a different, and perhaps more promising, way of keeping Black residents out of white neighborhoods. In the years after the Fair Housing Act, the valley's white polity sought to regain its position through institutional discrimination, symbolic claims to supremacy, and periods of intense violence, inculcated by leaders like Swift. Yet none of this was enough to restore the valley's hierarchies.

Over time, though, these disparate, grasping attempts to reassert the valley's hierarchies gave way to participatory forms of policing that allowed everyday residents of the valley to join in the work of surveilling, policing, and ultimately evicting their Black neighbors. Through these policies and practices, white polities transformed the right to exclude from a right expressed through market discrimination to a right expressed through policing. Policing synthesized the mob violence of Swift with the policy violence of CREA, the California Real Estate Association. In this way white residents of the valley rebuilt the symbolic value of property and re-established their full sense of property rights. As the conclusion of the chapter argues, the rise of participatory policing highlights not only the role of policing in racial segregation but the value of policing as a form of property, something to be used to denigrate and remove Black neighbors. Governing housing through crime has become a key way to reestablish hierarchies threatened by desegregation in housing.

THE FOUNTAINHEAD

Wesley A. Swift was born in New Jersey in 1913, the son of Methodist minister R. C. Swift. He was to follow in his father's footsteps, and he became a Methodist clergyman by the time he was eighteen. But in the early 1930s, he left the Methodist Church and New Jersey as well, moving to Echo Park in Los Angeles and eventually joining the nearby Angelus Temple, part of Aimee Semple McPherson's Foursquare Pentecostal church.[5] There he encountered British-Israelism, a set of beliefs that mixed white supremacy with religious predetermination, as well as religious and political figures like Charles Parham and Gerald Winrod who espoused it.[6] In time, Swift would transform British-Israelism from an obscure and fringe concept into what he called Christian Identity theology, a precursor to and influence on contemporary Christian Nationalism. Christian Identity espoused the idea that white Christians were locked in an apocalyptic struggle against Jews and their non-white allies in the United States and around the world—a formulation that has remained a powerful ingredient of right-wing politics in the decades after Swift's passing.[7] Over time, Swift began to expound on these ideas and develop Christian Identity into a popular and robust religious platform that would gain traction around the country and influence the American right for decades.

Although Los Angeles was a hotbed of Ku Klux Klan activity, Swift turned to the region's fringes to establish his ministry and political base.[8] By 1946, he had established the Church of Jesus Christ-Christian in Lancaster, where he would preach the ideas of Christian Identity for the rest of his life. The valley offered him a site in which to transform a religious strain of white supremacy into a playbook for violence. From the valley, he organized local Klan members into violence, traveled to Los Angeles to extol white supremacy, campaigned with local antisemitic and anti-communist politicians, and taped sermons to be distributed around the country. Mentored by Gerald L. K. Smith, Swift bridged important eras of white supremacist politics, mentoring in turn key figures in the white power movement of the 1970s and 1980s such as William Potter Gale, who founded the Posse Comitatus, and Richard Grint Butler, who inherited Swift's church and moved it to Idaho, where he started a violent white separatist movement. But as important as Swift was, he cannot be fully understood outside the context of the valley's larger fight for racial segregation.

Swift's Big Bear Lake endorsement of the Klan was soon noticed by California Attorney General Robert Kenny, who began an investigation aimed at shutting down the organization. Although Kenny found that Swift had been purchasing

FIGURE 13. Reverend Wesley Swift, April 12, 1946. Source: Bettmann via Getty Images.

weapons for nearly a decade, he did not find grounds to prosecute or otherwise penalize Swift. But the investigation did reveal that a sheriff's deputy had been serving as a bodyguard for Swift and his mentor, Gerald L. K. Smith. The association of police and white supremacists was deeply revealing, but so too was the Swift-Smith connection.

By the 1940s, Swift had become a regular figure preaching at local churches; by the '50s, his sermons were advertised in local papers. The sermons were viciously racist. Charlotta Bass's paper, *The California Eagle*, reported on one attendee, Ranita Whitney, who was assaulted by Swift protégé William Potter Gale as she was thrown out of the event after standing up to Swift and denouncing his racism.[9] Meanwhile, Smith had been a devotee of Huey Long and developed his supremacist ideas during his involvement with Long's political movement. After Long's death, Smith turned to recreating the America First Committee as the America First Party. He began a national magazine called *The Cross and the Flag*, and eventually took over Father Charles Coughlin's radio broadcasts. The two would pair up to push white supremacist politics in Los Angeles and beyond.

One key tactic that Swift and Smith employed was to intervene in national political issues. In the 1944 congressional elections, when liberal actress Helen Gahagan Douglas first ran for Congress in Los Angeles, Smith and Swift campaigned against her. Local Democratic party organizer Alvin P. Meyers recalled their campaign telling voters "You can't elect this woman that sleeps with a Jew," referring to her husband, Melvyn Douglas.[10] Douglas prevailed, but similar tactics would eventually help Richard Nixon defeat her Senate campaign in 1950.[11]

After the Douglas experience, Swift and Smith broadened their ambitions, contributing to McCarthyist Red Scare politics at the national level. In the 1940s, Swift founded the Anti-Communist League, and through it he helped instigate an investigation of Defense Department appointee Anna Rosenberg in 1950, accusing her of membership in the Communist Party's John Reed Club. Swift and Smith travelled to Washington, meeting with Mississippi Congressman John Rankin and pushing testimony against Rosenberg in the Armed Services Committee. The effort ultimately failed when the evidence presented against her began to fall apart and the key witness recanted.[12] The pair tried a similar playbook again in 1954, submitting testimony encouraging the Senate Judiciary Committee to reject Earl Warren's appointment as Chief Justice of the Supreme Court due to his laxity on communism.[13] Swift was reportedly the first person to testify at the committee's hearing.[14] Though their efforts proved unpersuasive, they gained news coverage and helped drag out Warren's confirmation, presaging the contemporary pattern of contentious confirmation battles.

In 1946, Smith and Swift relocated to Lancaster, where they founded paramilitary organizations the Christian Defense League and the California Rangers. They used Lancaster as a home base of sorts, traveling first to Los Angeles to give speeches extolling antisemitism and white supremacy, and then across the country.[15] Swift soon visited Utah, urging audiences to purchase guns and follow the lead of those in Los Angeles, where he claimed that twenty thousand men were ready to aid in a war against communists.[16] His growing profile helped him raise $10,000 from various white Christian organizations in 1949.[17] Throughout the 1940s, with help from Smith, Swift gave speeches in Northern California, Cleveland, Denver, and Minneapolis.

The pair continued to test their political power. In the 1950s, Smith and Swift became the beneficiaries of California State Senator Jack Tenney, the chair of the state's Un-American Activities Committee. Tenney was using his state and local platforms to espouse antisemitism and anti-communism. He was perhaps the most prominent public figure broadcasting ideas of a piece with the Christian Identity movement. To support his re-election campaign in 1954, Smith organized a meeting of another of his organizations, the Christian Nationalist Crusade. Swift chaired the meeting, and the two invited Tenney to be its featured speaker.[18] Over six hundred people were in attendance. Tenney lost his party primary, but in doing so had grown Smith and Swift's audience immensely.[19]

By the 1960s, Swift was a national figure. He had a weekly radio show in Los Angeles called "Crusade for Christ," and spoke frequently at the Embassy Auditorium in Downtown Los Angeles and the Hollywood Womens' Club. Wealthy businessman James Oviatt, a former member of the John Birch Society, gifted Swift's "Christian Defense League" with office space in his downtown building, from which Swift sent mailers and fundraised.[20] A 1965 investigation by Los Angeles radio station KLAC summarized Swift's new stature as follows:

> Swift's church is not, we've found, the only source of extremist thought, but is generally regarded by those of the Klan mentality to be purest . . . the very gospel. His mixture of biblical and historical distortion . . . fortune-telling and star-gazing, coupled with a smattering of legitimate conservative politics, and rolled from a silver tongue has become, as we said earlier . . . the fountainhead for extremist thought and action in California.[21]

While his public profile grew, Swift remained involved in the politics of the valley. In October of 1963, in Lancaster, Swift presided over the first meeting of the Christian Knights of the Invisible Empire (CKIE).[22] At the meeting, where thirty-eight members were admitted to the group, Swift explained that the organization was for all intents and purposes the same as the Klan but was operating under a different name because the Klan had been outlawed in California.[23] On November 5, CKIE met to discuss plans to burn down a television store operated by a Black businessman in Quartz Hill, just outside Lancaster. The shop, Wilson's TV Sales Service, was burned down using Molotov cocktails five days later.[24]

Swift's influence began to reach Los Angeles as well. Keith Gilbert, a Minuteman who had attended Swift's sermons, led a cell plotting to assassinate Martin Luther King, Jr., when he visited the city in 1965 on a tour that would include a public speech at the Hollywood Palladium. Gilbert's associates were arrested the day before King was to give the speech. The arrests led police to Gilbert's home, where they found 1,400 pounds of explosives that the group had stolen and planned to use to assassinate King while he spoke at the Palladium. Gilbert, already awaiting trial for the attempted murder of a Black man in 1964, escaped police custody.[25] He would eventually be convicted of stealing the explosives and spend five years in San Quentin before moving to Idaho to join Swift's successor movement, the Aryan Nation, led by Richard Grint Butler.[26]

Other Swift associates carried his influence farther across the country. Reverend Conrad "Connie" Lynch, of San Bernardino, whom Swift had ordained as a Christian Identity Minister and who served as a minister in Swift's Church of Jesus Christ-Christian, left Southern California to fight the Civil Rights Movement head on in the South.[27] Founding the National States Rights Party, Lynch became a leader of the Ku Klux Klan's prolonged violent campaigns against civil rights organizing in St. Augustine, Florida.[28] The *Washington Post* reported that

Lynch's speeches helped fuel nightly waves of Klan violence against the NAACP.[29] Swift also inspired J. B. Stoner, a Klan member who shadowed King throughout the South, leading rallies against the civil rights leader at his stops. As a young man he re-established the KKK in Chattanooga, Tennessee, and he later went on to serve in the leadership of the National States Rights Party. As the *New York Times* reported in his obituary, his philosophy was inspired by Wesley Swift.[30] In 1958 Stoner bombed the Bethel Baptist Church (led by Reverend Fred Shuttlesworth) in Birmingham, Alabama. Stoner would go on to serve on King assassin James Earl Ray's legal team.

Over time, Swift would increasingly shift strategy to focus on his national reach. By 1964, he had turned over leadership of CKIE to William Potter Gale, a retired army colonel who had served in the Philippines and returned to the United States an active white supremacist. Gale would take Swift's ideas around Christian Identity and fuse them with anti-tax ideas on the American right, founding the Posse Comitatus. Unburdened by the CKIE, Swift turned to recording and distributing his sermons. Although he had traveled across the South to rally against civil rights and his acolytes continued spreading his ideas throughout the region, mass-distributing his sermons proved to be a much more effective mode of influence. FBI files on Swift include numerous incident reports in which suspected white supremacists arrested in the South were found in possession of Swift's tapes.

Sam Bowers, the leader of the White Knights of the Ku Klux Klan, was reported to have "listened to Wesley Smith's Christian Identity tapes in Mississippi." Bowers was one of the key perpetrators of the 1963 murders of James Chaney, Andrew Goodman, and Michael Schwerner. Bowers's disciple in the White Knights, Thomas Tarrants, partnered with fellow Klan member Kathy Ainsworth to attempt a bombing of a Jewish synagogue in 1968. Ainsworth "had listened to Swift's tapes in her roommate's Mississippi home."[31] The two were confronted by the FBI, which killed Ainsworth and injured Tarrants, who went on to repent for his participation in the Klan. Swift's long reach from Southern California to the Southern United States was a sort of perverse parallel to the SAV-NAACP's efforts to fundraise for the Mississippi Freedom Fund. In the decades to come, Swift and his ideas would continue to carry weight on the American right, and his recordings continue to circulate online today.

FAIR HOUSING PREVAILS

While the Klan used physical violence to "hold the line of pure Americanism," the California Real Estate Association used the law. In 1948 business and real estate interests had successfully stopped the first Proposition 14, which would have driven state funds towards public housing construction. It then passed Article 34, which added new barriers to building public housing anywhere in the state. Now, conservative forces in the Antelope Valley played those notes again in their 1960s fights to preserve the right for property owners to discriminate against tenants and purchasers.[32]

As reported by the *Antelope Valley Press*, in 1963 CREA president L. H. Wilson gave a talk in which he declared, "It is time to launch a new crusade—a crusade for freedom to rescue the rights of the new 'forgotten man.' The cold war over discrimination has passed him by."[33] He continued, "Militant minorities have organized and vocalized for 'equal rights' . . . until 'equal rights' have almost become 'special privilege' and this forgotten man lies neglected. He is the great, patient, passive majority, the working majority that pays for expensive government. He is the American small property owner."

Wilson went on to introduce a campaign for a Property Owner's Bill of Rights, intended to head off the Rumford Act (California's 1963 statewide fair housing law) before it was passed. That the response to a ban on discrimination was to assert that property rights were being diminished is to concede that racial discrimination was an essential part of the white conception of property rights. The rights CREA outlined included a number of unobjectionable and uncontested demands—the right to choose your own friends, for example—but also clauses starting that property owners should have the right to discriminate in the sale or rental of their properties. That the right to discriminate could not be forthrightly stated is an indication of the defensive nature of white politics by the 1960s. Yet as the Rumford bill came closer to a vote, its opponents' complaints grew louder and clearer. Writing in the *San Bernardino County Sun*, David Lawrence suggested that banning discrimination was not just a diminishment of property rights, but actually constituted a confiscation of property itself: "The Constitution plainly says that no person shall be deprived of his property without due process of law, 'nor shall private property be taken for public use, without just compensation.' Do the suggested restrictions mean that if the government supervises the sale of property, it is, in effect, 'seizing' private homes?"[34]

The Rumford Act passed anyway. Not long after it did, CREA president Arthur S. Leitch spoke to a regional audience of realtors including more than two dozen from the Antelope Valley. On behalf of CREA, he warned that the state would be "set back 50 years" if the Rumford Fair Housing Act was allowed to stand, whipping up support for a new Proposition 14 that would overturn it in defense of individual rights—not the right to purchase or rent housing, but to rent or sell it in a discriminatory manner. Proposition 14 had taken elements of CREA's crude Property Owner's Bill of Rights and turned it into legislative language securing property owners' unfettered rights to discriminate.

In advocating for Proposition 14, CREA leaders repeated the association between discrimination and rights. In a letter to the editor responding to an earlier column published in the *Los Gatos Times/Saratoga Observer* in April 1964, Shelley Williams, the president of the Los Gatos-Saratoga Board of Realtors, wrote, "In your judgment, the CREA initiative places property values over human values.

In our judgment, owning and disposing of property, in a free society, is a human right."[35] These words illuminate the conjoined nature of racism and capitalism in the context of housing markets. The ability to dispose of property (that is, to sell it) is one of the characteristics that helps define something as property, and so when a realtor exalts that right and demands it be unfettered by anti-discrimination law, that represents the inscription of discrimination as a property right. Thus, to limit a property owner's ability to racially discriminate was to diminish their property and its market value. Though Proposition 14 was often framed in non-racial terms or as a response to "forced" housing, its genesis illustrates that discrimination was fundamental to white property rights. Williams's claim exposes the reality that no group that viewed the right to discriminate as of paramount importance could simply accept the loss of that right without a fight.

The South Antelope Valley NAACP countered CREA's Proposition 14 campaign with their own organizing. In May, the Southern Area Conference of the NAACP met in Littlerock to map out organizing plans. Ruby Williams, the Pasadena NAACP leader, visited the Unitarian-Universalist Fellowship of the Antelope Valley to speak on civil rights,[36] while campaigners took out an ad in the *South Antelope Valley Press* tabled for 'No on Prop 14' at the Antelope Valley Fair, and organized an essay contest whose prizes included a typewriter and personal letter of congratulations from Governor Edmund Brown.[37] And in October, Sun Village NAACP held a voting workshop in advance of the November election.

The first Proposition 14 had ended in a 2–1 defeat of the pro-public housing referendum. Now, the second ended with CREA having nullified the Rumford Fair Housing Act by a 2–1 margin.[38] The measure passed with 65 percent of the vote statewide, and 67 percent of the vote in Los Angeles County. But in Palmdale, voters approved the measure by an even greater landslide, with 79 percent in favor.[39]

CREA then turned to battling the legal challenges to Proposition 14 that rapidly emerged. The *Antelope Valley Press* reported that between its passage in November 1964 and May 1965, CREA was fighting eight legal challenges to Proposition 14, and warning of a ninth. In July, the paper printed CREA's opposition to comments made by the State Fair Employment Practices Commission that challenged CREA's practices of including racially restrictive housing listings in its real estate listing services.[40] As the legal challenges mounted, CREA floated new ideas like a new initiative more directly aimed at overturning the Rumford Fair Housing Act.

Ultimately, Proposition 14 was overturned by the California Supreme Court in 1966. CREA reacted by petitioning the Supreme Court to review the ruling,[41] formally endorsing another initiative to repeal the Rumford Act in 1966,[42] and urging the California Attorney General to weigh in with the court as well.[43] Meanwhile, local realtors mobilized to stop fair housing legislation at the federal level. The Civil Rights Bill of 1966, which principally sought to defend civil rights workers from violence in the South, was effectively killed in the Senate over its fair housing provision (a national version of the Rumford Act).[44] In fall 1966 Joe Rodgers, head of the Property Owners Division of the Antelope Valley Board of Realtors, led a fundraising drive to support the National Association of Real Estate Boards (NAREB)'s campaign to prevent the fair housing provision from being raised in the next congressional session.[45]

Sun Village residents spent those years fighting for the right to live anywhere in the valley while also continuing to build Sun Village. In 1964, the Sun Village Chamber of Commerce began recruiting investors to build $8,000–$10,000 homes ($66,500 in 2020 dollars) in the subdivision.[46] The low-cost homes were envisioned in circular plots with space for a children's playground and swimming pool—amenities Black residents of the Antelope Valley had historically been denied. In 1965, after years of effort, Sun Village residents succeeded in getting Los Angeles County to install streetlights at thirty-seven Sun Village intersections.[47] Jackie Robinson Park opened to fanfare in 1965 and was running full schedules of public events soon thereafter. In a report to the Chamber of Commerce at the start of 1967, Daisy Gibson noted that Sun Village had built more homes in 1966 than in 1965 and had very few vacancies. Other homes were being remodeled, and additional water mains had been installed to extend municipal services to new residents. The growing population of Sun Village, approximately two thousand at the time,[48] needed improved roads. The Chamber planned to spend 1967 focused on that issue, and continuing to build up social services, including Head Start programs. At Jackie Robinson Park, the Chamber had gotten crosswalks installed to increase pedestrian safety, and begun adult literacy and math programs as well.

The period of community flourishing was not restricted to Sun Village. Beginning as early as 1967, the Antelope Valley American Indian League (AVAIL), led by Marion Rawlinson, began organizing regional powwows, with participants and attendees coming from as far east as Daggett, as far north as Barstow, and as far south as Los Angeles. Events were held at "Totem Pole Ranch" in Littlerock, less than ten miles south of Sun Village.[49] Reports on the events appeared in the *Navajo Times* in the late 1960s and early 1970s, and included description of aid efforts organized at the powwows for Native communities across the region.[50] In 1968, Rawlinson would testify to the Public Forum Before the Committee on Urban Indians in Los Angeles, California, of the National Council on Indian Opportunity, insisting that resources be immediately provisioned to support Native communities in the valley and beyond.[51]

These steps, however, weighed against larger political headwinds against civil rights and social services. Although the courts had struck Proposition 14, its passage by overwhelming margins was unforgettable. In a February 1967 address to the Sun Village NAACP, Mrs. Tarea Pittman, the NAACP's national Special Contribution Fund Director, decried "trouble" in the Antelope Valley and California, warning of Governor Ronald Reagan's cutbacks to social spending in high-poverty areas and his call for the repeal of the Rumford Fair Housing Act. And she reminded her audience that the state's electorate had voted overwhelmingly against civil rights in the Proposition 14 fight.[52]

Pittman's warnings were prescient. In October, at CREA's statewide convention held at the First Methodist Church in Los Angeles, the organization announced its push to get the state legislature to repeal the Rumford Act and replace it with a commission which would supposedly remedy racial discrimination in housing through education and counseling. Governor Reagan keynoted the convention, opening his talk by reaffirming the "human rights" of all people "regardless of race, color, religion or creed." Reagan went on to say, "Make no mistake about it. There are no such things as property rights in the connection used by some. There are only human rights and some of those human rights are the rights involving property. These rights affect all our citizens, regardless of their color, their race or their social status."[53] Reagan went on to reaffirm his opposition to the Rumford Fair Housing Act, situating it as an expression of a consistent principle of respect for property rights rather than a preference for racial discrimination, but spent much of his speech warning CREA that it would not be easy to repeal, only to claw back one inch at a time.

How far CREA and Reagan would have gotten with these efforts to repeal the Rumford Act or render it toothless is unknown. The assassination of Martin Luther King, Jr., on April 4 sent shockwaves through American society, temporarily demobilizing opposition to civil rights. CREA announced on April 7 that it would not pursue a new initiative to repeal Rumford. The fair housing provisions that had been stalled in 1966 were reintroduced and voted on within days. Although the Fair Housing Act passed by a large margin in the House, the Antelope Valley's congressional representative, Ed Reinecke, was one of fourteen Republicans from California's congressional delegation to vote against the bill. Reinecke issued a statement reading in part:

> I favor meaningful civil rights legislation but the time has come when we must stop kidding our minority populations. The new Civil Rights Bill, hastily strong-armed through the unusual house vote yesterday, contained many, many imperfections, particularly concerning the open housing clauses, which perhaps could have been purified in a House-Senate conference. . . . House members deserve the right to give the important matter their thoughtful consideration and suggestions outside the atmosphere of riot and unrest.[54]

President Johnson signed the bill on April 11. In the span of a week white property owners saw their worlds turn upside down. Federal law now prohibited the use and disposition of property in ways that were fundamental to their established understanding of property itself. The Antelope Valley re-elected Reinecke in 1968, and Reagan appointed him Lieutenant Governor of California in 1969. Reinecke's political career ended after he was convicted of perjury related to the Watergate scandal in 1974, but his vote against the Fair Housing Act was an indicator of the local politics of the Antelope Valley.

As the 1960s ended, CREA moved on to the new political touchstones of the right—its Make America Better program focused on fearmongering about urban crime, poor schools, and high taxes.[55] The Antelope Valley Board of Realtors made peace publicly with fair housing, blaming property owners and real estate agents for not getting the message that fair housing was the law of the land.

Other evidence seemed to confirm a change. Lynole Williams, who grew up on Edwards Air Force Base, recalled to me that in the 1980s Black children and families from the base would come to the cities to buy groceries, shop, and eat. When they were mistreated or denied service in the cities, the Air Force would threaten local businesses with an informal boycott. "The military base basically told them, okay, you mistreat ours, they're not coming shopping, they're not getting gas . . . our people aren't coming and they know that if our people aren't coming . . . this little town is going to dry up." The next decade saw more examples of progress. Bishop Henry Hearns was elected to the Lancaster City Council in 1990 and became the city's first Black mayor in 1991.

WHITE POLITICS IN DISARRAY

Perhaps the greatest evidence of change came in the form of two news articles printed on page 2 of the October 11, 1970 edition of the *Antelope Valley Press*. Above the fold, the paper announced, "Dr. Wesley Swift, Noted Conservative Leader, Dies." Swift had been in poor health and died of a heart attack while convalescing in Mexico.[56] Below the fold, the paper reported, "Picture of Angela Davis Stirs College Controversy," explaining that a poster in support of Angela Davis during her eighteen-month incarceration had been taken down by the administration of Antelope Valley College. The incident was part of a broader mobilization of radical and anti-war politics in the valley.[57] Swift's body was returned to Lancaster and his funeral service was held at Mumaw Funeral Home. That Swift was dead, and the Free Angela Davis movement was alive, suggested just how clearly the valley's social order had shifted. The valley was no escape from Black civil rights struggle, and now more radical and internationalist demands had reached it too.

Nevertheless, Swift left three legacies. First, he had authored the religious foundations of white nationalism that continued to influence organizations around the country decades after his death. Reports about Swift link him to a dizzying array of right-wing groups during his lifetime, to some degree a product of his penchant for fabrication but also a reflection of how deeply influential he was on the evolution of the right outside of the Republican Party.

Second, Swift served as a bridge between the Depression-era right and its more contemporary stewards. Through his mentor Gerald L. K. Smith he was influenced by Henry Ford and Father Coughlin; through his mentorship of Richard Grint Butler and William Potter Gale he influenced the next generation of the white supremacist, militia, and neo-Nazi movement in America. Gale's legacy appears in sovereign citizen and contemporary militia movements today. Butler was a Lockheed employee in Lancaster whom Swift mentored into a Christian Identity pastor, and who served as the head of the Christian Defense League from 1962 to 1965. After Swift's passing Butler moved to Idaho, founding the Aryan Nation organization and opening a new branch of Swift's church. Butler spearheaded the white separatist movement that hoped to create a white homeland in the Northwest, building a compound that would become an international meeting site for white supremacists and a font for violent incidents around the country, including the notorious Ruby Ridge standoff.[58]

Third, he influenced his community at home, including the followers who attended his church, and the families and friends they influenced in their own lives. Whether they knew it or not, children born in the year he died went on to revive American Nazism in Lancaster in the late 1980s and early 1990s.[59] To show how the valley got there, I trace the afterlives of the segregated system that produced Sun Village. These were to be seen in employment, education, and housing—spaces where the valley re-engineered hierarchy among less spatially separate Black and white communities. Disparate and disorganized but nonetheless powerful incidents and structures of discrimination arose in the 1970s and 1980s. After the valley's economy collapsed in the early 1990s, I describe two social processes that followed—the rise of white supremacist violence and the growth of racist policing—showing how they were synthesized into a participatory form of policing in the 2000s.

By the 1970s, racial discrimination was entrenched in the valley's major employers. Defense industry employers were widely understood to be discriminating against Black employees and tracking them into low-level jobs. In 1977, the Antelope Valley NAACP pushed the issue far enough to secure a meeting with Edwards Air Force Base's administration. Attorneys and advocates pressed the Flight Test Center on systematic and widespread discrimination, charging that the center's workforce comprised only 4 percent Black workers (86 of 2,300 people), who were completely shut out of top-level policy and decision-making positions. Other Black employees reported harassment and demoralization linked to being denied promotions over the course of several decades, while white employees enjoyed steady rises in status.[60] At various times, papers reported concessions by the main defense industry employers, but the work was piecemeal and never appeared satisfactory.

The educational system was also a site of near constant battles over educational content, discrimination against Black students, and racist symbology. In the 1960s, public criticism of California's textbooks mounted after the Congress on Racial Equality (CORE) criticized the state's textbooks for their demeaning portrayals of African Americans, and blinkered portrayals of American history more broadly. New educational materials were written and proposed for adoption in California schools, intended to better integrate race into public education. *Land of the Free* was one such textbook, written by John W. Caughey, John Hope Franklin, and Ernest R. May. Alongside revising the portrayal of non-white peoples in

California's textbooks, the work offered a more clear-eyed history of the country and its social struggles. Its appearance in California classrooms in the late 1960s was met with vigorous conservative efforts to remove it.[61] While protests against the textbook originated in Los Angeles, they blazed in the valley.[62]

In the April 1968 edition of *The American Teacher* magazine, reporter Larry Tomlinson wrote a dispatch about the campaign to ban *Land of the Free* from schools in the Antelope Valley. Tomlinson noted that the valley had been "inundated with propaganda against the text, much of it evidently coming from John Birch Society front groups or organizations which lean heavily toward the Birch-conspiratorial frame of mind." Tomlinson described a filmstrip and tape recording, titled "Education of Indoctrination?" authored by an anonymous "Publius & Associates" of Pasadena California (JBS had used Publius as its pen name before). The materials lied about the contents of *Land of the Free*, attempted to portray it as biased, and labeled it responsible for trends of drug use and liberal social attitudes among college students. Tomlinson noted, "The filmstrip is widely available in Antelope Valley and its proponents [are] eager to lend copies to service clubs, parent groups and even teachers." "Education or Indoctrination?" was given a showing and panel discussion at Antelope Valley College. Right-wing organizers targeted their outrage at the valley's local school boards, and in 1967 the Palmdale Board of Trustees adopted a resolution calling the textbook negatively biased against the nation, and proposing that educational materials should instead promote loyalty and love for the country. The Board sent the resolution to Governor Reagan, "who wrote back that he would support state legislation to give districts the authority to reject state-adopted books."[63] This incident of manufactured outrage and censorship presaged coming battles in higher education as well. The next major incident occurred as even Los Angeles's farthest peripheries became part of the Free Angela Davis movement.

Student mobilization in support of Davis reached Antelope Valley College in 1970. It was only one part of a longer battle in the educational system. The year prior, students had joined the national Vietnam War Moratorium protests, and opposition to the war and the valley's deep involvement in it continued to bubble up on campus afterwards. Though campus administrators appeared to manage these controversies as they arose, their removal of the Davis poster sparked reactions that could not be contained. The student government voted to invite Black Panther representatives to speak on campus, as a way to make up for the administration's censorship. In a telling reaction, other members of the student government proposed inviting members of the American Nazi Party, for balance. Administrators considered whether they had to allow the student government to invite any guest speakers at all. Meanwhile, public backlash grew, with protests being mounted in opposition to even the consideration of inviting a Black Panther speaker. At one, a mother of an AVC student was reported to have shouted, "If those black bastards come here, I'll be on the front lines with a gun!" Finding that they could not legally bar the student government from inviting a Black Panther speaker, the administration instead took over the event, and reorganized it so as to bury the Black Panther speaker amid speakers from CORE, the NAACP, and the Urban League.[64]

In the 1980s, Quartz Hill High School and the nearby Quartz Hill Elementary School adopted Confederate mascots and school symbols. The high school mascot, a Johnny Rebel figure carrying a Confederate flag and sword, was printed on clothing, stationary, and other school materials, while the elementary school labeled itself "Home of the Junior Rebels."[65] Until the late 1980s, the high school kept a homecoming tradition known as "slave day" in which "students auctioned off other students to raise money for clubs."[66] By 1995, the issue rose to public prominence as students, community members, and the Antelope Valley NAACP led by Linda Thompson Taylor organized to persuade the school board to mandate changes at the high school, later focusing on the elementary school's "Junior Rebels" iconography. The high school dropped the Confederate flag and changed its letterhead the following year, though the Johnny Rebel mascot and Rebels school name lasted until a new wave of protest and scrutiny that had coalesced around the killings of George Floyd, Breonna Taylor, and Ahmaud Arbery finally toppled it in June 2020.[67]

Finally, in housing, the dynamic flipped from a more explicit and publicly understood form of racial segregation to one hidden in the rental process. In the 1980s, Investment Concepts, Inc. was alleged to have developed a system of racially discriminating against Black renters. Employees were asked to mark rental applications made by Black applicants with a smiley face, so they could later be denied. A whistleblower, Annette Caracciolo, refused, and claimed she was fired for it, sparking a group of employees to file the lawsuit. Perhaps most strikingly, the employees who filed the complaint after refusing to participate in the marking scheme stated that every lawyer they contacted in the Antelope Valley declined to take their case. The case was taken by Bert Voorhees, whose team was eventually contacted "by a little more than 100 Blacks and Latinos who [the company] turned down for housing."

One mixed-race couple, the Reeses, recounted their experience when applying for housing in one of the company's properties. When Anna, who was white, applied, she was told of several openings, but when she returned the next day with her husband, Johnnie, who was Black, those openings suddenly disappeared. Investment Concepts settled for $1.1 million, the largest fair housing settlement in the country at the time, and a sum which included funds to fair housing groups for the purpose of auditing rental practices for evidence of similar discriminatory tactics.[68]

These types of racial discrimination served the ends of re-engineering anti-Blackness inside the Antelope Valley. Before 1968, hierarchy was achieved by keeping Black residents outside Lancaster and Palmdale; after 1968 it needed to be achieved by making them unequal within Lancaster and Palmdale. As vicious as these tactics were, they were superseded by much more visceral and violent forms of white supremacy that emerged as the valley lost its economic engine and entered a period of sustained decline.

The end of the Cold War marked the end of the valley's empire-fueled prosperity. The early 1990s saw a major recession in Southern California, driven by the decline in aerospace and defense industry activity. This marked a turning point in the valley's economic relationship to the rest of Los Angeles County, transforming it from an area that was wealthier than the rest of the county to one that was increasingly poorer. As William Finnegan described the recession,

> Los Angeles alone lost more than half a million jobs, and property values throughout the region collapsed. Few places were hit harder than the Antelope Valley. Housing prices fell by as much as 50 percent, land prices by as much as 90 percent. Abandoned housing tracts began to dot the subdivided desert. Boarded-up shopping centers and bankrupt school districts followed, along with a wave of personal financial disasters so severe that *USA Today* dubbed Palmdale 'the foreclosure capital of California.'[69]

Yet despite this economic collapse, the 1980s and early 1990s saw the valley's population continue to grow. This growth included a slow but steady rise in the Black population of the Antelope Valley. As Finnegan describes it,

> Between 1990 and 1994, Palmdale was the second-fastest-growing city in the United States, Lancaster the sixth. As a rule, the valley's newest residents were poorer and darker than their predecessors, lived in more crowded lodgings—new home construction having essentially stopped—and were more likely to rent. Still, the valley remained, in a county where whites were a minority, overwhelmingly white (68 percent), home-owning, and dominated politically by conservative Republicans of the pro-growth, anti-tax stripe.[70]

Finnegan describes the contradictory trends of population growth and economic decline as an environment in which "widespread white insecurity and downward mobility intersected with significant black and Latino upward mobility—an intersection that made for an altogether different kind of social friction."[71] Mike Davis described the public's attitude as follows: "In their increasingly angry view, the landrush since 1984 has only brought traffic jams, smog, rising crime, job competition, noise, soil erosion, a water shortage and the attrition of a distinctively countrified lifestyle." Davis described the valley's older population as "frantically trying to raise the gangplanks" against those making an exodus out of Los Angeles.[72]

How the Antelope Valley tried to raise its gangplanks exemplified a social process that has occurred throughout the nation. Governments turned to policing—not just the policing done by law enforcement, but also a form of policing which enfolded residents into the work of surveilling, reporting on, and punishing their Black neighbors. For the valley, this participatory policing would become a way to empower its favored residents while also slowing or reversing the racial integration of its once white neighborhoods. This would be what Ocen would come to label the new racially restrictive covenant, a system whereby policing could replace the mechanisms of segregation struck down by the Fair Housing Act.[73]

The valley arrived at that moment through two processes that began to occur in the 1990s. Locally, residents and government officials fruitlessly tried to make the valley fit the dream of a white middle-class utopia. Meanwhile, at the federal level, the governance of housing through crime control policy created a set of legal tools that would enable the mass and participatory policing of housing. All it would take was local leaders finding and implementing those tools to create a perfect storm, whereby valley residents might participate in policing the homes of their Black neighbors, to evict and repel them from the valley. In the balance of this chapter, I will trace these trends, first showing how both bottom-up and top-down movements to conserve white supremacy foundered, and second, how the policy apparatus of participatory policing grew in the meantime. Participatory policing synthesized the mob and the state in the service of redeeming racial segregation.

THE MOB

While earlier decades saw the valley's social institutions and corporate actors trying to raise the gangplanks through discrimination, the 1990s saw a rise in violence by white youth. When the state could not ensure a white valley, they took that effort into their own hands. The process was documented by William Finnegan in his narrative nonfiction book *Cold New World*, which chronicles the social consequences of the valley's de-development in the 1990s— including the rapid growth of white supremacist groups among the valley's youth, including the racist skinhead group known as the Nazi Low Riders. Finnegan described young people addicted to crystal methamphetamine engaging in petty burglaries and forming gangs in an "apocalyptic" environment where they saw no economic future for themselves.[74] As Kathleen Belew documents, what was happening in the valley was being repeated across the country as white power leaders sought to incorporate skinheads into their movement.[75]

The gangs rampaged throughout the valley in the 1990s. A group of Nazi Low Riders threatened to blow up a Lancaster coffee shop because it served minorities; a Latino individual was beaten outside a 7-Eleven; a group of white supremacist students stabbed a Black student at Antelope Valley High School; Black motorists were shot by three young white men in a racially motivated attack; and a homeless Black man named Milton Walker, Jr., was brutally murdered by three avowed white supremacists in 1995, at least one of whom was a member of the Nazi Low Riders. That final case was closed after a cursory investigation by the Los Angeles County Sheriff's Office but reopened two years later after a federal intervention discovered witnesses to the case and evidence of racial motivation.[76] In 1996, racially motivated hate crimes against Black men in Los Angeles County were reported to have been 50 percent higher than in 1995, with a cluster of crimes located in the Antelope Valley. A summary of the report stated, "the increase 'does not say it had become open season on African Americans' but reflects increased hostility as blacks move to areas populated by other ethnic groups."[77]

In 1993, two young white men from Lancaster planted a six-foot-tall, four-foot-wide wooden cross in the front yard of Eleanor and James Pate (ages sixty-three and seventy, respectively). The cross was covered in "KKK" and white supremacist slurs and prompted an NAACP request to prosecute the incident as a hate crime. In 1994, "vile racist flyers exhorting their readers to violence in defense of a white and pure nation" were found throughout Los Angeles County, especially in San Fernando Valley, Santa Clarita, and the Antelope Valley. The fliers often contained anti-Black, anti-immigrant, and antisemitic sentiments and were made by groups like "White Aryan Resistance." They encouraged readers to take action, join white supremacist groups, and donate money to such groups, and were distributed in grocery stores and shopping centers in the Antelope Valley and nearby areas.[78]

While it may be tempting to see these violent white supremacist youths as exceptional, alienated, or solely a product of the valley's economic decline, they were also responding to the valley's politics, echoing the ideas and attitudes printed in the newspaper and voiced by their political representatives. And whether they knew it or not, they were following not only in the region's long history of white supremacist organizing, but also in the national trend of skinheads as the vanguard of the white power movement in the late 1980s and early 1990s.

Yet, white supremacist youth represented only one trajectory of young people's politics in the valley; a rich tradition of youth anti-racism also existed in the region. In the mid-1950s, a young Frank Zappa organized a high-school R&B band, The Blackouts, made up of white, Mexican, and Black youth from Sun Village. The band practiced in Sun Village. They faced backlash from Antelope Valley high school students and local police when trying to play public shows, but as Zappa recalls, their heyday came in 1957, when they played at the NAACP Festival of Stars event at the Shrine Hall in Los Angeles.[79] Zappa's later music would offer fond reminiscences of Sun Village ("Village of the Sun") as well as sharp critiques of white supremacy and authoritarianism, locating it not just in government but in everyday people (see, for example, his lyrics in "Plastic People").

A generation later, Finnegan also chronicled resistance to the white supremacist skinhead culture in the valley. These were the S.H.A.R.P.s: Skinheads Against Racial Prejudice. The young anti-racist youths embraced skinhead culture—its music, clothing styles, and working-class orientation—but insisted that this tradition be an anti-racist one. Finnegan chronicles their social lives and their repeated violent confrontations with their racist counterparts (the Nazi Low Riders) as they sought to define skinhead culture as anti-racist and protect their members. The S.H.A.R.P.s serve as a reminder that the valley's white supremacy was never the product of white consensus, that some working-class people and youths dissented from it at great risk, and that these lineages of struggle extended across local and national borders.[80]

Despite this contestation, white power politics persisted. It grew after the police beating of Rodney King in Los Angeles, and the subsequent uprisings in response to the acquittal of the officers. A Washington state cartoonist named Chris Britt drew a cartoon depicting a Ku Klux Klan member lynching a Black man while holding a newspaper with a headline about the acquittal of the men who attacked white truck driver Reginald Denny. Britt was part of a three-hundred-paper syndication network, allowing his work to be picked up by newspapers around the country. It was published in an Iowa paper in September of 1993, generating substantial controversy, and then published again in November 1993 by the *Antelope Valley Press*. The publication provoked outrage across the Antelope Valley, culminating in, among other things, a forty-person protest in Palmdale. The paper's editor issued a rationalization of the cartoon and claimed not to have been asked to apologize, despite the protest.

THE STATE

The valley's white supremacist politics extended beyond anti-Blackness and was implemented not just by the valley's skinheads but also by its elected officials. In the same year as the *Antelope Valley Press* published the lynching comic, State Assemblyman William J. (Pete) Knight, representing Palmdale, targeted the Antelope Valley's growing Latino population by writing and distributing an anti-immigrant poem. Called "I Love America," the five-stanza poem written in a mocking style tells the story of an immigrant who crosses the border illegally, goes on welfare, asks friends to help invade an Anglo neighborhood, and jokes that Americans are crazy to support them with their taxes.[81] Knight publicized the poem widely, and even read it into the California Legislative Record in 1993. Its lyrics included:

> Write to friends in motherland, tell them come as fast as can . . .
> They come in rags and Chebby trucks, I buy big house with welfare bucks . . .
> Everything is mucho good, soon we own the neighborhood.
> We have a hobby, it's called breeding.
> Welfare pay for baby feeding . . .
> We think America damn good place.
> Too damn good for white man race.[82]

Knight's actions provoked local and regional opposition. Latinos for Social Justice, recently established in the valley, organized heavily in response, including organizing a march for racial harmony to protest Knight.[83] More broadly, the Mexican-American Political Association of California deliberated calling for a Latino boycott of home purchases in the valley in response to Knight's actions.[84] Latinos for Social Justice, led in part by Richard Loa, would go on to organize community events, rally voters against California's anti-immigrant Proposition 287 in 1994, and criticize gang policing of youths in the valley.[85] But while Knight's behavior generated significant opposition, it also roused a groundswell of support, which became evident when a local talk radio show covering the issue found its phone lines overwhelmed with calls in support of his views.

Knight was not alone in elevating right-wing politics in the valley. The Antelope Valley Springs of Life Church reanimated the media playbook of Wesley Swift in its campaign to produce and disseminate media in its anti-gay campaign of the early 1990s.[86] It built a TV set and developed a weekly show advocating a Christian Right political agenda. The show featured guests including Pat Buchanan. A segment from the show called "Sexual Orientation or Sexual Deviation: You Decide" became a minor hit. The twelve-minute video was made by editing segments of an amateur gay pride parade video and was designed to stoke opposition to gay rights. The film was picked up by James Dobson of Focus on the Family, who shipped eight thousand copies around California, and it was screened in the Palmdale City Council as part of a successful effort to pass a resolution opposing a gay civil rights bill. Knight, who would go on to author California's Proposition 22 (2000) restricting marriage to men and women, praised the video. Seeing the potential of this media strategy, the church doubled down, producing a slick twenty-minute video called "The Gay Agenda" with lurid scenes designed to shock, stoke homophobia, and prompt viewers to oppose even modest attempts to advance gay rights. The film caught fire, selling more than twenty-five thousand copies around the country and being rebroadcast on religious television shows including Pat Robertson's *The 700 Club*. The *Los Angeles Times* reported that the film was "widely distributed in Congress and the Pentagon during the debate over homosexuals in the military."[87]

In 1994, State Senator Don Rogers, an Antelope Valley Republican, became the subject of another controversy when it came to light that he was scheduled to speak at the annual banquet of a white supremacist organization called Jubilee. Jubilee was part of the Christian Identity movement, which endorsed white supremacy and believed non-Northern European races were "mud people," the same phrase found on many of the fliers distributed throughout the valley in that year. Rogers was scheduled to speak alongside a former leader of the KKK and a member of the Aryan Nation, but refused to cancel the talk, claiming that the organization was composed of patriotic Americans simply "working to preserve and restore individual rights and freedoms."[88]

It took until 1997 for the federal government to intervene in the valley's white supremacist violence. Only thirteen hate crimes cases had been prosecuted in the Antelope Valley between 1993 and 1997. In 1997, the Federal Bureau of Investigation reported seventeen race-bias incidents in Lancaster, a figure that was surpassed by only six cities in the state, each of which had populations at least three times larger. Federal investigators told the *Los Angeles Times* they were targeting three groups in the Antelope Valley—the Nazi Low Riders, Palmdale Peckerwoods, and

Metal Minds. Local police estimated that the Nazi Low Riders had between two and three hundred members as of 1999, when two of them, Shaun Broderick and Christopher Crawford, beat a Black Wal-Mart employee outside the store.[89]

Federal authorities said they were "concerned that white supremacists [were] trying to frighten minorities away from the area's working-class suburbs."[90] But Lancaster mayor Frank Roberts refused to acknowledge it was a problem. Roberts had first been elected to the city council in 1992, after serving, among other roles, as Dean of Administration of Justice and Criminology at Antelope Valley College.[91] Now mayor, Roberts turned the anti-gang crackdown from one focused on white supremacists to one focused on Black youth. In 1998 the city announced it had secured $1.5 million in funding for a Gang Violence Suppression program that marked the start of a decade of anti-Black politics articulated through the controlling image of the Black gang member.[92] Two years later, a Black family in Palmdale awoke to find racial slurs and swastikas written in chalk on their driveway, and the tires on their car slashed. Later that day in Lancaster, a six-foot swastika was chemically burned into the grass at a park where a multi-ethnic celebration was about to be held.[93]

As the valley largely declined to police its white supremacists, it turned instead towards policing Black and Latino residents. Lacking their own police departments, the cities had contracted with the Los Angeles Sheriff's Department (LASD) for police services. The valley was an assignment with benefits and drawbacks—far from Los Angeles and not prestigious, but a place where law enforcement could do as it pleased with little oversight. The deputies sent to the valley were sometimes members of two of the notorious LASD "deputy gangs," the Rattlesnakes and the Cowboys, which inculcated a culture of violence against Angelenos.[94] As a 2013 Department of Justice investigation would report, they sorted the valley by race and targeted Black and Latino residents for additional stops, searches, ill treatment, excessive use of force, and property seizures. These findings are discussed in more detail in chapter 6, but these policing practices were designed to impoverish, incarcerate, and demean nonwhite residents. They reflected only part of the story of how policing came to remake white supremacy in the valley.

THE SYNTHESIS

So far I have drawn a distinction between the Antelope Valley's citizens and their government, which took diverging paths to reassert white supremacy in the valley. This dual-channel approach is hardly new: the history of racial residential segregation in the United States is one of alternating forces and actors who substitute for one another depending on social, legal, and political circumstances. In the early Jim Crow era, Southern white society was able to keep neighborhoods segregated entirely through its own collective action—effectively discouraging its members from selling or renting to Black residents. But as that power waned, they turned to local governments to pass legislation mandating segregation, what would come to be known as the municipal segregation ordinances.[95] This classic example of substitution echoes through history. As the segregation ordinances were struck down by 1917's *Buchanan v. Warley* decision, they were substituted for by restrictive covenants, and once those were defeated by *Shelley v. Kraemer* in 1948, they were replaced with real estate association rules that concretized segregation,[96] exclusionary zoning,[97] and onwards through history. Even after the passage of the Fair Housing Act, the same pattern appeared. As Jeannine Bell documents, individual and collective violence rose to replace tools of segregation that the Fair Housing Act had eliminated.[98] Conducted by individual white perpetrators in response to Black residents moving into white neighborhoods, move-in violence became the third most common form of "hate crime" in Boston during one 1980s study.[99] Though the city coded these incidents as individual hate crimes, it is perhaps more accurate to think of them not as individual acts nor as hate crimes, but instead as a form of mass segregationist politics expressed through violence. Between 1990 and 2010, Bell found 455 of these incidents across the country, appearing as vandalism, harassment, verbal threats, cross burnings, arson, physical attacks, shootings, and homicides within days, weeks, or months of a Black family's move to a predominantly or all-white neighborhood.[100] This violence was not categorically separate from the state. For example, in *Campbell v. City of Berwyn* (1993) a Black family that had moved to the nearly all-white Chicago suburb Berwyn experienced racial violence and threats to their home. In response, police initially offered protection but withdrew it quickly, abetting segregationist violence.[101]

There are two factors, however, that limit the usefulness of a substitution framework for our understanding of the persistence of racial residential segregation. First, under democratic conditions, citizens and representative governments cannot be neatly disentangled. Second, the trend towards increased citizen participation in governance blurs the lines between the very actors who may be substituting for each other. Historically, this has been analyzed through the concept of delegation, whereby governments assign to individuals the power or authority to enforce the law or to enact power within its boundaries.[102] This has been central to creating a deeply unequal society, as K-Sue Park notes, because state delegation moved "the racial violence of creating and maintaining property in lands and people—and the racial order that sustained the state—to private interests."[103]

Since the 1960s, new forms of citizen involvement in governance have emerged and been theorized through the lens of participation. Consider participatory budgeting, whereby citizens are invited to help shape government budgets, or the many modes of audience participation in television shows and other media.[104] Law enforcement has followed these trends. One example might be "third-party policing," which examines how governments induce non-state, non-criminal actors to engage in policing, such as landlords compelled to evict tenants based on police activity at their units.[105] But most salient is the growth of Neighborhood

Watch, in which residents of neighborhoods engage in the work of surveillance, information sharing, and reporting to police.[106] These schemes empower participating citizens while extending policing and police legitimacy farther than its formal capacity would allow.

It is precisely this merger of state and citizen that has appeared in the Antelope Valley. Participatory policing is not about a substitution of one technique of segregation for another, but rather a synthesis of actors and techniques. Governing housing through crime policy offered the valley a way to synthesize individual action with state power, working around the Fair Housing Act to re-segregate the region.[107]

In what follows, I trace the evolution of the region's crude attempts to police housing in the early 1990s to a more sophisticated adoption of crime-free housing and nuisance ordinances that spread across the country in the 1990s and 2000s, formally putting the power of policing, eviction, and racial segregation in the hands of its residents. The development of crime-free and nuisance housing laws at the national level represented a merger of the war on crime with American housing policy and inaugurated a merger of civilian and police at the neighborhood level. By facilitating individual participation in the policing of their neighbors, these laws synthesized the individual and communal violence of the valley with the state violence of police and government agencies. Participatory forms of policing empowered, encouraged, and rewarded residents for surveilling and policing, and ultimately evicting, their Black neighbors. The synthesis began in the aftermath of the early 1990s recession and during the rise of Los Angeles's regional gang panic.

Billy Pricer, a retired sheriff's deputy and pastor at Lancaster's Springs of Life Church (the font of anti-gay media described earlier) was an early innovator of policing in the valley's schools. After a 1990s gang-related shooting, Pricer set up a "gang information hotline" in his home, the first steps in building a private policing enterprise in the region. Pricer's group, Operation Gangwatch, involved a heavy dose of citizen participation. It would answer calls, take down information, provide resources to callers, and pass on information to the Sheriff's Department, which boasted of having begun several investigations based on Pricer's information.[108] His nonprofit United Community Action Network would raise funds from government and private grants. As George Salas, then head of Latinos for Social Justice, explained, the UCAN developed symbiotic relationships with the Sheriff's Department and the local school system. "One of the things we've been watching real closely," Salas explained, "is the issue of the schools' truancy program, and the Sheriff's Department doing sweeps and then turning in all the students to UCAN."[109] Salas noted the appearance of a conflict of interest; Pricer's retort was that his funding was not dependent on the number of truant students (though one might claim that the panic itself was dependent on a perception of truancy). The city of Palmdale cut its funding to the group when it was learned that the organization was spending half its income on its four staff members, two of whom were Pricer and his wife.

Pricer would soon take his punitive ideas to the Palmdale School Board, proposing that students should be asked to participate in random drug tests. When his proposal was denied, he ran for the board, earning the most votes in the 1991 school board election, and soon becoming board president. He withdrew Palmdale from statewide tests he deemed "anti-family values," and developed a program offering a $25 reward to students who turned in their classmates for crimes. Pricer's local innovations around gang policing would resurface in the late 1990s and early 2000s.

Meanwhile, the *Los Angeles Times* described the valley in the aftermath of the recession in the terms it most feared, describing its rental neighborhoods as "so rife with crime, drugs, and violence that they resemble urban ghettos."[110] In reaction to the crash, Lancaster launched what it called "Operation High Desert Storm." Named after the first U.S. invasion of Iraq that was ongoing at the time, Operation High Desert Storm was the city's housing policy for its poorest residents. It diverted state redevelopment funds marked for promoting low- and moderate-income housing towards purchasing and demolishing apartment buildings in disrepair. To its south, Palmdale launched a "Partners Against Crime" program, which brought sheriffs together with city code enforcement to both police residents of poor neighborhoods and push building owners to either rehabilitate, sell, or forfeit their properties for demolition.[111] In its reporting on these nascent programs, the *Los Angeles Times* noted that Palmdale was considering further steps, such as "a law making it illegal to loiter in areas with identified drug problems, another law forcing landlords to evict tenants involved in drug activity, and a possible program to send warning letters to owners of cars seen lingering in the area."[112] These strategies drawing together police, municipal code enforcement, and housing are part of the early history of what scholars and civil rights advocates now see as one of the biggest threats to fair housing in the country today—crime-free and nuisance housing ordinances.

First pioneered inside the American welfare state, these ordinances and the enforcement mechanisms behind them allow cities, police departments, housing authorities, and individuals to deny entry to, surveil, regulate, police, and evict Black residents—reestablishing the racial hierarchies threatened by the civil rights revolution of the 1960s. These policies' development, implementation, effects, and opponents will be the focus of subsequent chapters of this book.

Policing Public Housing

If you break the law, you no longer have a home in public housing, one strike and you're out. That should be the law everywhere in America.
—PRESIDENT BILL CLINTON (1996)

With the overwhelming support of a Democratic congress, Ronald Reagan passed the Anti-Drug Abuse Act of 1988 to broaden and deepen the war on drugs by increasing criminalization and criminal penalties for drug possession. In his signing statement, he declared that "drugs give a false high. They feel good only long enough to weave a web of addiction. And once trapped, the user is drawn into an existence from which nothing good could come."[113] Reagan ensured that this was true by engineering the immiseration of those he portrayed as victims of drugs. The law expanded the war on drugs and deepened its effects, authorizing local housing authorities to adopt leases allowing the eviction of tenants from public housing on the basis of suspected criminal activity even if committed outside the home, and even if committed by a guest of the tenant.

Eight years later, President Clinton rebranded Reagan's eviction law as an even crueler "one strike policy." Instead of allowing housing authorities to evict tenants on the basis of criminal activity, Clinton's 1996 Housing Opportunity Extension Act mandated their eviction. And rather than necessitate a conviction, Clinton's legislation allowed eviction to occur based on the belief that a tenant had violated the law.[114] In 2002's *HUD v. Rucker* case, the Supreme Court blessed these practices, which had led to the eviction of sixty-three-year old Pearlie Rucker on the basis of her daughter's possession of cocaine three blocks from Rucker's public housing building.

During this period, Reagan and Clinton inaugurated not just the increased precarity of public housing tenants, a new pathway to their eviction, and ever steeper life consequences for even being associated with criminal activity, but also a reduction in the constitutional rights of public housing tenants. As Alexis Karteron describes, low Fourth Amendment standards for stops and searches, combined with broad powers to regulate conduct in public housing, combine to create a situation where "Fourth Amendment protections usually associated with the home are virtually unrecognizable in these places."[115]

In the decades since Clinton's statement, the power to deny someone a lease or evict them from their home based on criminal legal system involvement has spread from public housing into the private housing market, becoming one of the nation's strongest tools of racial segregation. It now operates through two legal mechanisms, crime-free housing law and nuisance property law.

Crime-Free and Nuisance Housing Law in California

Crime-free housing ordinances originate from the 1980s-era turn towards increased criminalization and punitive governance of public housing.[116] Though their language can vary between jurisdictions, they are generally understood to give police power to influence or even decide who can or cannot live in a home, neighborhood, or even city. They train landlords in conducting background checks, allow or mandate the rejection of rental applications based on past criminal history, and empower and even mandate landlords to evict tenants who have even the most anodyne interaction with law enforcement.

When they are introduced to cities, news coverage often emphasizes the relationship between the ordinance and property values. But when Liam Dillon, Ben Poston, and Julia Barajas examined the circumstances present at the adoption of these ordinances, they found an association between increases in a city's Black and Latino population and the subsequent passage of a crime-free housing ordinance. For example, "Among the 20 California cities with the largest increases in Black residents since 1990, 85% have approved crime-free housing policies . . . includ[ing] the fast-growing suburbs of Lancaster, Moreno Valley and Victorville. For communities that saw the largest increases in Latino population, 75% have approved the policies."[117] Reviewing public comment and minutes of city council meetings in these cities, the journalists documented numerous references to a city's changing racial composition as the reason that the laws needed to be implemented.

While crime-free housing laws encourage landlords to bar and evict renters entangled with the criminal legal system, another legal innovation at the intersection of policing and property is designed to ensure landlords comply with these pressures. Nuisance property ordinances allow the criminal legal system to force private landlords to evict their tenants or have their properties designated as chronic nuisance properties. Such a designation can make the landlord subject to fines, revocation of a rental license, or other penalties.

For example, Peoria, Illinois, passed a chronic nuisance ordinance that established a blanket rule mandating the eviction of tenants in "chronic nuisance" properties—a definition triggered by three or more police calls tied to a property within a 365-day span (or two calls for "serious crimes").[118] Once these thresholds are met, the police department may compel a landlord to propose a solution (generally, eviction) that would abate the nuisance. There are no stated enforcement mechanisms against non-rental properties. The ordinance was only enforced as a result of police discretion or resident nuisance complaints about neighbors. Thus, despite evidence that more than ten thousand properties across the city would qualify for nuisance abatement, the law was enforced only on roughly 1 percent of those properties, mostly located in neighborhoods with high rates of Black residency.

The creation of broad categories of vulnerability that are only enforced on a much smaller set of tenants is common to the expansion of policing power in public housing, crime-free housing ordinances, and nuisance ordinances. White homeowners in the city might implicitly understand that these statutes are unlikely to be evenly enforced, and that instead, broad regulations act as a vehicle for them to enforce those rules against others.[119] Sometimes, however, cities are quite open about who they are for: the mayor of Bedford, Ohio suggested his city's nuisance ordinance had solved its "Section 8 problem."[120] Regarding their nuisance abatement program, police officers in Peoria stated, "It says to the law abiding, good people in the area, 'we have heard your complaints and we want to help you stop the chaos.' It says to the thugs and the miscreants, 'You have dedicated your time to make life miserable for your neighbors, we will now dedicate our time to give you a taste of what that feels like.'"[121]

This type of participation in the policing of a neighborhood represents the redemption of the right to discriminate. Rather than directly discriminate against Black residents on the basis of color, it leans on the racial disparities in the nation's policing and punishment systems to discriminate racially through the proxy of police contact. And by putting complaint-making power in the hands of residents, it empowers white neighbors to police their Black counterparts, knowing full well that their Black neighbors have less access or ability to rely on police. The effects are predictably devastating.

In Riverside, California, Terrance Stewart was enrolling at UC–Riverside when he found that all the housing options available to him were covered by the city's crime-free housing program, which would deny him a lease based on his prior drug conviction. Stewart and his family were forced to move ninety minutes away.[122] In Faribault, Minnesota, Selma Jones's neighbors called the police eighty-two times to complain about legal, everyday activities such as a barbecue, children's birthday parties, and children playing on a trampoline.[123] Those calls triggered police visits that found no criminal activity, but Jones was evicted by her landlord on the instruction of the police based on the city's crime-free housing ordinance. Even baseless complaints that resulted in no finding of wrongdoing put her in violation of the ordinance's ban on having too many police visits.[124]

To understand how much of a shift this represents in property rights, consider that during the height of the Jim Crow era, courts across the South rejected nuisance property lawsuits filed by white property owners that sought to prevent Black residents from moving nearby on the basis that race was a type of nuisance. Courts were generally loath to decide between a white landlord renting to a Black tenant and a white neighbor seeking to stop them. But they generally found that nuisance law should not be used proactively, and did not rule that race was a nuisance. Thus, in this instance, property rights could not be extended to include dictating the race of one's neighbors.[125]

Today, however, cities across the country have created elaborate systems that effectively allow what those Jim Crow–era courts denied. They have found ways to preemptively exclude criminalized people and have sided with the nuisance property claims of white residents that allow them to functionally treat Black neighbors as nuisances. For white residents unable to leave what—in their parents' generation—was a destination for white flight, policing serves to re-establish a racialized status gradient within a diversifying neighborhood. Here, policing is a form of political and racial subjectivity itself: to engage in policing is to occupy a superior social position.

In the next chapter, I return to the Antelope Valley to study the contemporary wave of Black migration through public housing's successor program, Housing

Choice Vouchers. I show how the polity turned to policing as a means of accomplishing what a prior generation did before the Fair Housing Act. I show how policing is both a means of re-segregating the region, and a form of social citizenship that imbues those who engage in it with psychic rewards of status and power.

As a result, in the Antelope Valley, policing itself became property.

3

Apartheid's Afterlives

We used to think this area was the end of creation . . . but it's home now.
—JOE DAVIES

Harass? This is police city, man.
—VOUCHER TENANT

In the dusk of the Cold War, when the nation's military industries moved on to different technologies and different geographies, the valley saw its aerospace industry begin to wither. Although the valley had needed war, war didn't need the valley. But local leaders believed that they could survive it, and that the region had outgrown its dependence on the volatile, contract-reliant aerospace industry, described as a "boom or bust" or "yo-yo" economy in the *New York Times*.[1] Part of their self-belief may have been attributed to Ronald Reagan, who campaigned for re-election in Palmdale in 1984, touring a Rockwell International B-1B bomber hangar and intimating that his re-election would bolster defense industry spending in places like the valley.[2] By the late 1980s, city officials told the Associated Press that they "see no end in sight to the population boom, which has been fueled by a steady stream of young families fleeing the sticker shock of Los Angeles basin real estate prices."[3] By then, Palmdale was ranked the fastest growing city in California, and Lancaster ranked fifth. A Palmdale city councilman explained, "Our biggest business is building homes. . . . Eighty percent of the people buying homes are moving up here and commuting."[4]

In its early years of growth, the valley built housing in service of its economy. Now, as its economic fortunes shifted, it would turn that formula on its head, making housing its economic engine. This chapter is about the costs of that transition for the valley's white polity, for whom housing offered a solution as well as a new problem: a second major wave of working-class, non-white migrants, who arrived to fill that housing but whose presence was seen as a threat to its value. The prior chapter traced the valley's unfruitful search for ways to reassert racial hierarchy after the 1960s, and posited that, at a national level, policing became a powerful tool of neighborhood exclusion and eviction. Now, in the context of another economic downturn, I show how a participatory system of policing was developed in the valley and deployed against incoming Black tenants.[5] While the hostility was broad, it began to land on specific figures who would serve as stand-ins for whole populations. The trend started with public focus on gangs, but eventually transitioned to the figure of the "Section 8 tenant" in ways akin to the public disgust aimed at welfare recipients in the 1980s. The cities of the valley devised an enforcement program in partnership with the Housing Authority of the County of Los Angeles and the Los Angeles County Sheriff's Department to target voucher tenants for additional inspections. The program was both a partnership between agencies and jurisdictions, and a partnership of sorts between the government and its citizens, as valley residents were asked to participate in policing.

POLICING AS PROPERTY

As I interviewed private homeowners and renters in the valley, I heard them couch their hostility to voucher renters in terms of the negative effects these tenants were presumed to have on property values, an echo of the older claim that racial integration would damage property values.[6] But as local residents described both their attitudes towards voucher tenants and the actions they took against them, another relationship between policing and property seemed to emerge. The ways that these residents participated in policing, the functions that policing served, and the way it changed citizenship in neighborhoods all suggested that this wasn't just a story of policing protecting property, but rather policing *being* property. It had become something possessable and wieldable, and in the process, it gave its owners value while remaining outside the possession of voucher tenants.

In this chapter I trace how policing was used in the Antelope Valley, how that usage fits a legal analysis of property, and what we might understand about the maintenance of neighborhood racial hierarchies by thinking of policing as property. To do so, I first summarize three understandings of property—traditional, relational, and active.

The traditional view is that property is discrete, objectifiable, and immutable. It is accompanied by four traditional markers: usability, status, exclusion, and disposal.[7] First, if one can use a thing, that is an indicator that it might be one's property. The second metric is that something might be property if owning it confers a different status upon its owner. Third, something might be property if one can exclude others from its use. And fourth, something might be property if it can be given from one person to another.[8]

But as Claire Herbert and Jay Orne remind us, "property is not merely a relationship between a person and a thing, it is a complex social relationship that mediates our interactions with one another and with the state, often in unequal and exploitative ways."[9] Following their argument, we can think of a second perspective on property: the relational. Nicholas Blomley, for example, argues that property is "an organized set of relations between people in regards to a valued resource."[10] As capacious as this definition is, it turns out that this relational view can still fit the four traditional markers described in the preceding paragraph. Cheryl Harris illustrated this in her analysis of how whiteness could be considered property.[11] Whiteness, she showed, could be possessed, gave its holders social status, could be held back from some and given to others. The point is not just that narrow definitions of property are insufficient to capture how property works, but also, and perhaps more importantly, that race and property intersect in critical ways.

Third and finally, property is active. The traditional four metrics, as Carol Rose notes, require actions—possessing, using, changing, excluding, disposing—in order to be made real.[12] These actions, Blomley adds, can include violence, and "this is particularly so when we remember that property is fundamentally concerned with legally defined and policed relations between individuals."[13] If, as Blomley argues, property is centrally defined by the right to exclude, and exclusion is backstopped by violence, then law enforcement—through whom the state enacts the legitimate use of violence—is a key actor in constituting property.

As this chapter will show, law enforcement officers were not the only ones engaging in the work of policing; residents were too. This participatory form of policing is useful for both police and non-police participants. It broadens police legitimacy, and expands the pool of labor involved in policing a community beyond the formal ranks of law enforcement. But for everyday people, something more is at stake.

To understand what people who participate in policing gain from it, we might turn to W. E. B. Du Bois's observations in *Black Reconstruction in America*. There, he catalogs a series of public policies created by Southern states to induce unequal citizenship between whites of all economic statuses and their Black counterparts. The goal was to break solidarity between poor white and Black people whose shared interests—when recognized—might be a foundation from which a new South could be built. Du Bois noted that these produced the public and psychological wages of whiteness—social status elevations exclusive to whites alone. Here, the return to a traditional property analysis is clear: whiteness is a form of property in the sense that it is possessed by those racialized as white, excluded from those who are not seen as such, and provides its holders with status rewards lucrative enough to break other solidarities.

In making his claims about the public and psychological wages of whiteness, Du Bois includes examples of advantages offered to whites exclusively, including public deference, access to segregated public resources like schools, leniency from the courts, and, most crucially for this analysis, policing.[14] He noted that "the police were drawn from" the ranks of whites, giving them exclusive employment opportunities and the advantage of never having to experience policing by a member of a racial group not their own. Nikhil Pal Singh identifies this as policing's role in shoring up the "value of whiteness" or in turn producing and protecting whiteness as property.[15]

But today, as the ability to engage in policing has diffused in ways that make private participation in policing possible and popular, Du Bois's mechanism merits the corollary that the ranks themselves can engage in policing. This complicates a view of the relationship between policing and race that sees police as an external factor that affects racial experience. Participation suggests a different direction of flow between people and policing, but with the same outcome: drawing the power of policing into oneself is a way to elevate oneself over others, creating what Singh has described as "policed social relations."[16] This is what I believe played out in the valley as it developed its participatory system of policing. In what follows, I will trace how a regime of participation in policing was created, how the Antelope Valley's non-Black polity engaged in that policing, and how their actions fit a property framework.

Building from the previous chapter's overview of national trends in crime-free and nuisance housing laws, this chapter will trace a two-part process of policing voucher tenants in the valley. One part is at the level of local policy, as the cities of the valley constructed a partnership across agencies and jurisdictions to marshal resources and information required to police voucher tenants. The other part is at the level of everyday people, as the policing partnership also included mechanisms by which individual residents of the valley could participate in policing through surveilling their neighbors and making formal complaints that lead to the punishment or eviction of tenants.

In this way, the valley created a form of policing that fit the traditional markers of property described earlier. Policing became as usable for local residents as a tool in a toolbelt. Participation in policing conferred social status, especially relative to the subjects of policing. Policing is exclusionary in a narrow definition, as voucher tenants are functionally excluded from participation in policing or even asking for police services. And it is exclusionary in a broad sense, as it works to evict and push out voucher tenants such that they are excluded from the valley altogether. Finally, policing is disposable, or transferable, as neighbors appoint or rely on others to perform the work of surveilling and policing the block.

Thinking about policing as something that individuals acquire and do represents a shift in the conception of property and property rights. Residents I spoke to—often but not entirely white—routinely spoke of voucher tenants as affecting their property in other ways, such as harming their property value or diminishing their sense of ownership of the valley itself. They imagined the voucher population as double, triple, or quadruple its real size, expressed fears that their community was being overrun, and despaired over the changes they and their leaders apparently would not or could not stop. They were losing something they felt belonged to them and feeling the value of what they had left diminishing. In *Darkwater*,

Du Bois described this as not so much the fear of poverty, but the "death of their rising dreams."[17] The dream of a middle-class, economically self-sufficient valley was being burst by the reality that the valley remained derivative of Los Angeles. Once, the metropolis boomed, and the valley reaped the rewards; but when it entered recession, the valley felt it too.

The ability to police is something that the valley's leaders gave to its residents to make up for these losses. The valley could have instead offered its residents economic assistance, jobs programs, or other remedies addressing the causes of the valley's problems: the collapse of its major industries and the absence of new ones to replace them. But policing was nevertheless a powerful salve, a way of re-establishing the value of longtime residents' property—not just in the monetary sense but in the sense of meaning, rights, and powers that are bound up with property ownership.

Showing how policing resembles property in the valley is more than just an academic exercise; it points to something real about personhood and race today. Policing's evolution into something akin to property is changing the nature of citizenship. Grace Hong notes how "subjectivity is defined by the ability to own," fundamentally oneself. As Craig Willse mobilizes this point, it is one's ability to own in the context of housing.[18] If one is only free if one can own property, then freedom and property rights are coterminous in a regime of what Ananya Roy calls "propertied citizenship."[19] And when policing functions as a form of property, then engaging in policing may work as a form of increasing one's citizenship or sense of personhood. Notably, as Willse reminds us, this is at the expense of those without or dispossessed of property.[20] In addition to substantiating personhood, police as an institution and policing as a broader social practice also make race.[21] As Rinaldo Walcott points out, when either being "deputized" into the ability to police or instead subject to policing by others falls along lines of racial difference, the difference helps constitute what race means.[22]

This, then, is why a property analysis of policing is important. It can help us understand why people participate in policing their neighborhoods and communities, what this turn to policing represents in terms of alternative economic and social paths not taken, and how participation in policing obviates other possible solidarities between those living in the valley. To demonstrate how this process unfolded, I turn back to the 1990s to trace the fate of the valley after the decline of its Cold War industries.

REPERTOIRES OF RECESSION

When the recession first mentioned in Chapter 2 hit California in the late 1980s and early 1990s, the valley faced the strongest test of its economic transition. The recession was driven in part by declining military investment, meaning that the valley was particularly vulnerable to it. At the time, Palmdale and Lancaster were home to 225,000 people. They lost 40,000 aerospace jobs alone: one job for every six people. The effects were devastating, and helped explain why the region became the "foreclosure capital of the United States."[23]

After the crash, the valley rebuilt itself along the same lines it had been pursuing before—mowing down the Joshua trees, paving the desert, and building cheap single-family housing. The *Los Angeles Times* estimated that Palmdale alone quadrupled its housing stock between 1980 and 1995.[24] But although its leaders hoped to follow the path of Orange County—a similar commuter neighborhood that transitioned towards building its own local economy—it found no foothold to do so.

Elsewhere in the state, cities had been turning to incarceration as a means of creating local employment.[25] But the valley struggled to join them. It had a long-standing detention center, Mira Loma, but this had never been a steady site of activity or employment. In 1945, it was a vocational school where the California Youth Authority conducted job training for juvenile defenders. About a decade later it was repurposed into a medium-security facility, and continued that way until it closed in 1979. It was reopened again in 1983, this time repurposed for female inmates and called the "Mira Loma Female Honor Ranch." That lasted only a decade, and it closed again in 1993. In 1997, U.S. Immigration and Customs Enforcement acquired Mira Loma for use as an immigration detention facility, which it remained until it was again closed in 2012.[26] Plans to renovate it into a Women's Detention Center failed and it sat empty. A mile to the north, Lancaster did manage to ride the prison wave, opening the California State Prison of Los Angeles County in 1993. The institution, which cost over $200 million to build, employs roughly 1,500 people, less than 5 percent of the aerospace jobs lost in the early 1990s recession.[27]

And so the valley again raced off its self-made cliff. In 1990 Palmdale had been the nation's fastest growing city with a population of at least 50,000. Six years later its 27 percent foreclosure rate was the highest in the country.[28] The result was a fundamental transformation of the valley. The *Los Angeles Times* reported on it in 1996 in a sprawling multi-page feature titled "Class Struggle Unfolds in Antelope Valley Tracts."[29] Reporter Sonia Nazario's descriptions and interviews hinted at the reality that the valley was enduring a prolonged economic restructuring, yet the class realities of the valley were obscured in the paper's frame.

For example, while the report's infographics documented a tenfold rise in Palmdale's population, it only showed a 10 percent rise in the number of residents on welfare, belying the thesis of an explosion in welfare usage. Nevertheless, the report's substance was about the threat of welfare recipients to the valley's middle-class way of life. The paper's infographics also showed that 48.7 percent of welfare recipients in the valley were white, suggesting that public assistance was helping longtime white residents of the valley to survive its crumbling economy. Nevertheless, the paper interviewed middle-class whites about their fear of welfare-receiving

FIGURE 14. Oda Hutchison, left, and her daughter, Carol Ann Wagner, stand inside barred entrance to their home on 13th Street. Source: Bob Carey/*Los Angeles Times* via Getty Images.

Black and Latino migrants. Finally, while the valley's own economy had collapsed, the report framed economic decline as something brought to the valley, quoting a resident claiming, "These are not problems created by Palmdale. They were brought to Palmdale."

The paper documented dehumanizing rhetoric such as police referring to the freeway connecting Los Angeles to the Valley as "the Sewer from LA," and the mayor referring to "families from hell," but largely accepted the basic framing of the issue as the valley as a victim of Los Angeles, quoting one resident complaining that "they have moved all the people on welfare from L.A. to Palmdale."

Local fear led to extreme acts of securitization. Raytheon quality assurance inspector Gene Mandel got the city to install barricades at the end of his street. He told the *LA Times* that he slept with a gun on his nightstand. Carol Ann Wagner and her mother Oda Hutchinson had a "heavy black iron cage" built around their front door, virtually imprisoning themselves within it. The scenes described in the paper were reminiscent of Octavia Butler's fictional Los Angeles suburb Robledo, walling itself off from those down below.[30]

Alongside these tactics, one could see the valley turning to policing as a solution. The Antelope Valley Mall imposed bans on three or more youths walking together or any customer sitting on a mall bench for more than fifteen minutes. And the cities began to create gang policing programs, such as a school anti-gang probation officer, and a Gang Violence Suppression program in partnership with the Hard Core Gangs Unit of the Sheriff's Department and Billy Pricer's gang hotline. Praising the coordination between agencies, "Lancaster spokeswoman Anne Aldrich explained, 'This is a really big deal for the Antelope Valley. . . . Coordinating the efforts of all of the different agencies that have been working independently against gangs will make all their efforts more effective.'"[31]

Ultimately, the paper reported white residents seeking to sell their recently purchased tract homes at significant losses. Susan Kerpan, a UCLA administrator who had moved to the valley for its affordable housing, was an example. She purchased a home for $110,000, but by 1996 had stopped making mortgage payments and had listed the property for $79,500. The $30,000 discount attracted no offers.

Skipping forward just a few years, however, we find Palmdale and Lancaster in another building boom. They expanded outward and westward—away from the older nucleus of 1950s-era homes built by the war economy. New styles, larger plots, whatever it took to convince Los Angeles residents that the move would be worth it. This time, the housing boom was induced by changes to mortgage banking that incentivized the construction and selling of mortgages even to buyers who could not actually afford them, using tactics like interest rates that started small and ballooned later. The schemes caught on like wildfire. Craig, a construction worker I interviewed in 2015, told me he moved to the valley to work in the early 2000s housing construction boom, experiencing both its rewards in terms of plentiful work and risks in the form of a housing market that threatened to quickly price him out:

> Back in the early 2000s I was delivering roof tile when the housing market was sky high and in 2001 or 2000. . . . I can't remember exact what year we bought this house, but this house, it was like $190,000 and the prices were going up. Like every week the prices were going up. If we wouldn't have qualified for this house I think our—the most I qualified [for] was like $195,000 and this house was $190,000 something. If we wouldn't have qualified for this one houses this size would have been $200,000 after. I was busting off my ass off, man, I was working 60–70 hours a week.

In the meantime, lending banks chopped up and sold these subprime mortgages to other banks and financial institutions. The financialization of the boom helped get thousands of Angelenos situated in the desert. It also ensured that when the unpayable payments began coming due, the consequences would be widespread and devastating. Once again, the Antelope Valley became a foreclosure hub: at the peak of the 2008 foreclosure crisis, Lancaster and Palmdale occupied two of the top three spots in the ranking of California cities by foreclosure rate. This marked the third time in twenty years that the valley was devastated by economic crisis and waves of foreclosure, and the combined effect was to invert the valley's relationship to Los Angeles—where it had once been Los Angeles's prideful superior, it was now its inferior.

It is into these circumstances that Housing Choice Voucher tenants were moving. As the program grew nationally, the valley saw its total number of residents in the voucher program grow from roughly five thousand in 2000 to just over ten thousand in 2006, and over fifteen thousand in 2016. As theorized in the introduction, they came because the economic structure of the voucher program gave them little choice—they were made into agents of the spatial fix that allowed Los Angeles to offload its priced-out tenants into spaces that would economically benefit from their presence. The price that the county would pay to landlords on behalf of voucher tenants (the fair market reimbursement rate) was calculated over the entire county. That meant that it was too paltry to convince landlords in wealthy areas to accept it, and so generous that landlords in struggling neighborhoods often affirmatively searched it out. Because Antelope Valley rents were roughly 20 percent lower than rents in the rest of Los Angeles County, the geography of available rental units for voucher tenants skewed towards the valley.

Like so many others, Craig purchased his home in the valley at near the maximum of his credit range and just as the market was beginning to peak. This made him especially vulnerable to the recession. When the housing market eventually crashed, Craig's own fortunes took a downturn, as he no longer had much work delivering roof tile. His family lost ownership of their home in 2009, but, as he put it, "we've just been here, they haven't foreclosed yet." He compared his situation to that of the average Section 8 renter, speculating that those renters would be more attractive to landlords because their rents were guaranteed by the government while his ability to make rent depended on getting a steady income.

> Say they foreclose on me and I gotta move out. I got no—I went bankrupt, I got no credit, I got really nothing. I work and my wife works, but someone that has a house that's gonna rent it out to me; would they rather rent it out to me when they don't know me from Adam, or they'll give it to some guy that has Section 8 because they know they're gonna get the money from the government?

Craig knew that his economic position put him at a disadvantage compared to voucher tenants, whose rents would be paid on time every month. To a landlord his economic precarity would make him look like a risk. But the idea that he too could sign up for a voucher never came up. Perhaps he knew, as I did, that, for lack of funds, the waiting list was closed.

Between 2011 and 2014, I interviewed forty voucher tenants in the Antelope Valley. Many voucher renters I spoke to came to appreciate the valley after they got there—I did too—but almost none that I spoke to said they had wanted to move to the valley when they got their voucher. People did it because they needed a place to live. When they received their voucher from the Housing Authority of the County of Los Angeles, either they were given a list of landlords willing to rent to them, or openings were taped to the walls of the housing office, or they checked a website marketing listings to people with vouchers, or they set out on their own to find a landlord willing to rent to them in the limited time tenants have to secure housing. One way or another, tenants found that they definitely could use their vouchers in the Antelope Valley, but that it would be harder to use the voucher elsewhere. Even so, they became segregated within Lancaster and Palmdale, pushed into its older east side and steered away from the newer, wealthier, and whiter west side.

Voucher holders being steered to older homes on the valley's eastern side meant that they were moving into the homes that had originally been built for the white workers staffing the aerospace economy of the nascent Antelope Valley.[32] These had been homes built at the request of the military and its defense contractors, and with the kind of federal financial backing that was never made available to Black families. What started as a form of public housing had become so again, and in so doing extended the military's role in shaping Black Los Angeles's geography.

The system was ripe for exploitation by landlords, because voucher tenants were desperate to find places that would take them before their vouchers expired. Some used the opportunity to overcharge tenants. Andrea told me, "Get a newspaper or go online to Craigslist. The ones who take Section 8 [charge rents] much higher than the ones who don't. It could be actually the same identical house. You know how they do them in tracts? This one is $1,600, but this one that doesn't take Section 8 is $1,100, or $1,000." Others placed tenants in uninhabitable homes. Jordan recounted such an experience, explaining, "the landlord rented me a house that was just burned down and we didn't know anything about it. You know, we were in desperate need of a house. They moved us in, but then, like, a month later we started having all these problems. The city came out and said that the house was condemned. It wasn't livable, they should have never rented [it] out."

NOTHING STARTS RIGHT AWAY

Racial backlash theory in the social sciences generally defines the term as "the politically and electorally expressed public resentment that arises from perceived racial advance, intervention, or excess."[33] The concept suggests an acceptable status quo ante in which backlash is not present; this is then disrupted by social change. One voucher tenant I interviewed, Nate, reflected on the contemporary politics of the valley in a different light: "Nothing starts right away, so it must be something that's been lingering along going out here, and people that's been out here since the late '70s, '80s when it was unincorporated, pretty much ran the town. So, you probably have generations of people who have those type of racist views that instill it in their kids and their grandkids and their grandkids."

From this perspective, the backlash concept obscures more than it illuminates. As the prior chapter recounted, there was no moment of 'normalcy' in the valley whose disruption led to backlash. Indeed, the violent enforcement of the valley's hierarchies has been the metronome of the region's twentieth-century history. So if the backlash was always there, then the term itself loses coherence. Instead, we might say that what the valley experienced was a long struggle over its social hierarchies, a struggle whose terrain shifted from location to location: employment, housing, schools, gangs, and more. To see these fights together is to see that, although the terrain of the struggle had shifted to the voucher program, the stakes remained the same.

In 2015 and 2016 I returned to the valley to interview forty-three local residents about their views on the voucher program. I chose neighborhoods with high rates of voucher tenancy, and walked door to door on Saturdays and Sundays in the summer to conduct interviews.

In August of 2015 I interviewed two of the older tenants in my study, Linda and Dorothy. We sat at a small table in Linda's kitchen and they told me about their long histories in the valley. Linda's husband had been a flight test engineer at Edwards Air Force Base. After he died, she sold real estate. "It was just wonderful. Everybody sold real estate. It was great until about the last of the '80s, I would say. You could just see, I mean cars would roll off the freeway. Well, why wouldn't they? They didn't have to pay a dime down on a house." She lived in one of the neighborhoods built in the 1950s, and which had recently seen a relatively high rate of voucher movement (by this I mean it's likely that one or two tenants were in her vicinity). She hated the program, and like Nate had speculated, she anchored her understanding of it in the fight her community had lost fifty years prior.

> There was a community east of Palmdale called Sun Village. In those days, most of them lived there. Now the people who were here then, the black people, they were high-class people. I mean they didn't go around selling drugs and getting in jail for the most part, at least the ones I knew. And the children, not many, were here in school but the ones that were, were very nice. Then came—I think the riots in LA in 1966. That was the first indication I had of how horrible it really was. . . .
>
> Well, I can just tell you that for the first time a black family moved into this neighborhood, there went the neighborhood. And that was about 1988, I think. I know [that] was not the first family. We had a lovely family, they owned a religious bookstore. . . .
>
> I think it was a law passed that there had to be a black family in every block. They were gonna put a Black family in every block in Lancaster. That started during the '60s. This was the NAACP. And they did it.

From the historical injury of civil rights, everything else followed. The destruction of her neighborhood was not triggered by the decline of the aerospace economy, but by the mandated placement of Black families on every block. Crucially, this was not Linda's memory, because it never happened. It was instead, a backward-facing fantasy that justified her contemporary views. It illustrates what Camilla A. Hawthorne and Jovan Scott Lewis describe as "the ongoing production of race and racisms via the production of space," as Linda's contemporary racism is infused by a past comity with Sun Village and the breaking of that comity by civil rights law.[34]

Dorothy had arrived in 1958, during the boom years of the valley. Her husband was a trucker. But when I asked her about the voucher program, her reply turned sharp and bitter. "I'm here fifty-ish years, tried to make it at home and how do you think I feel when I see some of these people that their Humvees sitting in their yard and not in their garage at the Section 8 houses over there, and $300.00—$400.00 for a $2,500.00 a month house? To me, that is a problem."

I don't know if the neighbor Dorothy was referring to was actually renting their home using a voucher. But as a thought experiment, we can assume she was correct in order to reverse-engineer the set of conditions under which she would accept the tenant's presence. In this case, perhaps if a voucher tenant drove a sufficiently cheap car, or hid it so as not to offend anyone, their presence could be accepted.[35] But another interviewee, Ashley, opposed the voucher program "because when you see someone who's able to buy a lobster because they don't have to pay rent. . . . I don't get lobster." Add "no lobster" to the list of acceptable conditions for voucher residents. Yet another local resident surmised, "They're just kinda—I don't know. They feel entitled, I think." Add to the list, "don't make people feel like you feel entitled." Dorothy claimed, "They're living in better houses than we are." As my interviews continued, it became harder to see any correct way to be a Black voucher tenant in the Antelope Valley. One voucher renter I spoke to named the futility of trying to fit in: "They don't want you next door for some reason. No matter how gracious you are."

Late one afternoon, I was walking down the street after conducting an unremarkable interview with a woman at her door. As I walked away, her partner, who I will call Michael, arrived home, and learned of the interview. He got back into his car and drove down the street to catch up with me, eager to make his views known too. We did his interview in the road through the rolled-down window of his car. Unsurprisingly, Michael spoke extensively and energetically about his attitudes towards voucher tenants. When I asked him about his attitude towards the voucher program he explained, "It's not the Section 8 woman that lives there. That's fine and all that." But as he continued speaking, this sympathy quickly melted away.

> *Michael:* But it's all the fucking riff-raff they bring with them. All the 98s that come up here from LA and hang out in the yard and fucking barbecue, couches, all that shit in the front yard.
>
> *RK:* What's a 98?
>
> *Michael:* Ninety-eight is security code for blacks . . . it's not like saying black. You know what I mean? . . . It's a neutral term.

> *RK:* So you're saying that the tenants can be good but there's other people that come in with them—
>
> *Michael:* Tenants can be okay, like it's just the momma and the little couple of kids or whatever, that's fine. But that's not what you get. You get all the cousins staying overnight, you get the drug dealing, all the bullshit. I've seen them. Go down to the Section fucking 8 office and watch them. . . . Watch it. Watch what happens. You can see them all. They're all the same size. They all eat the same. Go ahead.
>
> *RK:* And this is based on your personal experience—
>
> *Michael:* It is the fucking reality! My experience is reality.

Michael started by dividing voucher tenants into good and bad—the good mothers who unfortunately can't be tolerated because of the bad people around them. But within a few sentences, he communicated what he really thought and the evidence he used to substantiate his intolerance—go to the Section 8 office and look at the tenants. His comments reveal how central surveillance is to producing racialized emotions of hostility and superiority that undergird the policing and punishment of Black tenants.[36]

Michael continued to unravel his analysis of Black mothers, who are often the face of the voucher program. He commented on their cooking and their dietary practices, suggested they were "professional" welfare recipients, and claimed that voucher holders simply "wait about four years and then squeak out another one, so they can always stay on the program." These comments are echoed by other respondents who commented on voucher tenants' sexual practices, number of partners, manipulation of pregnancy or disability to qualify for welfare or housing support, and parenting practices. One explained the program by saying, "If a woman gets pregnant and has a child she has everything paid for. Her boyfriend lives in the house. They get [a] free house. Free rent. If she goes to college they get more money, and they have another child, more money and they get this, that and the other." In another interview, a respondent echoed the welfare-queen myth, stating that they opposed the voucher program because "my friend goes and gets her welfare check and she sees people pulling up in their Escalades to go collect bills." It was Pete Knight's anti-immigrant song described in the previous chapter, but now sung in the key of anti-Blackness.

These attitudes on excess are consonant with many of the other local residents I spoke to, and with a half-century of how policymakers have thought about poor people, poor Black people, and poor Black women and mothers in particular. Just as policymakers have used these ideas to dismantle the welfare state and fuel mass incarceration, the Antelope Valley searched for ways to materialize its opposition to voucher renters.

During my conversation with Linda and Dorothy, they summarized the stakes of their opposition to the voucher program. Linda explained, "I'm last of the originals here in this neighborhood, and so for a long time I said well, they're not gonna run me out. I'm gonna stay." For them, and increasingly the valley at large, staying would come to mean fighting back.

TURNING ON TENANTS

Lancaster Mayor Raymond "Rex" Parris, Jr., was born in Palmdale in 1954, the third of Raymond and Jeanne Parris's four sons. But his father left the family when Rex was eleven, and Jeanne, a waitress, was left to raise the boys alone. The household sometimes relied on welfare assistance to get by.[37] But as he described in a phone interview in 2019, the family had other support too, like someone who helped by "taking us to the snow and doing stuff like that you do with kids."

When we spoke, Parris recounted to me a time in the early 1960s, before his father left, when "an African American family moved next door to us." He spoke proudly of his parents' reaction: "And my parents were the only ones to go over and meet them, you know, bring the traditional pie or whatever [it was] you do to welcome people when they moved in. . . ." He told me, "The rest of the neighbors were really upset. But I think they were more upset about the impact it might have on home values."

Parris's memory of his neighbors' opposition to integration being based on home prices is instructive. Then and now, home prices are not just marked to real values of material, labor, and land, but also to relationships. The racial exclusivity of a place like Palmdale would give each home within it additional value, at least for other whites seeking the same. Break the promise of segregation, and you'd break the housing market.

As a young person, Parris suffered from severe social anxiety, but he overcame it in high school, running for freshman class president and remaking himself as R. Rex Parris.[38] After briefly becoming addicted to drugs and dropping out of high school to work full time, Parris went on to enroll in junior college, then UC Santa Barbara, and eventually Southwestern Law School. He would return to Lancaster to begin what would become a wildly successful personal injury firm. The firm became the launching pad for public service, and, eventually, a political career.

But as he rose to personal and political success, Parris would come to occupy the role of his neighbors rather than his family in the valley's new battle over integration, voicing hostility when a new generation of Black tenants arrived in the valley. He wasn't the first to oppose voucher tenants, nor was he the only mayor in the Antelope Valley to build an infrastructure to oppose it. But he made himself the face of the campaign, directing the construction and coordination of a massive anti-housing voucher campaign, arguing for it in public venues, and defending it when challenged. If the valley was a modern-day Newburgh, NY, site of early opposition to welfare, Parris was its Joseph Mitchell.[39]

To achieve his business success, Parris bucked convention. Defying the informal regional agreement among personal injury lawyers not to advertise, he

FIGURE 15. A billboard advertising Lancaster Mayor R. Rex Parris's namesake law firm. Source: Kim Stringfellow © 2017.

purchased billboard advertisements targeting motorists driving into the Antelope Valley on Highway 14 and kept a steady cycle of them for years.[40] They drowned out his competition and helped him land lucrative cases. Alongside his class action suits, he pursued cases advancing social and economic justice. In 1994, he represented a Black security director at Palmdale High School, George Jenkins, whom the school yearbook had portrayed as "Buckwheat" from the 1930s television show "Our Gang." Despite being alerted to its racial offensiveness and asked to change or remove it, the school published the material anyway, leading to the employee being targeted with racial slurs, harassment, and ridicule.[41] In 2000, Parris and his brother sued Michelin Tires for providing training seminars to auto accident investigators that encouraged them to mislabel crashes caused by defective tires as driver error.[42]

By the mid-2000s, Parris had turned his attention towards anti-crime measures, starting volunteer associations and organizing anti-crime meetings in Lancaster. The crackdown on voucher tenants started as early as 2006, when there were only about 3,500 voucher-holding families in the Antelope Valley. Then, Lancaster passed a nuisance ordinance, and by 2007 was beginning its first steps toward using policing to govern voucher tenants. Quoted in the *Los Angeles Times*, Parris justified what was already known to be a racially discriminatory scapegoating of voucher families. "Our community is dying," he said; "the reality is we're going to have to suffer a certain amount of injustice to fix this."[43] A community town hall on neighborhood issues like vouchers was reported to have amassed three thousand attendees; at its conclusion members declared a "war on gangs and crime," which they vowed to enact through "limiting the number of Section 8 tenants in the Antelope Valley." Bishop Henry Hearns, now Lancaster's first Black mayor, largely supported the voucher crackdown, noting that after they failed to bring in their trash cans, he personally confronted and then arranged to have evicted a neighboring Black family he suspected was using a voucher. The next year, Lancaster's City Council passed a crime-free housing ordinance that fined landlords if they did not evict tenants who had been the subject of more than five police calls.

It was into this environment that Parris launched his mayoral campaign. Focusing on issues of crime during yet another period of economic unraveling (this time nationally), Parris easily won Lancaster's mayoralty in April 2008. He quickly made gangs his public antagonists, passing a measure through the city council that would mandate neutering pit bulls and Rottweilers, portrayed as the favorite pets of local gang members. As Parris explained, "I want gangs out of Lancaster. . . . I want to make it uncomfortable for them to be here. Anything they like, I want to take it away from them. I want to deliberately harass them." When asked why gang members wouldn't simply adopt other breeds, he responded, "If they move on to cats, I'm going to take their cats."[44] Parris found flashy ways to place himself between Lancaster and the specter of gangs. When the Mongols motorcycle gang booked a local hotel for its annual summer gathering, Parris had the hotel padlocked for failure to pay back taxes.[45]

In a way, the strategy was a victim of its own success, running out of steam after Lancaster and the LA County Sheriff's Department coordinated a mass arrest of suspected members of the Mexican American Lancas 13 gang. Accompanied by a televised press conference, Parris and Sheriff Lee Baca declared victory over gangs.[46] The *Antelope Valley Press* splashed its front page with "AV reaches turning point in war on crime."[47] The city erected a billboard thanking Baca. And, to put icing on the cake, Arizona State University's Herman Goldstein Center for Problem Oriented Policing gave Lancaster and the LASD its 2010 Award for Excellence in Problem Oriented Policing.[48] The center published the submission packet that accompanied the nomination, and within it was included maps of crime and Section 8 housing, illustrating how police and city leaders thought of the rental assistance program as intertwined with crime.[49]

Now, having declared victory over gangs, Parris's focus would shift to low-income renters.[50] As the campaign of security against crime ran out of road, it would be transformed into a campaign of security of property, placed in the hands of valley residents themselves. Mark Neocleous suggests that this association of security and property masks "an underlying insecurity at the heart of the bourgeois order—the insecurity of property—which is deeply connected to the question of class."[51] Indeed, as the property value and class position of valley residents became more unstable, the commitment to security, and by extension policing, only increased.

In a 2008 City Council meeting, Parris announced that it was "time to go to war" against Section 8. "Make no mistake," he told the audience, "this City wants to limit the number of Section 8 units that are placed in this community." To legitimize efforts to stop voucher renters, Parris asked the Housing Authority of the County of Los Angeles for data on the "impact" of voucher renters on the city. When told that no such data existed, he echoed the neighbors of his childhood, explaining, "I'm more interested [in] what the neighbors think. I mean, we're assuming that these homes are having a detrimental impact on the morale of the neighborhood, for lack of [a] better word, for the character of the neighborhood."[52] But as Parris told me years later, there was simply no evidence that voucher tenants had a detrimental effect on the valley: "There was one and a half percent of this, actually, people who were creating problems. That was all, yeah."

Nevertheless, by 2009, Parris was publicly expressing frustration about the city's inability to curb the program. In the City Council's March 24 meeting, he had the following exchange with the lead administrator charged with carrying out city policies, City Manager Mark Bozigian,

> *Parris:* I am tired of working with these people. I want to see those numbers drop. I want us to be proactive in dropping those numbers. . . . I want us to set the goal in this City of how many thousands of Section 8 we are going to get rid of, and then we can at least start being, be accountable to ourselves as to whether or not we are moving in that direction. What I [am] unwilling to do is talk about this anymore. We know as much as we need to know. Let's figure out what the number, this is the number we will reach, and then we will be able to evaluate if we are doing things in a direction that is moving us into a successful conclusion. . . . And I think we should be absolutely honest and transparent, or whatever word you want to use, to the entire world: we are going to get rid of this many, this number, Section 8, from our community, and that is what we will devote all of our efforts to until it happens. When can I have that number? When can you present something to the Council that this will be the goal of the City?
>
> *Bozigian:* We could do that right now. Our goal, initial goal, is to get down to the County average, which is half of what we're at right now.
>
> *Parris:* So now we know that the goal of this City is to get rid of half of the Section 8, right?
>
> *Bozigian:* Yes.[53]

Lancaster began trying a series of strategies to achieve its goal of reducing the voucher population. One idea that Lancaster and Palmdale jointly explored was to split from the Los Angeles County Housing Authority, escaping their jurisdiction and allowing them to limit the number of voucher tenants who could move to the valley from Los Angeles. The strategy was the reverse of a quiet trend happening in Los Angeles, where tenants under the City of Los Angeles's Housing Authority were "porting" their vouchers to the County's Housing Authority to give them more access to available rental units. In 2008, Lancaster established a Section 8 Commission to look into the feasibility of creating its own housing authority. Ultimately, the strategy was dropped, because it was too expensive and administratively complex to create a new housing authority, and because departing from HACoLA would mean forfeiting tens of millions of dollars in other forms of housing assistance funding.[54]

Another idea was to find ways to limit the supply of rental housing available to voucher tenants. If it could not find practical ways to prevent voucher renters from choosing to move to the valley, it could restrict the ability of property owners to rent to them. The strategy responded to a widespread understanding that real estate speculators were purchasing homes at low cost, and renting them through the voucher program while waiting to eventually flip them when the market rebounded. As Parris told me by phone, "Certainly, you know, far more houses were being purchased for the purpose of renting them out than living in them . . . it was both companies and individuals . . . I know there's companies doing it. [I] never actually identified them, but I did identify some of the individuals, and, you know, they were friends of mine." Parris named an example, saying, "I think they own close to a thousand rental properties. They did most of it with Section 8, I guess."

To curb these practices, the city passed a Rental Housing Business License ordinance in 2007 that made all owners of rental properties acquire licenses from the city.[55] To acquire a license, property owners had to agree to be subject to inspections by the city. With the license system in place, the city looked into the viability of capping the number of business licenses issued for rental properties. A one-year moratorium on business licenses for single-family homes was proposed in 2009, but not enacted. Since business licenses for single-family homes would be used almost exclusively for renting homes either on the private market or to voucher renters, this strategy would have created a one-year moratorium on most new Section 8 rentals in Lancaster. The city would later return to this strategy of supply-side enforcement through the municipal code structure. This reveals a novel mechanism for local governments to restrict voucher renters from moving in. Rather than pass discriminatory policies that could be read as such and be struck down by a court, this strategy simply shrinks the possible supply of rental property by making business licenses a necessity and then capping them to restrict growth. For a city so dependent on its homeowners to consider curtailing their economic power during an economic crisis suggested just how important limiting vouchers was to its leadership.

Lancaster and Palmdale also considered a plan to steer voucher renters away from the valley and towards other locations in Los Angeles County. As Parris told me, "I was deliberately saying things to discourage people from moving up here on Section 8. I thought we were getting our unfair share of them."

Parris's statements were one thing, but Lancaster's Section 8 Commission asked HACoLA for permission to make presentations to voucher renters, and included police and code enforcement officers in the planned presentations as well. The presentations were intended to "inform them of what the cities expect from them as residents of both cities."[56] The content of the presentations was a stream of negative information designed to persuade renters not to rent in the area. One example included emphasizing high costs of home heating and cooling that voucher renters might not consider when looking at the cost of renting in the valley. Although the matter was discussed seriously, HACoLA ultimately declined the requests. The cities also asked HACoLA to "produce an ad campaign to dissuade voucher participants from moving to the Antelope Valley by falsely suggesting that there were no jobs, no services, and that the cost of living was high."[57] This too was declined.

A final strategy floated by the city in its efforts to restrict voucher renting was to direct enforcement through schools. In 2010 the mayor proposed to HACoLA that the city could begin a program whereby voucher renters with children would have their vouchers revoked if their children missed school. The plan was brought up multiple times. In an October 26, 2010, city council meeting, Parris formally proposed it to a HACoLA administrator. HACoLA responded by saying it had no authority to terminate the vouchers of parents whose children were truant. The city also pushed for state legislation that would empower HACoLA to terminate parents of children who missed school; HACoLA's response was that it had no interest in such legislation. "Some district attorneys' offices actually bring child-neglect charges," Parris argued, implying that the practice could be seen as a precedent to follow.[58] In 2011, Lancaster officials asked State Senator Sharon Runner (R-Lancaster) to write legislation that would allow housing authorities to terminate vouchers based on children's missed school.[59] Runner filed SB 660 in February 2011. The bill received a negative analysis and did not pass.[60]

This series of dead ends might appear to be failures, but the message they sent to the valley was clear. To private renters and homeowners, it kept the issue alive in the papers on a regular basis, constantly focusing attention on the tiny percentage of valley residents using the voucher program. It put those residents in constant fear of eviction. As avenue after avenue proved fruitless, the city consolidated its efforts around policing as a way to govern and remove voucher tenants and restore the lost social status of private renters and homeowners. As mentioned earlier, pastor and community activist V. Jesse Smith described the role of policing as part of a transition in strategies of racial segregation: "They just changed the way in which they were going to go about segregating people of color. In Sun

Village they were blatant, they were open about it. It was quite explicit: we don't want you here. With Section 8, they tried to do it through legislation, and tried to use crime as a new form of segregation."

THE POLICING PARTNERSHIP GROWS

The turn to policing began with Lancaster, Palmdale, the County of Los Angeles, and the Housing Authority creating a new enforcement program focused on voucher tenants. But it evolved into a form of participatory policing that enfolded residents of the Antelope Valley into the work of policing their neighbors.

The seeds of the enforcement program date back to a 2004 Memorandum of Understanding between Lancaster and the Housing Authority that enabled their cooperation in investigating tenants. The agreement was expanded in scope and budget 2006 and 2009. Palmdale also participated in the program. In 2009–2010, Parris expanded the Memorandum of Understanding undergirding this relationship such that Lancaster paid $121,266 for expanded investigations of voucher renters. This was matched with $284,000 from County Supervisor Mark Antonovich. This funded the salaries of inspectors and analysts whose job was to visit the homes of voucher renters to perform spot inspections of units for violations of HACoLA rules and city laws. This enforcement staff was given office space in the Los Angeles Sheriff's Department stations in the Antelope Valley (there is no local police force in the Antelope Valley: rather these services are contracted out from LASD). LASD officers accompanied the inspectors on their visits. HACoLA used its administrative time to liaise with the cities' enforcement program, providing the inspectors with names and addresses of voucher tenants in the valley. As Gary Blasi, Professor of Law at UCLA and a key figure in the effort to end the policing of voucher tenants, explained, "They were basically supplying them a target list once a month. Like, these are the people you should be harassing now. I don't know what else they told them, but they told them anywhere they lived. They knew everything about them, because they had their files."

The inspection regime was brutal. "Anywhere else in the county, if they were going to do an inspection, they were civil about it," Blasi said. "They would make an appointment to come talk to you and that sort of thing. They didn't surveil you as [the Antelope Valley fraud inspectors] did. I mean, literally, they did stakeouts on people to see if some guy showed up." The system was not confined to trying to find reasons to evict tenants based on purported violations of their rental contracts; it extended to terrorizing them as well. Speaking about fraud inspectors' practices of parking near voucher tenants' homes to surveil them, Blasi surmised,

> He was probably there to signal that people were being watched. And that's the way that stuff works. It isn't what they actually do, so much as what they communicate that they're going to do. So you have this anxiety all the time, and it's very

stressful. Particularly when he talked about Child Protective Services, and the implication that not only we're going to evict you and make you homeless, but we're going to take your kids away from you.

As Smith recalled, sheriff's deputies also asked people about their voucher status during police stops, including young people the deputies suspected of being children of voucher holding parents. "They stopped them right on Lancaster Boulevard and asked them, we know your parents are on Section 8. If you don't tell us what we want, if you don't give us what we're looking for. . . ." Smith elaborated that deputies would try to get children to answer questions in a manner that could implicate them in gang activity, which could then be used to jeopardize a parent's voucher through the crime-free rules. Smith explained, "They were using any way possible to get them out of Section 8. If they can get their Section 8 vouchers revoked, they would use the kids to do it. That literally would happen."

But the cities also extended their policing of voucher tenants beyond the new investigatory staff and sheriff's deputies detailed to this work. They began to make a concerted effort to involve residents of the Antelope Valley in the policing of their neighbors. This participatory policing had several advantages: it expanded the number of people surveilling and filing complaints about voucher tenants far beyond the government's capacity, it satisfied angry residents and gave them a sense of empowerment (rebuilding the lost morale Parris referenced earlier), it allowed for discrimination to run rampant as long as it was being done by everyday citizens, rather than the government, whose role was simply to accept and investigate complaints, and it offered the possibility of evicting voucher tenants and resisting the integration of once-white neighborhoods.

In newspapers and online, people spread the word about the HACoLA Fraud Hotline, a number that anyone could call to report a voucher tenant's suspected violation of Housing Authority rules. Around this time local residents started a Facebook group called "I Hate Section 8," in which they would discuss the program, denigrate its participants, encourage policing, and doxx suspected voucher tenants. Even on a mundane website like city-data.com, where people generally carry on unremarkable discussions about their cities, ask and answer each other's questions, and share trivia, threads could become singularly focused on the voucher question. Posters discussed where to live in the valley that would have no Section 8 tenants, bemoaned the waiting list being reopened, discouraged their peers from renting their property to voucher tenants, and encouraged each other to report Section 8 tenants to the program's fraud hotline, even without proof. A user employing the name of Palmdale's lead voucher fraud inspector, Gary Brody, replied to comments about the voucher program with reassurances that he was leading the efforts to police voucher tenants and encouraging angry residents to be patient as the system worked to remove them.[61] As a voucher tenant named Andrea described, these ideas were present in the media as well:

But [it's] the whole culture of the Antelope Valley. You can go to the *AV Press* any day of the week and you might see something, if you feel like somebody on your street is on Section 8, call this number and you think they're not complying. So that starts with them. Then you hear the city officials talk like that. Then you hear—when I say hear, you see them on T.V., you hear them in the newspaper. So that's what kind of culture we live in.

The results were predictable. In 2008–2009 for example, 414 calls were made to the fraud hotline regarding voucher tenants in the Antelope Valley, 40 percent of the total 1,084 calls made across the entire county in the same time period. It was a remarkable number given that the valley was home to just 17 percent of the voucher tenants in the county.

A staff report from Lancaster's Section 8 Commission to the City Council summarized the results of these efforts. Fueled in part by neighbor calls, the report noted, "Code Enforcement, County Housing Investigators, the Los Angeles Sheriff's Departments tasks forces, LAN-CAP, Community Oriented Policing Services team, (COPS); and Target Oriented Policing team (TOPS) and High Impact, Parole Officers, and Probation Officers have been working as a unit going house-by-house, block-by-block, and neighborhood by neighborhood to eliminate all disorderly tenants. This strategy is working and many citizens in several neighborhoods are beginning to feel the effects and see the positive change."[62]

THE WAGES OF POLICING

What accounts for such enthusiastic participation in the policing of one's neighbors? By creating pathways for individuals to participate in policing, the Antelope Valley was making policing into a form of property, something that would be used, and which could increase the status of its user. Policing restored the right to discriminate that was so diminished by the Fair Housing Act. And that right is one with powerful implications for the symbolic value and meaning of property. Being able to police elevated the status of those who possessed that power. Actually engaging in policing took that process farther, because it also diminished the status of those being policed. As Nick Blomley argues, property is not just about our capacity to use something; things are made property through their use.[63] Its not just that residents could engage in policing, or that they used it to protect property values, but that policing had become a form of property. This perspective does not rely on the stated attitudes of white residents (though they were overwhelmingly hostile to voucher tenants); rather, it explains their actions by considering what was at stake for them. In what follows, I show how local residents came to participate in policing and the effects it began to have on the neighborhood.

The "war on Section 8" was a war to regain property by dispossessing voucher tenants. The city paired the creation of enforcement capacity targeted at voucher tenants with legal moves empowering residents to file complaints against their neighbors. This moved the locus of discrimination down from the city itself to the individuals enforcing city rules. The system, according to The Community Action League (TCAL)'s complaint, originated "after Lancaster's mayor specifically asked the City Council to —[l]ook into a means for making it very easy for neighbors to file nuisance lawsuits with the assistance of the City against . . . Section 8 housing."[64]

The city's nuisance ordinance provided "enhanced penalties where there are multiple calls to the police or public safety entities for service—even where there is no actual criminal activity." The ordinance defined nuisance as: "Anything which is injurious to health, or is indecent, or offensive to the senses, or is an obstruction to the free use of property, so as to interfere with the comfortable enjoyment of life or property by an entire community or neighborhood, or by any considerable number of persons." This broad definition is not unique to Lancaster, but clearly can be used maliciously by anyone seeking to punish a neighbor based on a subjective interpretation of the code. Finally, and perhaps most importantly, the municipal code was also amended to state that if a rental unit was the subject of five nuisance complaints in one year, both the tenant and the landlord would be subject to fines and other penalties, which the landlord could avoid by evicting the tenant.

In sum, the city had created a system for local residents to police voucher renters. It both set up a way for individuals to make complaints that result in severe enforcement and encouraged the creation and use of neighborhood watch programs under the broader context of this policing. To really bring it all home, the city created a "Good Neighbor Guide" which informed residents of the municipal codes, gave them examples of complaints they could make, and walked them through the process of making a complaint. The cover illustration depicts a clearly African American figure standing in the middle of a home, surrounded by a racially diverse group of figures each holding on to a piece of the building (for example a roof, or a wall). The illustration nominally portrays the neighbors as helping to build the home, but given the guide's content and context, one might also interpret the image as the neighbors collectively dismantling it. The guide told residents, "When a problem landlord, tenant or homeowner becomes responsible for five or more nuisance calls within a 12-month period, each additional call will entail a stiff penalty of $1,000. When a neighborhood has a persistent problem, residents now have the ability to hit the property owner where it hurts, in the pocketbook."[65] This helped to ensure that the changes were not just made in the law, but that local residents opposed to Section 8 knew about them and knew that they should take advantage of the new codes. It made policing usable, fitting the first marker of property.

FIGURE 16. The City of Lancaster's
Good Neighbor Guide.
Source: City of Lancaster.

Some local residents were clearly empowered by the city government's hostility towards vouchers. Jim is a retiree who had moved to Lancaster after leaving the Navy in the mid-1970s. In my conversation with Jim he explained how reassured he felt by Parris's election and his efforts to give citizens more abilities to police their neighbors: "When we got R. Rex Parris in office that was the change up time because he stood up to the mongrels. He stands up for what he believes—he's against Section 8 himself and bottom line is he's got the Sheriff's department working with him where—I got a Deputy Sheriff on speed dial on my phone. I call him every time I've got a problem on the block. I don't put up with no crap."

One can easily read this in the language of property by seeing how acquiring more ability to police translated into increased status for Jim. This participation may generate its own empowerment, or what Du Bois called "wages." Here we can begin to see the fulfillment of the status marker of the property definition.

The city and its residents fueled each other, with city officials engaged in racist and anti-voucher speech and implementing vicious tactics to evict tenants, and local residents supporting the city ever more while feeling empowered to take the law into their own hands. They did so by surveilling neighbors they believed were using vouchers, dispatching police and city agencies to visit their homes for possible infractions, and directly confronting voucher tenants to assert their preferences and control over the neighborhood. The actions are legible from the lens of policing as property.

When private residents interacted with voucher tenants, it was from an assumed social position of superiority, rather than as neighbors. Patricia, a middle-aged Black tenant, explained, "When I came up here, people don't speak to you . . . they're really disrespectful. When you do speak to them, they try to figure out why you're speaking to them . . . they treat people however they want to treat them, they talk to them however they want to talk to them."

Andrea described her neighbors in a similar light: "My neighbors haven't been aggressive towards me or my family, but they're not very friendly. . . . Just—they're very cold if you speak to them. Many of my neighbors turn their head. I'm like, oh my God. What was that about? Did I do something wrong?" John added that one local resident overtly told him of his resentments. The local resident stated that while he paid $1,600 for his home, he knew John only paid $400. His statement that "I could pay your rent" suggested a superiority over John and other voucher tenants.

These interactions demonstrate two processes occurring at once; the denigration of Black residents of the neighborhood is tied to the assertion of a superior social status of private renters and homeowners. But the ability to weaponize these feelings through policing allowed local residents to further elevate their social status while diminishing that of voucher tenants. This is one reason why residents might participate in policing. Through participatory policing, local residents are enfolded into the act and practices of policing by their local government. It represents a synthesis between the mob and the state, in which the state empowers residents to act in ways that it knows are racially discriminatory but which it can claim to simply neutrally respond to and enforce. Local residents are empowered to participate in this policing because it furthers the ends they are invested in— removing Black residents from the neighborhood and asserting their superiority to them.

Local residents used their ability to police to surveil the neighbors who they believed were voucher renters, using crude race-class shorthand. The surveillance practices themselves delivered a first blow to voucher tenants, making them feel watched and unsafe in their homes and neighborhoods. Alicia explained her experience as a voucher tenant. At the time of our interview, her neighbors did not know she was a voucher renter. Nevertheless, she explained: "They stare. They call the police for anything. Not on me but my neighbors across the street. . . . They call the police on them like if they park their car in front of the mailbox, they call the police. That's ridiculous. They have too many cars in their driveway, they call the police. That ain't your business."

Another voucher tenant explained that they experienced surveillance by neighborhood watch, rather than just individuals acting alone: "There's something like—what is it? Not the policemen, the watchers. So for any little thing, they want to make a complaint, you know. They must want to get rid of us. They pretty much disagree with a lot of us that are on Section 8. You know, like I said, that's because they think that we're minimal or less of a person. . . ."

As these tenants attest, the purpose of surveillance is to generate opportunities to file complaints, call police, and otherwise trigger moments of state intervention that might result in the eviction of voucher tenants. Only a small number of local residents actively investigated which of their neighbors might be using a voucher. But by sharing this information with neighbors either informally or through the neighborhood watch, they effectively expanded the effects of surveillance much farther. These activities helped some residents reassert a feeling of control over their surroundings and laid the groundwork for further policing.

In multiple cases, respondents being interviewed at their front doors would point out the homes on their block which they knew were rented to Section 8 tenants and describe something about the tenants who lived there—whether they were noisy, how recently they had moved in, why a rental unit might be vacant, and so on. Jim explained in detail the various strategies he employed to identify voucher tenants:

> *RK:* And how do you know when a house is Section 8?
>
> *Jim:* How do I know? First place, I know every owner of every house in this block and I've got their number. And when someone rents a house and moves in, I ask them.
>
> *RK:* Okay. You ask the renter or the—
>
> *Jim:* I ask the owner. Is this Section 8 or are you just renting it out?
>
> *RK:* Oh, okay.
>
> *Jim:* And you can always go to the courthouse and find out if it's a Section 8 rental or not.

Jim later explained that he not only worked hard to know when and where voucher tenants were living in his neighborhood, but that he actively worked to organize his community to be aware of and assist in monitoring these tenants. This type of information sharing was not uncommon. Russell, a retired-by-layoff former aerospace employee who had been transferred to Lancaster by his former employer in the 1990s, explained how he benefited from these surveillance networks:

> *Russell:* We have a neighborhood watch here, one guy, and he always knows what's going on all hours of the night.
>
> *RK:* Oh, okay. So he kind of keeps an eye on things?
>
> *Russell:* Yeah. Makes the complaints.

Russell was effectively giving his policing power to a neighbor, perhaps someone like Jim. The act fits the marker of property known as disposal—the ability to give something away suggests that it was one's property. Russell did not need to go to the same lengths as Jim to discover voucher renters because he actively benefited from one of his neighbors' efforts to collect that information and share it among local residents. In this way, residents like Jim had an outsized effect on the neighborhood, as their information diffused through networks such as preexisting friendships between longtime residents or organizations like the neighborhood watch. These networks provided Russell with enough information to allow him to stand at his doorway and point out the homes within eyesight he claimed to know were rented by voucher tenants—adding the tidbits of information he knew about the renters as well.

In some cases, this surveillance and coordination operated through the local neighborhood watch, which served as both an information exchange and a tool of intimidation. Jim explained that they played a symbolic function: "I'll do anything I can to keep the signs up because that's a good preventative." Although he was frustrated by the scope of territory that required surveillance and disappointed that public participation was inconsistent, Jim remained adamant about doing his part, saying "I walk my block once a day or twice a day," and added that he would always watch the houses of those who made a good effort to participate in the neighborhood watch. In an interview conducted down the street, another respondent referenced him as a source of information about voucher tenants, an active monitor of the block, and a person who could be relied upon to call the sheriff or the city's code enforcement office. Another older resident on a different block expressed thankfulness for the good people on her street that monitored the "comings and goings," again suggesting that while only some residents engaged in very active surveillance efforts, their work had wide effects and was appreciated by others.

Returning to markers of property, something is property if its possessor can exclude others from its use. By watching supposed voucher homes, local residents could then call the local office of the Los Angeles County Housing Authority (which could investigate or evict voucher holders for violation of program rules), the city's code enforcement hotline (which could investigate or fine the property owners renting to voucher holders for violating city rules), and the police (who could make arrests and issue citations). Even if no formal punishment occurred, the inspection or police visit itself was a form of punishment for the tenant and could also function to intimidate them. Deploying these agencies constituted an important part of fighting back against vouchers and provided a sense of agency to local residents.

According to Russell, the motivation to make these calls was the promise of evicting unwanted neighbors: "Yeah, well I heard someone tell me that if you rent to someone and there's five complaints about them then they're evicted, and you can't rent no more." Russell's version was near the truth; it closely resembled the terms of the nuisance ordinance adopted by the city and described earlier in this chapter. One striking aspect of Russell's comments is how well he understands the city's new municipal codes, despite relying on a neighbor to make complaints. Whether his knowledge was a product of his social network informing him of these rules, online forums and message boards where opposition to Section 8 is discussed, or the Good Neighbor Guide that the city distributed widely across Lancaster, he knew exactly how many calls were required to evict a voucher tenant and place maximum pressure on his or her landlord.

Just a handful of local residents I spoke to volunteered to me that they made these calls, but they indicated that they made the calls in high volume and often on behalf of others on their block. Jim spoke with pride about the power afforded to him by this dynamic: "I got the Section 8 people thrown out because I was calling Code Enforcement every day. Every day Code Enforcement was over at that Section 8 house." Returning to the exclusion marker of property, to get someone "thrown out" of their home is to exclude them from the neighborhood, and by extension to exclude them from democratic participation in that neighborhood, including the ability to engage in policing if they wished.

But what was tacitly understood about this system of policing is that although the law is written in a facially neutral manner, it is really only meant to work in one direction—private renters and homeowners policing their subsidized and/or Black neighbors. Voucher tenants themselves stated that they did not want to call the police for service because they believed that doing so would mark them as a potentially problematic tenant in the eyes of HACoLA. It was rational not to want to increase the chances that they might lose their voucher, but that means that voucher tenants were excluded from possessing policing in the ways their neighbors possessed it.

Later in his interview, Jim detailed one incident in which he called the code enforcement hotline to inform the city that a neighbor had violated housing code when fixing part of her home. The tenant begged him not to file a complaint, but he said he did so anyway in order to send a message to others that violations would not be tolerated. When confronted by neighbors who claimed he was being too harsh, he recounted telling them to, "Take your neighborhood watch and shove it. Next time you see somebody messing with your mailbox, call a sheriff. Don't call me to call the sheriff." Here, Jim revealed his role as a local resident who made complaints on behalf of many of his neighbors and illustrated how seriously he took this informal role—either he would be allowed to enforce it as fully as he desired, or not at all. When other respondents stated that they were glad someone was making complaints or that they knew someone was keeping an eye on things, they were likely referring to a small number of individuals like Jim, who played this communal role.

In his 1985 study of Canarsie, Brooklyn's, resistance to racial integration, Jonathan Reider found that, although "a larger minority of the community approved of, or tolerated, vigilante-style actions, many residents, probably a majority, were only vaguely aware of them."[66] Rieder argues that the actions of these vigilantes had an outsized effect on the neighborhood because they intimidated Black families who rightly suspected they could be next, and because they shaped the broader public's perception that anti-integration violence was representative of the neighborhood's character.

The actions of respondents in the Antelope Valley seem to fit this schema—few were actively hostile to voucher tenants, but they enjoyed a large base of social acceptance or approval of their actions. One key difference, however, is that in 1980s Canarsie, anti-Black hostility was expressed through moments of criminal violence, while through its structure of policing, the Antelope Valley had created an environment of virtually constant harassment, but this violence had been endowed, embraced, and emboldened by the law. Because it imbued white renters and homeowners with the status benefits of being able to police their Black neighbors, they had every reason to keep it going, regardless of whether even the perceived threat of Black residency remained convincing.

In a lecture at UCLA in 2012, David Shorter discussed his experiences being stopped at checkpoints as he drove to conduct fieldwork with Yaqui communities in Mexico.[67] Shorter noted how checkpoints have a Janus-faced nature to them. Every checkpoint is a place where a soldier both checks you and themselves. People passing through checkpoints are checked both for the presence of unallowed physical objects, and for their docility and willingness to cooperate with the rituals of degradation that occur at the stops. Meanwhile, and perhaps more importantly, the officer conducting the search is simultaneously checking that they remain capable of asserting power, status, or dominance over passersby. In her work on anti-immigration attitudes, Cristina Beltrán has called the capacity to enact cruelty a form of citizenship in the United States.[68] Here, too, the processes Shorter and Beltrán discuss are in operation. The capacity to enact cruelty, violence, or eviction against another is valuable not only for its effect on its target, but also as a measurement of one's own personhood.

To understand the full consequences of the imbrication of policing as an enactment of social citizenship, I turn to Black voucher tenants to understand how they experienced, understood, and survived these forms of policing.

4

Unmaking Home

I don't know if things changed or if I've changed after being out here so long. When I first came out I saw things. At first, I saw the beautiful landscape and grass. The more I lived here I saw—started seeing the dirt.

—ANDREA

Outside the Housing Authority offices in the summer of 2015, Andrea agreed to speak with me. Usually I recruited interviewees at my little folding table on a grassy patch of the parking lot, and offered to call people at a time of their choosing. But Andrea wanted to talk now. She walked me to her car, where she sat in the driver's seat, leaving the door open so that I could stand beside it. It was going to be a long conversation.

"If I had known beforehand I never would have moved here," she said. "It's very racist." Thinking back to her early days in the valley, she recalled seeing Confederate flags in the neighborhood. "And I kind of didn't even know what they were. I had to do a little research. Like what's that about? . . . Are these patriots? What's that about?" The longer she stayed, the clearer things became. "And then I moved closer into the city of Lancaster and there was a skinhead meeting at the local Walmart, which I didn't know about, but my boys knew. I said hey, can you run across the street to Walmart? They said mom, we can't go today. It's Wednesday, and it's dark." Not understanding their meaning, she asked, "What does that mean? It's right across the street." To which they replied, "Mom, the skinheads is out. Like that's them." At this point it clicked: "Oh my God," she recalled thinking. "For real? At that time, I heard about stuff in the paper about crosses being burned, and people that's running for election who was part of the skinhead movement. I said 'oh my God, it's racist out here.'"

Years later, the skinheads had receded, but the city's hatreds had not. As public ire turned to the voucher program, and the policing program lurched into action, Andrea got a knock on her door. She had been expecting her annual compliance check the next day, so the arrival of an inspector that day was a surprise. Perhaps it was a strategy to catch tenants unaware. Andrea recalled, "So when the man knocked at the door I could see his badge, and I'm like 'Why are you here? I have a reinspection tomorrow.' I was expecting him, but the next day. He goes 'Oh, you've been selected for reinspection—I mean for a compliance check.'"

It is unclear whether the inspector had been hired by the city or was from the housing authority, but at the moment, it was a distinction without a difference. He was accompanied by armed officers. Andrea asked him,

> 'Why are all these police here?' My heart was beating so fast it was about to bust out of my chest. He said, 'They're with me.' And I said, 'Well, you can come in. I don't have nothing to hide, but they can't come in. They don't have a warrant and they're not coming in here.' He told me 'If they don't come in, then you're going to lose your Section 8. They go where I go.'

What can anyone really say to a person flanked by armed sheriff's deputies? Andrea nevertheless pushed back once more—asking why they needed all these deputies just for her and her children. The official's response was telling: "Well, that's up to us to figure out." The inspector had made it clear that he wanted to evict her, and was here to figure out how to do that. And so they began to enter and search her home. As Andrea described it, "They came in with shotguns. They came in in vests. They came in in riot gear, and they held guns on us like we were wanted criminals."

Room by room they went. "They went in my drawers. They held guns on my kids. They went in my kitchen drawers." They were finding nothing, so they kept going. They went to her son's room, and rifled through his drawers. Andrea recalled, "They pulled out an ID and some money and said bam—threw it across the table at me and said 'Hah, who is this?' That's what the officer said. 'Yeah. We got her. Who is this?'"

From her seat in the car on that hot day in Palmdale, Andrea conveyed the glee that she remembered in the officer's voice: he thought they had found something that would substantiate her eviction. If Andrea was harboring a resident who wasn't on the lease, even if it was her child, she could be evicted and have her voucher terminated. But she had all the documentation she needed to defend herself and her son. "I said that's my son. He's on my contract, and that's a little change from his Walmart job. What?" When they checked her voucher contract, the officer said "Oh yeah, yeah. She's right." You can still hear it on the recording, the dejection she attributes to the cops when they realize they have nothing on her.

That she had survived this eviction attempt could only be partial comfort. Speaking to me that day, long after the raid was over, she described the short and long-term consequences her treatment has had on her life. That day, the raid wasn't just happening in her home. It was a public spectacle for the neighborhood. She despaired that, "as if things weren't bad enough, I got all my neighbors on

FIGURE 17. Lancaster Sheriff's Deputies, LA County Housing Authority investigators, and parole agents search Section 8 apartments and homes in Lancaster, March 29, 2007. Source: Photo by Michael Robinson Chavez/*Los Angeles Times* via Getty Images.

the line, mostly white, and they're looking at us. All I know is after that day they never spoke to me again. They never said good morning—ever. Ever again." The immediate violence of the raid was accompanied by the slow violence of its social aftermath.[1] The inspection might not have succeeded in finding a reason to evict her, but it did succeed in degrading her in front of her neighbors. Perhaps it had been instigated by one of them calling the housing authority or city.

That day, Andrea was at risk of being evicted for having an unauthorized tenant—her child. The unauthorized tenant rule states that no one who is not on the lease can live in the voucher tenant's unit. Visits are permitted, but stays of an extended length would subject tenants to termination of their voucher. The rule, however, is weaponized to prevent tenants from even having the semblance of another person present, because someone complaining to the Housing Authority can just assert that the rules are being broken, triggering a more formal investigation. It is one of the easiest ways to evict voucher tenants.

What Andrea experienced, an unannounced inspection of her home conducted by a government official and often accompanied by armed police, is perhaps better understood as a home raid. Home raids are an important mechanism of urban governance, have persisted throughout the twentieth and twenty-first centuries, and are enacted against Black residents, particularly women, across both private and public housing. Though they are enacted upon the home, their target is the person who occupies it. In the prior chapter I explored policing's property function—namely, increasing the social status of those who might wield it. Here, the policing of housing functions to decrease the social position of those subject to it—taking away key elements of privacy, safety, autonomy, family, and more that are tied to home and that help to substantiate one's personhood.

THE HOME RAID'S PLACE
IN URBAN RACIAL GOVERNANCE

While the policing of Black homes stretches back to the slavery era, one early manifestation of the home raid appears in the post–Civil War era. Kidada E. Williams documents the night riders, vigilante collectives abetted by law enforcement that raided Black homes in the South to kill and terrorize Black families out of their homes.[2] They targeted Black men for the worst of their violence, and Williams notes that some slept away from the home to protect their families and selves. It would not be long until these extra-legal practices were absorbed into public policy.

Saidiya Hartman traces an early manifestation of the home raid as public policy to New York's 1901 Tenement Act, ostensibly passed to support the poor by attacking problems of unsanitary and uninhabitable tenement housing.[3] As Hartman documents, its most manifest effects were to increase the surveillance of Black homes and the arrest of young Black women.

This occurred because the act "identified the diseased home as the incubator of crime," and as a result sought to increase state power to enter and assess homes for their unsafe or unsanitary conditions, both in terms of physical conditions and overcrowding.[4] Rather than use economic redistribution to solve those issues, the state sought to police the home into a proper condition.

Thus, over time, as Hartman traces, the act mostly managed to 1) create a public and legal association of Blackness and prostitution, 2) criminalize vagrancy and define it as a product of prostitution, and 3) create an easy means for police to enter Black homes and charge tenants with prostitution. These charges no longer needed proof—all that was required was suspicion, based on officer testimony. And a wide variety of noncriminal activity was recoded as criminal. As Hartman notes, "any young woman residing in a tenement who invited a man into her home risked being charged with prostitution."[5]

Just as the legal bar to charging a tenant with a violation of the Tenement Act was virtually nonexistent, the police power to conduct searches under the act's auspices was equally unbounded. The key mechanism used to enact the Tenement Act was the "jump raid," a practice by which officers knocked at a door and then broke in when a resident answered. The widespread employment of jump raids physically and symbolically degraded Black homes, created a statistical association between Blackness and disorder through the circular logics of the law and its enforcement, and contributed to racial segregation and dispossession as landlords faced fines for their tenants' violations of the law. Ultimately, poverty was not addressed nor were building conditions repaired, but Blackness was policed and punished, and the practice of the raid was strengthened. When the tenements were torn down to be replaced with public housing, the raid reappeared as a way of governing its residents.

The jump raids' successor in mid-century public housing was the "midnight raid" of the 1950s and 1960s.[6] These followed the legal and social templates of the Tenement Act and its enforcement. States passed regulations that mandated the searches of welfare recipients' homes to ensure their compliance with the rules of the Aid for Families with Dependent Children program. Because only single mothers with children were eligible for AFDC, the state had a nominal interest in ensuring compliance by certifying that the women who received this aid were indeed single. The regulation came to be known as the "man in the house rules," and evidence of a man's presence (not just a male person, but even shoes, a coat in the closet, etc.) could immediately disqualify a mother from AFDC.[7] Because AFDC recipients often also lived in public housing, women faced a termination of benefits and housing.[8] The state's inspections took place at all hours, earning them the "midnight raid" moniker. Though those specific practices were stricken in 1968's *King v. Smith* ruling, the basic dynamic echoes into the present.[9] Raids on public housing tenants, including raids flagrantly in defiance of Fourth Amendment protections, continued after *King v. Smith*.[10]

In 1984, police killed Eleanor Bumpurs while evicting her from from her home in New York City public housing.[11] Four years later, the Chicago Housing Authority and the Chicago Police Department coordinated massive raids of public housing properties, with armed officers bringing drug-sniffing dogs into homes without warning or warrants.[12] The raids were portrayed as exceptional, and challenged by legal aid groups as unconstitutional searches, but after these highly visible moments, as Beth Richie documents, Chicago police continued to raid homes in public housing as a punitive and exploitative practice, using raids as occasions to threaten, steal from, sexually assault, and extort tenants.[13] As Richie notes, these practices were all the more possible given the impending demolition of buildings they raided: broader structural abandonment empowered specific violence against tenants. Today, public housing authorities continue to employ these practices from Indiana[14] to New York City.[15]

Home raids have also been a key historical part of the racial and urban governance of Los Angeles. Kelly Lytle Hernández traces the 1927 LAPD home raid of Clara Harris, during which officers murdered her brother Samuel Faulkner, and the protest movement that arose in response to it. As she notes, the LAPD preyed on South Central, "collecting pay-offs, conducting raids, and harassing people."[16] Despite the social movement that grew in response to the killing, police continued to invade homes to, among other things, enforce evictions spurred by development and business interests. Marques Vestal illustrates how these processes continued by illuminating the 1938 case of George and Cora Farley, who resisted being evicted from their home as part of the city's effort to expand the roads connecting their subdivision to other industrial areas nearby. George Farley killed the police officers who attempted to evict him and his wife.[17] The story has been turned into LAPD mythology—a story of valiant officers who sacrificed everything to enforce the law, rather than a story of the police role in unjust evictions. The story of the Farleys echoes through LA history; in 1979, LAPD officers Lloyd O'Callaghan and Edward Hopson killed Eula Mae Love at her home over a delinquent water bill.[18]

The raids were an important ingredient in reshaping early Los Angeles for capital and white interests. Operation Hammer, an outgrowth of the mass arrest style of policing implemented during the 1984 Olympics, illustrates the ongoing continuities of LAPD's degradation of the home. In 1988, "88 LAPD police officers raided two apartment buildings located on the corner of 39th Street and Dalton Avenue." The raids were an occasion to deface the homes. Police "caused massive property damage, including smashing furniture, punching holes in the walls, and destroying family photos." To assert their dominion over the homes of South Central residents, "police sprayed graffiti messages such as "LAPD Rules" and "Rollin 30's Harlem Crips Die.""[19] In the valley, too, police routinely used battering rams to break down front doors of suspected parole violators or gang members, and boasted of going to the homes of suspected gang members to give them "early morning wake up calls."[20]

The home raid is an important tactic of urban governance because it stretches the gap in how home is experienced between people at different ends of the nation's social hierarchies. It is among the many tactics that help widen a spectrum of experiences of freedom as it relates to housing.

On one end is a set of policing practices that make home unfree. For example, law enforcement uses no-knock home raids with impunity, killing Breonna Taylor and Amir Locke in recent years, and subjecting Anjanette Young to a humiliating search of her self and home, despite not being the target of the search. As a report on Young's case describes, Chicago police are able to conduct no-knock raids of homes without oversight or accountability. House arrest programs often use camera surveillance to enforce their rules, subjecting individuals to having their homes and private lives filmed. As Susila Gurusami shows, re-entry programs, managing people post-release from prison, routinize the pernicious inspections of homes as part of probation officers' powers.[21] And both the valley (as seen in the previous chapter) and the City of Los Angeles use nuisance property law to mandate evictions in majority Black and Latino neighborhoods.[22] For tenants exposed to these practices, this is an unfree, carceral form of housing.

On the other end of this spectrum, the right has increasingly asserted a vision of home centered around the capacity for violence. This trajectory builds on Oscar Newman's 1970s-era theory of defensible space, which argued that public housing failed because its architectural design encouraged crime and that increasingly atomized and inaccessible housing would naturally help defend against crime. Today, the home is not just a place to be defended but a platform for violence. The policies and practices discussed earlier in this book are complemented by the nationwide rise of neighborhood policing applications like Nextdoor and Citizen, as well as technological accompaniments like video doorbells. In addition, legislation to increase the powers of homeowners to "protect" their dwellings has spread across states, often anchored in what is known as the "castle doctrine." Dating to British common law, the doctrine permits someone to use deadly force to stop another person from intruding into their home. It envisions home as a place that can be defended, and that is permitted to be defended with violence.

The castle doctrine is being used to justify extreme violence that in other contexts would likely be prosecuted. In Texas, for example, Joe Horn saw his neighbor's home being burglarized and called the police. Because Horn was safe inside his own home, the police advised him not to engage the burglars, reassuring him that police had been dispatched. Nevertheless, Horn told the police that he was going to kill the men. Defying a 911 dispatcher's entreaties, he left his home and shot them to death. Horn was white; the men he killed were Colombian. Whereas leaving your house to kill other people might in other times and contexts be easily recognized as murder, Horn faced no consequences because of Texas's broad application of law around the castle doctrine.[23]

Just a few years after the Horn incident, Marissa Alexander fired a warning shot to defend herself from domestic violence in her Florida home. Her stand-your-ground defense, however, was rejected, suggesting to many the racially conditional nature of the castle doctrine. In this way, raids—who can summon them, who is subject to them, who can defend themselves against intrusion—widen the gulf between the empowered and disempowered when it comes to the meaning and rights attached to their homes. They make Black homes indefensible spaces by eroding the meanings, rights, and possibilities we might attach to the meaning of home itself. In that sense, this chapter will argue that the home raid is about devolving home into something lesser—mere shelter.

This chapter is based on the experiences of tenants across the Antelope Valley, including both plaintiffs in *The Community Action League et al. v. City of Lancaster and City of Palmdale* (hereafter *TCAL v. Cities*) complaint as well as forty tenants I interviewed between 2011 and 2015. I focus on seven tenants: five I interviewed between 2011 and 2015 (pseudonymously named Maxine, Barbara, Keisha, Andrea, and Shirley) and two whose testimonies appear in TCAL's litigation (plaintiffs Sheila Williams and Jaquinn Davis). I supplement these extended narratives with additional information from other interviews. These accounts reflect what tenants across the Antelope Valley experienced while the multi-pronged policing regime outlined in the previous chapter was at its peak. It was an effort to surveil and police them, but also to degrade the status of their homes through the raid, to transform their homes from something reliable, stable, and safe, into something permeable and tenuous.

This happened through many avenues. As we have seen, neighbors could pick up the phone and call the city, complaining to the nuisance hotline, or call the housing authority, complaining to its fraud hotline. Or city inspectors, empowered to police tenants, could choose to initiate inspections. Or the housing authority could do so, seeking to verify that tenants were complying with program rules. Regardless of which avenue was pursued, there were two possible ways in which a tenant could lose their housing: 1) either the landlord would evict them, forcing them to find another landlord willing to accept their voucher, or 2) the housing authority would terminate their subsidy, leading to their eviction if they could not come up with the entirety of the rent on their own.

Tenants describe government agencies relying on three housing authority regulations to generate evictions.[24] The first is the unauthorized tenant rule, which stipulates that only the authorized voucher tenant and the members of their household specifically on the lease may inhabit the home, and that violation would open a tenant to punishment or voucher termination. The second is a set of crime- and drug-free housing rules, the contemporary implementation of the long process of moving the war on crime into the realm of housing described in chapter 2. The third is the anti-fraud rule, which commits tenants not to deceive the government by participating in the program when their incomes are above its limits. By initiating queries as to whether these rules were violated based on small pieces of evidence that can be interpreted subjectively, neighbors, city investigators, police, and housing authority staff can initiate lengthy and difficult administrative processes that put the burden of proof on tenants and put them in jeopardy of having their voucher terminated. In total, between June 2007 and July 2010, the Housing Authority received 904 fraud hotline complaints, began 1,377 investigations, and terminated at least 496 tenants in the Antelope Valley. For comparison, in the rest of the county 1 in every 100 voucher tenants had their lease terminated, but in Palmdale, that fraction reached 1 in every 12, and in Lancaster, 1 in every 22.

This pressure affects tenants' lives at multiple levels. Their selves, romantic relationships, family relationships, and social lives all became eviction liabilities in the eyes of city and housing authority inspectors. At a broader level, however, the reality is that their status as Black women made them evictable; the specific justifications inspectors used were essentially pretextual—a way to justify evicting people who the valley long ago decided were not to be allowed.

In cataloging the effects of the Tenement Act and jump raids, Hartman noted that Black families tried to stay under the police radar in order to avoid arrests and prosecutions—sometimes splitting up families by sending a daughter to live elsewhere. At every instance, the valley's system of policing housing produced similar incentives. Tenants were pushed to become atomized—to not socialize with others, to not have family over, to not pursue love or friendships, to not be too visible, and to not present themselves in a manner that fell outside the subjective expectations of neighbors and governments.

In this chapter, I detail the aspects of life that are turned into eviction liabilities by neighbors, police, housing and other social service agencies, and the local government. We might take home to be a place where one can expect some level of safety, a space to be yourself, a refuge for romantic relationships, or a foundation for family relationships and community support. The policing of housing destroyed these expectations, devolving the places tenants lived into something that no longer was home.

HOME AND SAFETY

Sheila Willliams's experiences were recounted in *TCAL v. Cities*. For her, the safety that a home offers was obliterated by the policing of voucher tenants. Rather than a space protected from violence, the valley used "protection" as a way to police and potentially evict her.

Williams was a Black single mother and preschool teacher who had been living in Lancaster since the early 2000s. She had always been careful about revealing her voucher status to others, but that fear was heightened as public hostilities, particularly from city leaders, escalated, and word circulated that other voucher renters were being evicted. By October 2009, those trends reached her door.

"Sheriff's deputies came to her home one day while she was at work, allegedly responding to a call about a potential burglary. There was no burglary; Ms. Williams' son and his friends were at the home." The deputies determined that the home was a Section 8 unit, so rather than leaving once it was clear that there had been no burglary, they called a city-funded housing investigator named Allen Mullins and flagged the home to the Department of Children and Family Services. Mullins and the deputies searched the entire home. Her son called her at work to tell her about what was happening. She came home immediately, but by then the deputies and investigator had left. But her home had essentially been marked. Her neighbors, having seen the raid, now saw her with suspicious eyes.

Not long after, she received a notice terminating her voucher, presumably the outcome of the raid on her home. But she successfully defended herself in an administrative hearing at the Housing Authority. But Williams had only survived the first round. Soon after,

> A marked Lancaster City car, with what appeared to be a HACoLA staff person in it, began driving past her home at least two to three times per week. Sometimes it parked in front of her home for a period of time. Ms. Williams felt she was under constant surveillance, and the presence of the City vehicle made her family even more suspect in the eyes of her neighbors. In addition, after the investigation,

Ms. Williams found that her landlord no longer wanted her as a tenant because the City was monitoring the property closely, and the landlord had apparently been fined under Lancaster's nuisance ordinance. Thus, the landlord began sitting outside of Ms. Williams' home and monitoring Ms. Williams' family.

Williams had done nothing wrong. But the false report about a burglary was a sufficient opportunity to push her out of the valley. The report served as the opportunity, not so much to protect her, but for multiple government agencies to coordinate with each other, search her home, invade her privacy, frighten her family, degrade her status publicly, and attempt to terminate her voucher. Williams's case is a reminder that voucher tenants in the Antelope Valley not only experienced specific forms of policing targeted at them, but also the broader climate of racist policing in the valley at large.

HOME AND PERSONAL PRIVACY

Maxine is a mother of two living in East Palmdale whom I interviewed in 2011. She had moved there from Los Angeles in the mid-2000s. Maxine described a broad climate of hostility to voucher tenants that had blanketed the valley. "It's been splattered all in the newspaper. If you read the newspaper you're always hearing, okay, this is going on with housing, and they're trying to hire more investigators to go in to find out who else lives there." Maxine explained, "I have a gut feelin' that these people in Lancaster are very racist. The harassment alone would drive a person away from the community. I never had problems like this when I was in LA." Maxine explained that her comportment as a tenant was irrelevant, saying, "if you took a survey, if you went up and down the street and nobody knew I was on housing and you asked them how am I, they would say, oh she's a good neighbor. But at the same time, because I know I am on housing, when I read about housing, well, you know, it's like they don't want me here."

That rejection manifested not only through neighbor interaction but also through how voucher tenants were policed, and how Black residents were policed more broadly. Over the course of the interview, Maxine described persistent police harassment that substantiated her feelings of alienation. During one incident, she and her son were pulled over for a speeding ticket. Minutes after being issued the ticket they were pulled over again by the same police officer down the street, this time for a broken light. She was frustrated by what she perceived as a malicious second stop. She explained, "They do harass you a lot. You really have to be careful about what you do around here."

Although her landlord wanted to rent to her, she noticed that "the housing program itself seems like they don't want you on housing. It's kinda weird, it's like a catch-22. So out here they make it a practice to try to get people out of here. They look for things."

This "looking for things" translated into a broad practice of pretextual investigations that appear as though officials decided they wish to evict a tenant and then looked for charges that could be used to facilitate that eviction. The practice is inherently bad faith, but because of the power imbalance between tenants and government actors, and because the burden of proof is routinely placed on tenants to prove they are not in violation of the law, the strategy is brutally effective.

Given these circumstances, the idea of home as a place of refuge from scrutiny becomes even more important. Under these circumstances, Maxine felt it was important that her status as a voucher-user was hidden. "You might not even want your company to know you're on a housing program," she offered. "You might not want anybody to know. I know I don't."

That self-protective desire to remain unknown serves as important context when considering the ways a tenant's personal privacy is shattered by the regulation of the voucher program. Consider Barbara's experiences, for example. Barbara had been living in Lancaster for just over a decade when I interviewed her by phone in 2011. She recalled being visited by the police for a noise complaint while she was moving into her current rental. She asked the officer, "How am I supposed to have loud music playing when I don't even have any furniture or anything?" When she asked the officer where the complaint originated; he responded that a neighbor had called it in. Since she moved in, the same type of police visit has happened three times. Through these visits, Barbara has become hyper-aware of all the ways she can be evicted. As was the case with Andrea, one of the easiest ways to evict voucher tenants is through the unauthorized tenant rule, which can be exploited through complaints to claim that temporary guests or visitors were in fact long-term guests in violation of the rule. The effect is to force tenants into simply never having guests.

Even Barbara's own clothing made her suspicious in the eyes of inspectors. "When I first moved up here," she said, "they came to my house and brought the housing authority with them to my house, because they were saying that a man lived in my house." The unauthorized tenancy of a man in the house would be prima facie grounds for eviction and termination of the voucher. But as Barbara explained, "Well, a man don't live in my house. I'm actually a lesbian. So yes . . . that's my stuff." For Barbara's case to be persuasive, she needed the property owner's support, something not always guaranteed. "And so my owner had to tell them, 'Yeah. She's a lesbian. I knew when I rented to her. This is how she came to me. This is her appearance when she came to me.'"

In this case, the state's presumption of heteronormativity meant that it interpreted the presence of male-presenting clothing in her closet as prima facie evidence that she was harboring an unauthorized tenant in her home. Even when she explained that the male-presenting clothes were in fact part of her own wardrobe, it was not sufficient to be believed. Barbara had to convince her landlord to testify on her behalf so she would not be evicted because of the clothes she wears. The level of power this gives the landlord is significant. If a landlord held discriminatory views, or even simply wished to rent to another tenant, he or she might just as easily have declined to offer that testimony.

While it was Barbara's closet that became the subject of scrutiny, for Shirley it was other personal possessions and the appearance of her home that brought suspicion on her. Shirley is a late-middle-aged Black former tenant. She was one of the only people I spoke to who had been evicted. She moved to the valley after her Housing Authority caseworker suggested that she could find a better home for her family there than in Los Angeles. Her life was initially unremarkable by most measures, but as anti-voucher sentiment grew, Shirley explained, things began to change. "They had a sign on [a prominent street] saying 'We don't want Section 8 here, we don't want Blacks in this area again,' saying all types of stuff for a long time before they took that sign down." Shirley soon found herself subject to the ire of a white neighbor who was convinced that her family was responsible for his car having its side view mirror broken (Shirley speculated that it had been broken by a passing car). He began calling the city and housing authority to complain about her, which she believed resulted in a fraud investigator doing checks of Shirley's home for program compliance. "They kept coming back and kept coming back," she recalled.

Those investigations often involved detailed examinations of a tenant's home, with the subjective perception of an inspector determining whether a tenant's home crossed unseen boundaries of appropriateness. Shirley explained,

> And they'd come in there and raid your house and all of this and then he's going to say, he's going to tell me, 'Well, how've you been living like this, like you're living out of a magazine?' Because I had everything so neatly and clean and . . . what am I supposed to do? Have stuff all over the house? Then that would have been a problem. Then that would have been a problem because now, oh, the new thing is your house can't be dirty. If your house is dirty, I think two times or three times, you lose your voucher.

Shirley must, therefore, calibrate the appearance of her home so as to not appear too dirty, which would appear to be disrespecting or even materially damaging the landlord's property (something the housing authority very much seeks to avoid), nor to appear too clean, suggesting that a tenant who could maintain a very clean home must not be in economic distress severe enough to truly need the voucher. The same care applied to objects in her home, such as a purse.

Shirley had been told by a friend not to have valuable items like a designer purse in her home. The presence of such an item would suggest that a tenant was committing voucher fraud, if they had an income sufficient to afford a luxury good. But as detailed in the next section, it could also affect romantic relationships.

HOME AND RELATIONSHIPS

Shirley explained to me how she now thought about nice items in her home. "So I'm dating a guy, and he bought me a designer bag. That's my business." She bristled at the idea that a city or housing authority inspector could hold the presence of a designer bag against her as evidence she was committing fraud. Someone had suggested getting rid of it, but Shirley resented the notion. "I say, yeah. I'm not going to go trade [it in]. Is you stupid? Come on now, that's stupid. . . . Any purse a woman gets . . . guess what . . . she's going to continue to use it. Why would she just throw it away?" It was not a choice she should have to make. The unspoken mandate to dispose of nice items if they might catch the suspicious eye of a city or housing authority inspector further reveals the ways that these inspections degrade the meaning and status of voucher tenants' homes.

Keisha is a middle-aged mother who has been using a voucher since 2007. During our conversation she explained her feeling of being spied on by neighbors and explained that her sister had experienced similar surveillance. Her sister was in a relationship, and her boyfriend sometimes visited her home or spent the night. It was unclear which party took note of this—aggrieved neighbors, city inspectors, or the housing authority—but they responded by attempting to terminate her voucher. As Keisha explained, "So they had a car sitting in front of her house for two weeks watching her house and it got to the point where my sister and her boyfriend were like 'hey I don't live here, this is my lease right here, you want you could follow me to my house, this is my girl, like I spend the night here, I stay here, this is my girlfriend's house, you know?'" That the boyfriend had to bring a lease to confront an authority engaged in surveillance reveals the extent to which tenants felt they needed documentation to enjoy any semblance of normality associated with home.

Telling this story jogged another memory. Keisha went on to describe the experience of a friend who lost her voucher simply because her boyfriend possessed a copy of her address when he was pulled over by police. Police found drugs in the car, and because he used her address, the housing authority attempted to revoke her voucher. As Keisha explained, "I mean, she said he didn't live with her but she let [him use her address]. But they never said you can't, that's just like if I have a uncle that's homeless and he says, 'Hey can I use your address for a mailing address?' That doesn't mean he necessarily lives with me because he used my address as a mailing address, you know?"

As this chapter will show, valid reasons to allow another person to use one's address can become eviction liabilities if they are read as evidence of unauthorized tenancy, or in combination with the program's drug-free rules. As each of these anecdotes suggests, tenants find their romantic relationships scrutinized by the public–private regime of voucher regulation, and this scrutiny can turn those relationships into eviction liabilities.

HOME AND FAMILY

Jaquinn Davis, a Black single mother, moved to Lancaster in 2010 in order to find a better quality Section 8 rental. Her son had asthma, and the unit they were renting in Los Angeles had mold. After their move, her son was bullied in elementary school in Lancaster. Other tenants I spoke to described this bullying in detail. They cited their children's experience being called "Section 8 moocher[s]." Another parent recounted how her child was told "if it wasn't for Martin Luther King, Jr., they wouldn't be here" (in the Antelope Valley), and one parent reporting that a group of children chose to dress as Ku Klux Klan members as a prank on career day. Yet another recounted that she was pleased her son could now walk to school, but worried that his repeated experiences of police harassment put him in danger when walking back and forth unaccompanied by her. Another tenant referred to her children as having to figuratively "fight their way through school."

So Jaquinn decided to re-enroll her son at his old school in Los Angeles, where he had been on the honor roll. They commuted to Los Angeles every weekday, taking the Metrolink train to Downtown Los Angeles where Davis's mother would pick up her son and take him to school, while she went to work at a beauty salon. She paid a heavy price for these sacrifices.

The Department of Public Social Services, from which she also received some support, opened an investigation into her family, believing that she was committing fraud by lying about residing in Lancaster. She had to prove to the fraud unit that she was genuinely commuting with her son for his school and her work. She was asked to, and did, provide a letter from the school confirming her son's commute from Lancaster, as well as "rent receipts, utility bills, train stubs, and a declaration" explaining her circumstances. The documentation satisfied DPSS, and they closed the case. But when they had initially flagged her case, they had also contacted officials in Lancaster, suggesting that she might be subleasing her Section 8 unit as part of the fraud it had once suspected. Now, having fought off one investigation, she would now need to deal with another.

In June 2011, she was visited by Inspector Mullins, who asked for permission to conduct a compliance check. Davis relented, fearing that to not give consent would be to risk her voucher. Davis asked why the search was happening, and Mullins replied that it was because DPSS had told him she was subleasing the unit rather than living in it. Davis explained that she had been cleared of the entire thing, and pulled out all the documentation from DPSS proving it. But Mullins replied that he already had all copies of it all. Knowing that she had been cleared, he was going to investigate her anyway. "Mullins conducted an inspection of the entire home—pulling out bureau drawers and looking through closets. Mullins expressed surprise that Ms. Davis' home was clean and well-kept, as though he expected otherwise. Unsurprisingly, he found no evidence that she was subletting the home."

Still, the next month, HACoLA summoned her to its Palmdale office and asked her to sign a copy of the Housing Authority rules, a sort of attestation that she had read them and could not claim ignorance if she violated them somehow in the future. Staff never explained why she had been called in, why she was receiving this warning and degrading experience, or what rules she might be breaking.

Davis was in an impossible situation; doing what was best for her child's health and education meant being exposed to a series of government agency investigations aimed at evicting her and terminating the public assistance she was receiving. Circumstances were heavily arrayed against her: government agencies could collaborate to punish her but would not collaborate to accept her innocence.

Other tenants spoke of their fear to help or even host family as visitors. Barbara explained, "I'm afraid, you know, if I have family visiting and they [inspectors] decide they want to come over, they might see a family member's toothbrush,[25] or they might see a family member's car. And you know, their whole assumption will go into 'oh you have an unauthorized tenant.' Do you understand what I'm saying? They just pick at that. So you know, I follow the rules. I don't want them kinda problems."

Under these circumstances, no tenant could feel safe having family over. Barbara recalled telling family, "You can't be here more than that many [a few] days. . . . They could terminate me!" As harsh as it might be to say this to family, Barbara feels trapped. "if they terminate me, how can I pay $1,650 for rent? If they kick me out, where will me and my kids go? How will we live?" The sentiment, of course, extended to social relationships more broadly. Maxine explained, "You're scared to have company because you don't want somebody pulling up saying, 'Do they live here?'"

Finally, the unauthorized tenant rule was not the only mechanism by which family members were turned into a jeopardy. Crime and drug-free housing rules accomplished the same ends by making it such that family members with criminal legal system entanglements were liabilities for tenants. Barbara explained, "For instance, if I have a son that went to prison, and my son got out of prison, and I'm his only family, do you know, my son could not come to my house because he's on parole?" Thus, even after a child has served time and been released from prison, parents still feel they cannot invite them into their homes for fear of a housing inspection that might evict them. Like the contexts of welfare and child services, where one's criminal background or drug use might render one ineligible to receive support or retain custody of one's children, in the voucher program a child's infractions may jeopardize a parent's access to housing.[26]

HOME AND AID

But this wasn't the end of Barbara's precarity. Mail addressed to the unit's prior tenant was still arriving in her mailbox occasionally, and there was little she could do to make it stop. She explained, "When the tenant's stuff comes in my mailbox, I just put it 'return to sender'. Because if they catch anybody else's address and they're not on your voucher, they will terminate you."

Barbara's fear of mail addressed to someone else comes from family experience; her sister was evicted because a housing inspector found a piece of mail addressed to someone not authorized to live in her home. "She was a lesbian also, but she had a girlfriend. And the girlfriend just happened to be there. And the girlfriend [was] using her address for a mailing address. The girlfriend didn't live there, but they took her voucher because of that. Just because of that."

Even though the girlfriend did not live in the home, the fact that she used the address to receive mail functioned as sufficient proof for the voucher holder to be evicted. In this case, mail addressed to someone other than the registered voucher renter is a cause for belief that the tenant is engaged in voucher fraud through harboring an unauthorized tenant. The personal relationship is thus transformed into an eviction liability. This anecdote reveals not just the depth of inspection that tenants are subject to—the contents of one's mailbox—but also the types of survival methods for poor communities that are rendered off-limits to voucher tenants. Mail addressed to someone other than the voucher tenant could arrive because a tenant is housing an unauthorized tenant, but it could also arrive for a number of other reasons. It could be misdirected, or it could be addressed to the previous resident. Or, as described earlier, the tenant could be receiving mail for another person as a form of social support, such as to assist someone during a period of homelessness or insecure housing.

DeAndre, an early-middle-aged father, relayed knowledge of a case in which his friends were evicted after they knowingly violated the housing authority's rules by opening their home to someone in financial distress. "I know two friends of mine that were incarcerated because extra people were in their house," he said, noting that voucher fraud could lead to criminal penalties. "You know, I'm not saying [the Housing Authority] weren't right, but I'm just saying . . . sometimes the economy is so bad, you've got to do what you've got to do." Los Angeles County is the center of the homelessness crisis in America, and housing family members or close friends is a common strategy for weathering financial crises. Although this mode of caregiving is denied to voucher renters, some choose to prioritize it over and above the rules imposed by the program.

A SECOND BANISHMENT

Towards the end of her section in the Community Action League's lawsuit against the cities of Lancaster and Palmdale, readers learn that "Ms. Ross is seeking to relocate to a home outside the Antelope Valley." It was the inevitable result of the process of expulsion initiated by the valley's people and its politicians. What Ross and tenants across the valley experienced was a sustained effort to devolve the places they lived in into something that no longer was home.

It wasn't only Michelle Ross who was forced out of her home. After a few months of harassment from her landlord and the housing authority, knowing that if her voucher was terminated she and her children would be homeless, Sheila Williams left her job, pulled her children from school, and moved out of the Antelope Valley. And while the third plaintiff in *TCAL v. Cities*, Jaquinn Davis, had not lost her home yet, she reported fearing that she would be evicted soon. Tenants I spoke to largely had not been evicted, but they expected it, and they spoke of life in the Antelope Valley in ways that illustrated that their homes were no longer such; they had been devolved into mere physical shelter. Tenants' circumstances should be understood in the context of how they arrived in Lancaster and Palmdale—racially banished from Los Angeles by its twin systems of segregation and scarcity. Now, in the desert, they faced a second banishment.

Before our conversation ended, I asked Shirley if she believed she had a right to privacy, given the depths to which her home was inspected. "No. No." She said, "The only way you have a right to privacy, you hit the lottery and get up out of here."

The lack of privacy Shirley spoke to reflected the larger process by which tenants could not rely on their homes to be a refuge from racism. It weighed heavily on tenants. Maxine explained, "How could you rest, how could you sleep at night, how could you relax? Even if you did what you are supposed to do, it's a very uncomfortable feeling that somebody could be down the street watching you, watching who goes in and out."

And Andrea still felt the effects of the raid on her home. "I think differently about the knock on the door now," she said. "I'm terrified. Like are they going to take my children? I don't have children now. So why am I still so scared that it's bam, bam, bam on the door? . . . Is this the police?" Noting the gulf between the rights attached to her home and those afforded to others, Andrea remarked, "They've got to have a search warrant, but for me they don't."

Knowing that peace of mind was not possible, tenants nevertheless tried to find ways to minimize the scrutiny of their neighbors and the city. As Barbara reflected on her life in the valley she described herself as withdrawing from her surroundings. "Now I just don't play any music, I try to keep the peace. No music, no company. Not that I had a lot of traffic anyways. I just try to stay to myself. It's been a few months since the cops have been out here."

Maxine explained her strategy to treat the valley as housing, but to pursue life back in Los Angeles. "Everybody I know and associate with don't live out here," she explained. "So I have to travel for my associations, have to travel to go to different events, and I come back home and this is where I sleep. And when I'm involved with different activities, it's never here, it's always away. I have to pack up and leave." These strategies can be read in several ways. At one level they are pragmatic ways to preserve shelter in the face of eviction. We might also think of them as forms of labor that are used to sustain one's ability to care for family, what Gurusami calls motherwork.[27] But we can also think of them as a form of resistance, a type of refusal, non-cooperation, or disengagement from a system of injustice.[28]

Finding ways to remain in the valley was not the only way tenants resisted—they also chose to leave it. Lakisha, a younger voucher renter, described her thoughts about leaving as she considered the impossibility of home in the Antelope Valley:

Lakisha: I'm gonna be honest and tell you the truth. I'm thinking about moving back to the city about—maybe next year—a year or two.

RK: How come?

Lakisha: I'm thinking about it. First of all, I miss my family and it get lonely up here. . . . Like I don't even know nobody. I stay to myself.

RK: Yeah. Yeah, that's hard.

Lakisha: And that's the best way to be.

MERE SHELTER

In *Neglected Stories: The Constitution and Family Values*, Peggy Cooper Davis shows that family was a central motivation for passing Reconstruction legislation and the Fourteenth Amendment.[29] Her historical account of legislative speeches and debates over these bills and amendments showed that Reconstruction legislators understood that the systematic violations of the integrity of the family that occurred during slavery would persist without constitutional protection. These texts surfaced an interpretation of freedom that required the autonomy of the family. As I read Davis's work, I saw home appear regularly throughout the speeches, testimonies, and records of the time.

In 1866, speaking about the homestead provisions of the Freedmen's Bureau Bill, Senator Thomas Eliot remarked that, "Slavery cannot know a home . . . where man and woman . . . are parted and sold at that owner's will, there can be no such thing as home. Sir, no act of ours can fitly enforce their freedom that does not contemplate for them the security of home."[30] Senator Jacob Howard, speaking in defense of Congress's right to enforce general citizenship rights on behalf of freedmen, again included the home as a central component of what constituted freedom. He asked, "Is a free man to be deprived of the right of acquiring property, of the right of having a family, a wife, children, home? What definition will you attach to the word *freeman* that does not include these ideas?"[31]

The frequent inclusion of home in the argument that freedom requires guarantees of personal and familial autonomy is revealing. Freedom needs a place in which to exist and grow. Or, as Ruth Wilson Gilmore has insisted, freedom *is* a place.[32] Such a place could be a city, town, or neighborhood, but as bell hooks shows, it could also be a home. hooks defines *homeplace* as a place of refuge from and resistance to racial oppression; a site, regardless of its physical form, of "radical political dimension."[33] She identifies the homeplace as a place to restore dignity, a space of healing and affirmation, a space that affords the opportunity to grow, and perhaps most importantly, a place of political possibility.

Reflecting on the era of the jump raids in New York City, Hartman observed that "The black interior fell squarely within the scope of the police."[34] The contemporary experiences of tenants in this chapter illustrate the continuity of this dynamic and the urgency of reversing it, and they are reflected in the experiences of subsidized tenants in cities like Houston, too.[35] Policing practices have increasingly created what tenants and scholars are identifying as carceral housing.[36] But considering the definitions of home developed above, one might say that the policing of home is antagonistic to home itself. As it eliminates the role that home plays in family liberty through casting family members as unauthorized tenants and forcing them apart, as it pierces the privacy of the home with surveillance to enforce its rules,[37] and as it enters it without restraint and turns family objects within it—like Shirley's purse—into liabilities for eviction, policing devolves home into something akin to mere shelter. As hooks warns, "when a people no longer have the space to construct homeplace, we cannot build a meaningful community of resistance."[38]

Yet despite the manifest attacks on home and person whose full scope and reality exceeds what is captured in this chapter, a community of resistance did exist in the valley and did work to halt and substantially beat back the policing of housing. Among the tenants I spoke to, many loved things about the Antelope Valley despite how unwelcome it made them feel. For some, the valley was quieter than the places they lived in before; for others, it was safer, or slower-paced, or had more space. There were things that made home in the valley worth fighting for. In what follows, I turn to an account of that fight.

5

The Second Sun

No longer will there be unannounced compliance checks. No longer will seven or ten sheriff's deputies show up at a Section 8 residence, armed and ready to invade the home. That is now finished.

—V. JESSE SMITH

One day, all the news articles about the policing of voucher tenants and community activism against it disappeared from the *Antelope Valley Press* website. It seemed that the paper had been bought by a new owner, who deleted the online archives and re-started the digital edition from scratch. One could be forgiven for the creeping suspicion that it benefited the powers that be to get rid of all the bad press. Thankfully, Pharaoh Mitchell had kept physical copies of the *Antelope Valley Press* editions that chronicled the multi-year fight against the policing and eviction machine targeting voucher renters in the Antelope Valley. He showed them to me one day after a lengthy interview about his experiences leading The Community Action League (TCAL) in the fight. To remember what happened is to work against agnotology in the valley, what Du Bois called "deliberately educated ignorance,"[1] or the effort *not to know* that is so central to maintaining things as they are.[2]

This chapter traces the struggle of Antelope Valley organizers to understand what was happening to voucher tenants and create a social movement capable of stopping that harm.[3] Organizers came together under the banner of The Community Action League to raise public awareness and pressure public officials. TCAL found allies in Los Angeles's activist legal community who developed a parallel strategy of litigation that would break apart the policing partnership that existed across city agencies. If the policing partnership was a three-legged stool between the cities, housing authority, and county government, the legal strategy was to knock out each leg. While TCAL's litigation focused on the cities, the Department of Justice's Civil Rights Division intervened as well, securing additional settlement terms that effectively knocked the County Sheriff's department out as well.

In all, the campaign successfully dismantled the policing partnership, a diminishment of policing in a region where it had only escalated for years prior. The campaign also successfully restored vouchers to many tenants who had them illegally stripped away and secured financial restitution to tenants. The movement also triggered broader investigations into racist policing across the Antelope Valley and a new settlement designed to remediate those practices. Not all these efforts were successful, and this chapter will explore how police reform was short-circuited. Nevertheless, this movement against the policing of housing built new social sinews connecting the valley back to activist lawyers in Los Angeles, remade and extended the legacy of fair housing work in the valley dating back to Sun Village, extended the legacies of public housing tenant activism, and overcame the voucher program's atomization of tenants with shared interests and problems.

BECOMING AWARE OF THE PROBLEM

V. Jesse Smith is a pastor, organizer, and union leader in the Antelope Valley. He became a leading member of the effort to undo the policing of voucher tenants through his work as an associate pastor at Solid Rock Bible Church in Lancaster. "Members kept coming up to me," he explained, "talking about how their homes were being invaded by the Los Angeles County Sheriff's Department, and that . . . it was maybe seven, eight [officers] showing up at their house, because they were on Section 8, with their guns drawn, knocking on doors, going into their homes, supposedly looking for drugs and looking for ex-offenders. Literally they were stopping their children, asking them, 'we know your parents are on Section 8, you better tell us what gang division you belong to,' and stuff like that."

The reports were shocking. "I was listening to them, I was like, this can't be happening. I went and set up a meeting with the Mayor, he didn't want to meet with me. . . . They had set up this commission which was the Section 8 Housing Commission. He'd given the decree, 'I want you to run this commission with an iron fist.' If you go back and read the archives and the newspapers, that's what his edict was. You're going to run this commission with an iron fist, and we're going to target Section 8 residents."

Meanwhile, Pharaoh Mitchell was part of a small group of community activists working on other criminal justice issues, including the misconduct by the Sheriff's Department described earlier. Mitchell said, "We saw that [Smith] took up the fight for Section 8, and was talking on behalf of Section 8 clients. So we said immediately we had to meet with him. . . . We met with him, and we formed a group. And we didn't know what the name wanted to be, so I said, 'Let's go ahead and name it The Community Action League.'"

Through TCAL, campaigners were able to create a single point of contact for organizing the voucher campaign. TCAL would soon become an organizing force in the Antelope Valley, bringing awareness about the issue and public pressure on the region to cease its practices. As TCAL member and longtime activist Emmett Murrell described the group, "TCAL saw themselves as one of the groups that was determined to show that . . . we could compete against these forces that pretty much dominated . . . the culture, but also [give people] hope for the type of justice we felt that had to take place. If we were going to alter and change that culture we had to be able to, we had to have a vehicle that we could all rally behind. Poor people needing a good place to stay and some of the things that were going on within the community at the time were just unacceptable. I think the politicians at the [time] were equally as hard on us. [They] were trying to combat what seemed to be a wave of the future."

In this way, the voucher fight became a way to struggle over broader conditions in the valley as well. "When it came to the police harassment, the unjust arrest," Murrell explained, "the two became merged as an equally dangerous issue. Section 8 itself became the foil that was going to determine where we were going to go and how we were going to get there."

At the local level, TCAL connected multiple struggles against the valley's racist practices. And regionally, TCAL became the node of connection between local activists and lawyers in Los Angeles who could support tenants' struggles. Their first connection was a law professor at UCLA named Gary Blasi.

ORGANIZING LEGAL SUPPORT
FOR VOUCHER TENANTS

Blasi had been teaching a fact investigation clinic at the law school, a type of course where law students gained skills in building real-world evidence that may support a legal case or the needs of a client. In the fall of 2010, students in the course had worked to dissuade the Los Angeles County Housing Authority from changing its administrative rules to make it more difficult for tenants with prior drug conviction histories to access housing support. The clinic was successful in its efforts, but as Blasi tells it, "towards the end of that class . . . I heard this story about one of the Section 8 tenants who was up in Lancaster and what had happened to them."

Alarmed by these reports of evictions, Blasi began reaching out to other organizations that might be able to help. Prominent among those was Neighborhood Legal Services and one of its lead lawyers, Maria Palomares. Blasi and Palomares began to work together, and Blasi made the work the subject of the next semester's fact investigation clinic. Next, they connected with TCAL. Per Blasi,

> TCAL agreed that at least Maria and I would become their lawyers for purposes of doing this investigation, and we got in our retainer agreements and stuff from them. And yeah, we just basically set about doing the work, but meanwhile as I was learning more, I was thinking I don't have a litigation clinic, but this is exactly what the fair housing laws and civil rights laws are for, is to stop this kind of stuff. I mean, this was not subtle.

As Mitchell describes it, the formalized partnership between TCAL, Blasi, and Neighborhood Legal Services was "what got all the balls rolling." As they gathered evidence over the next few months, it became clear that the case would require litigation. Neighborhood Legal Services had been representing some evicted voucher tenants, bringing four cases to Superior Court 2005 and 2007, and winning three.[4] Although the win rate suggested that the strategy could be successful, it would be difficult to pull off at a large scale. And other strategies, like tenants fighting the termination of their voucher benefit in the housing authority's administrative hearing system, would be just as unlikely to succeed at scale. Despite a handful of key legal protections, poor tenants face enormous obstacles to the enforcement of their housing rights.[5] Tenants may not always know their rights, may not have access to lawyers or legal aid, may not file cases in time, and face a civil legal system that reproduces race and class inequalities.[6] And the federal government does not recognize voucher tenants' rights to organize (though it does recognize this right for public housing tenants).[7] Most importantly, the climate of intimidation and hostility towards tenants affected their calculation about fighting back. One tenant described their concerns: "Okay, I can stand up for myself, and I'm going to sue them all. They knew they violated my civil rights. Then I thought about the other side. [I've got] kids to take care of. I cannot afford for those police to come in here and cause trouble. You know, is Section 8 going to kick me off?" In this way, the distance between tenants' rights and the remedies that would make them whole was simply too great.[8]

A better approach would be for a community group to sue the government on behalf of tenants. To pursue this course of action, there needed to be significant legal resources to gather and manage the volume of information that would be involved and staff the tasks required to mount litigation. Blasi built a small legal team with Palomares, Catherine Lhamon of Public Counsel, and other lawyers around the state with experience in fair housing who could help manage the case. This group would lead one track of litigation aimed at breaking up the policing partnership between the Housing Authority, the cities of the Antelope Valley, and the LASD.

In September of 2011, organizers held a Section 8 Community Forum, where Section 8 tenants and local residents spoke out about their treatment in the valley by the city, housing authority, and the Sheriff's Department. The *Antelope Valley Times* reported one such testimony from Jerome Reynolds, who told the story of an early morning raid on his family's home, based on a tip that drugs were being sold out of the house. "The Sheriffs came 8 cars deep and emptied everybody out of the house. . . . The Sheriffs never did find no drug paraphernalia and later apologized."[9] The forum showed how common these experiences were and how much more work had to be done to grasp its scale.

Not long after the forum, Blasi caught a lucky break. The head of the Department of Justice's Civil Rights Division at the time, Thomas E. Perez, was visiting UCLA, and Blasi was able to secure a meeting with him to describe what was happening in the valley. As Blasi recalls,

FIGURE 18. Residents pack the Center of Light Church in Lancaster to speak with attorneys and investigators from the U.S. Department of Justice, December 13, 2011. Source: *Antelope Valley Times.*

He was kind of noncommittal then, but the later conversations I had with him, or actually from people in his office, made clear that he had gone back to DC, and had put some really cracker jack people [on it]. . . . I mean, most of the lawyers in that division are cracker jack. It's a very elite group. But that was basically a one-way street. I mean, we fed them stuff, but they represent the government, and there's. . . . Other than giving them everything we had, we didn't get anything in return, but we understood that was the deal.

"And then," Blasi explained, "they were really admirable in terms of coming out here and spending a lot of time and having a big public outreach." Mitchell recalls, "The Department of Justice came on board, they gave me a call, and they called Darren Parker and they asked if we could put together a town hall event so that we could hear the complaints from the community."

Held in mid-December, the second town hall was a catalyzing moment.[10] Blasi said, "It wasn't easy to get individuals to come forward, because, well, because they were terrorized, which was the whole point of the policy." But TCAL and other groups, including AV Latino Education, spread the word and encouraged community members to share their experiences. Mitchell estimated that over three hundred people attended. The meeting took two and a half hours. People formed lines corresponding to the entity that violated their rights—one line for complaints involving Section 8, another for reports about the Sheriff's Department—with investigators and attorneys waiting to record their testimonies. Mitchell explained the town hall's impact on public discourse: "We told the newspaper 'See, it's not just us, it's not our imagination. . . .' From there, the newspaper started taking it seriously." That tenants, under such intimidating conditions, still gave testimony that would substantiate litigation, was a key component in galvanizing the work. TCAL had what it needed to build its case, and the DOJ Civil Rights Division left with its own plan for litigation.

From there, the campaign escalated, and TCAL began to see just how many tenants had been terrorized. "It had to be in the thousands," Mitchell said. "We were getting calls in our office every day. Every day, three and four. People who were even scared and moved out of town, were still reaching out to us." Handling this was not easy. As Smith said, it was "a lot of hard work. Endless nights, endless nights. I'm working at the same time, trying to take care of my family, doing community work, also part of the ministry, so yeah, it was a lot."

BREAKING UP THE POLICING PARTNERSHIP

Led by Palomares, the local team now moved to file its own litigation. As momentous a step as it was, there were also downsides to what Gautam Bhan calls the judicialization of resistance.[11] By filing litigation, TCAL and its allies would cede the organization of time to both their opposition and the legal system. This could slow-walk processes, deprive organizers of a sense of when steps would occur, and generally deprive tenants of the ability to affirmatively control the schedule of their opposition to the policing of their homes.[12] But the effort would also be a powerful act of resistance that put the parties policing tenants on the defensive, legitimized tenants' claims, and galvanized even greater public attention and support.

As Blasi explained, "our focus was to sort of defang this whole operation, and the fang was the sheriff. It's the guy with the gun that makes all this other stuff work. And that meant that we had to set up an information barrier between the housing authority and Lancaster, Palmdale, and the sheriff." If the information barrier existed, the city couldn't get names and addresses of voucher tenants from the housing authority for its target list, and couldn't give that information to the LASD or other public agencies to check if tenants had other enforceable infractions to pursue. And without the deputies accompanying city inspectors, the raids would be defanged.

On April 28, 2011, the team took its first step, sending a letter to Lancaster, Palmdale, and the County, which oversaw both the Housing Authority of the County of Los Angeles and the Los Angeles County Sheriff's Department demanding that they cease the policing program. The county, which represented both HACoLA and the LASD, responded positively to the letter. The team met with the county's lead lawyer, and, as Blasi recalled, "We just sort of laid out the facts. I remember just telling her some of the stories that we'd heard about. Particularly, I remember talking about a woman who'd been awoken with loud knocks on the door, and opened the door, and it was not only the housing authority inspector, but it was a code enforcement person, and a sheriff. I can't remember whether he had a shotgun or not, but it was a real display of force. And a Child Protective Services

FIGURE 19. Barbara Hawkins, 83, of Lancaster, joins others in raising their hands in agreement with a speaker, during testimony at the Los Angeles County Board of Supervisors on June 21, 2011 after she and a bus full of supporters of Mayor R. Rex Parris made the trip from the high desert to urge the supervisors to continue to allow Section 8 inspections in their city. Source: Photo by Bob Chamberlin/*Los Angeles Times* via Getty Images.

worker. Then they basically just ransacked the place and nothing ever happened. It wasn't just that they didn't find anything. There was nothing to find." The facts of what was happening on the ground apparently had an effect. "I think we walked out of that meeting thinking she was going to settle with us, and she did. I mean, she did the right thing. She thought that if what we said was true, she thought that was outrageous and the county should not be doing that and it was indefensible and she wouldn't defend it." After the county's lead lawyer met with the Board of Supervisors, they decided to consider temporarily suspending their participation in the program.

Palmdale and Lancaster, however, were outraged. They did want to defend these practices, and more importantly, to ensure that the county remained part of the program. The issue came to a head at the June 21, 2011, meeting of the LA County Board of Supervisors.[13] The meeting began with prepared remarks by local leaders supporting the policing program. Palmdale Mayor Jim Ledford assured the county that the practices were not racist, and that they were merely about enforcing the law. He was followed by Sherry Marquez, and then Bishop Hearns, who asked for the county to continue the policing partnership and assured the county supervisors that Lancaster and its mayor were not racist. Finally, Lancaster

Mayor Parris spoke, accompanied by a PowerPoint. He too insisted he was not a racist while accusing voucher tenants of crime, drug use, gang activity, and welfare fraud, and demanding that the program be maintained.

Ahead of the meeting, a bus had been organized for Antelope Valley residents who wanted to come to the meeting to give public comment. After Parris's comments, resident after resident supported the mayor and spoke in favor of policing voucher renters. At one point, one resident speaker explained that only people who supported policing voucher tenants had been allowed on the bus, and that she had personally witnessed a Section 8 tenant denied a seat and left behind in Lancaster. Indeed, three people who gave public comment disclosed that they were current or former employees of Mayor Parris, adding to the perception that the meeting had been stacked.

But TCAL had also organized. Chairman of the Antelope Valley Human Relations Commission Darren Parker called out the mayor's dog-whistle politics and denigrating references to "those people." He provided statistics about the spike in complaints about harassment and discrimination made to the commission. From virtually zero, the commission had now received hundreds of complaints from Section 8 tenants, while homeless residents' complaints doubled and complaints from people of color in the valley quadrupled. Pharaoh Mitchell described his own experiences in the valley and encouraged the board to see through Parris's presentation to understand what the city was really doing to tenants.

And tenants spoke out as well, though several testified remotely from the Lancaster public library, seventy miles away. One tenant gave detailed comments about how the policing program raided her house and drummed up false accusations designed to evict her. She accused the investigators of putting her family "through hell," and traumatizing her grandchildren. She recounted for the board how investigators accused her of drug use as a means to evict her, noting that the only drugs she took were for her high blood pressure and that in fact the behavior of the investigators had been so stressful that she experienced a stroke. Another tenant spoke of how investigators conducted a compliance check and used baseless accusations to evict her, leaving her homeless. And a local resident spoke of her disgust at the demonization of Section 8 tenants by the media and public officials.

When public comment ended, Supervisor Mike Antonovich dominated the board's discussion, arguing that the intense policing of Section 8 tenants in the valley not only was helping the valley, but should be expanded to the entire county instead of being rolled back at all. The moment illustrated the stakes of TCAL's fight: if the targeted policing of voucher tenants succeeded in the valley, it could easily spread county or even nation-wide.

Ultimately, Antonovich's position failed to win out. TCAL, in partnership with Public Counsel, Neighborhood Legal Services, and the state chapter of the NAACP filed litigation in U.S Central District Court in California on June 7, 2011, just days before the board meeting. It shifted the ground dramatically. Citing the experiences of tenants, the complaint asserted that the cities of Palmdale and Lancaster undertook a series of actions expressly designed to exclude and discriminate against Section 8 participants in their Cities, including: (1) subjecting current tenants to unwarranted, constant surveillance and harassment as well as frequent invasions of their homes under the guise of investigations and compliance checks; (2) attempting to dissuade landlords from renting to Section 8 tenants and subjecting those who do to increased surveillance and harassment; and (3) attempting additional action to dissuade would-be Lancaster and Palmdale residents from moving to the Antelope Valley.[14]

It had been one thing to voluntarily suspend the program in response to a demand letter, but formal litigation meant that the county had to decide if it would or could defend its role in the program. It decided the answer was no. The Board suspended its participation in the program for ninety days, temporarily ending its fiscal sponsorship of the city's investigators, and breaking down the information-sharing between HACoLA and other parties not legally entitled to tenant information. The effect was to dramatically restrain Lancaster and Palmdale from their policing of tenants.

For the next six months, the county negotiated with the plaintiffs on a settlement agreement. The Board formally voted (4–1) to settle on January 24, 2012, the lone dissent being Antonovich. The county agreed to put limits on deputies' ability to accompany investigators visiting tenants' homes, stopped the practice of HACoLA sharing tenant data with the LASD, Palmdale, and Lancaster, and guaranteed that no new agreements about enhanced investigation partnerships would be considered for three years. It was an enormous victory.

V. Jesse Smith explained its significance. "Here's the list, here's the money," he said, explaining the county's role in empowering Lancaster and Palmdale to police voucher tenants. Referring to the investigators paid for with county funds, Smith said, "Those individuals were brutal, they were hardcore, they were mean, they were nasty, they treated people in the worst of ways, simply because they have authority to do that, from the County Board of Supervisors, to Rex, to the city of Palmdale, and they let that nonsense go on." Cutting off the list and the money that paid the investigators, therefore, was monumental. "That's why I think this was a major victory when we got that funding cut off, that we implemented numerous laws that said, here's how Section 8 is going to be regulated from here on."

But Lancaster and Palmdale remained, and even without information and funding they were still dangerous. Blasi explained, "They could still do what they could do, but without their monthly target list. I mean, they only had the list of people that they already knew were on Section 8. Maybe they were doing their own intelligence. Maybe that's why kids were getting asked at school about their parents' Section 8 status."

Lancaster and Palmdale separately and unsuccessfully tried to dismiss the suit or sever themselves from it, but by February 2012, their attempts had been exhausted. Palmdale announced that it too was entering a settlement agreement. Crucially, it agreed not to use city funds to further investigate tenants, and allowed

FIGURE 20. Terminated Section 8 fraud investigators received commendations from Mayor R. Rex Parris at a Lancaster City Council meeting in July, 2012. Source: *Antelope Valley Times.*

the county to operate enforcement of Section 8 rules. Lancaster, then, was the main holdout. Mayor Parris lambasted Palmdale, saying that "their decision to acquiesce gives comfort to criminals perpetrating housing fraud in the Antelope Valley."[15] The Lancaster City Council attempted to essentially counter-sue the county, filing a housing discrimination complaint against the County of Los Angeles and the Housing Authority alleging that the county was injuring the city by steering voucher renters to it.[16] Next, Lancaster sued the Housing Authority to recover the funds it spent defending itself from TCAL's suit. None of these tactics worked, and Lancaster slowly found itself boxed in, having little choice but to enter settlement negotiations.

By October 10, 2012, Lancaster and TCAL had agreed on a settlement. Lancaster's terms were different from the other parties, and included stipulations that the city would cease conveying that Section 8 tenants were not welcome in the city, and would post on its website language welcoming people regardless of the type of housing they lived in. The city also agreed to create a Community Working Group to promote cooperation between the city and plaintiffs' groups. V. Jesse Smith summarized the victory:

> There was a judge in the original lawsuit that demanded that we get to the table and try to settle this thing, because it was going to be unfavorable towards Palmdale [and] Lancaster, because the statistics were just overwhelming. When those statistics

came out and it showed, wow, Section 8 people have been targeted. . . . When that came out, and then the DOJ came and verified even more what we were saying, we were like, we've been vindicated. We've been vindicated. It wasn't just a matter of perception, it was a matter of reality, this is really happening.

Ultimately, according to Smith, those legal realities won out. "I think that's what changed it, and that's what made Rex come to the table. He's a lawyer. He knew he had a losing battle there, he knew it."

THE DEPARTMENT OF JUSTICE INTERVENES

Blasi's initial meeting with the DOJ's Civil Rights Division head Thomas Perez had created a parallel track of investigation, one formally begun two months after TCAL filed its litigation. Its focus was on the LA County Sheriff's Department, focusing on both its broader policing practices and its targeted policing of voucher tenants. It covered 35,000 LASD documents, records on deputies' contact with voucher tenants, statistical analysis of 49,000 stops, and interviews with police, city employees, staff, government officials, and approximately four hundred community members in the valley. The community outreach was centered on two community meetings, organized by TCAL and others—one in September 2011 in Palmdale, and the other in December 2011 in Lancaster. On the basis of this work, the DOJ issued a findings letter to the LASD outlining its evidence that the agency was violating the law in its policing practices in the valley.[17]

The report meticulously reviewed police practices through the sequence from stops to searches to seizures and the use of force. The report found that Black and Latino pedestrians in Palmdale and Lancaster were stopped at rates 33 and 38.5 percent higher than they would be if there were no racial differences in policing.[18] Black residents were disproportionately stopped for things like "crossing against a traffic light, jaywalking, failing to yield right of way, or walking on the wrong side of the street." The DOJ further found that Black pedestrians in Lancaster were 25 percent more likely than their white counterparts to be stopped for a discretionary offense, with stops leading to "questionable pat downs and consent searches." Issues extended to cars as well. While the DOJ did not find racial disparities in vehicular stops, they found that, controlling for intervening factors, Black drivers and their vehicles were searched at rates roughly 10–15 points higher than white drivers, with many stops concluding without a citation or explanation.

Stops were more than just chances to search for evidence of crimes; they were also occasions to humiliate and assault Black and Latino civilians, what scholars have called degradation ceremonies.[19] As the DOJ explained, "The most common tactic was detaining a stopped motorist in the backseat of the police car during a stop for a minor traffic infraction or while an officer wrote a traffic citation." One sixth of all civilian complaints about police treatment in a one-year period reviewed by the DOJ were about backseat detentions during vehicular stops. Detentions were also opportunities for police violence; the DOJ cited cases of police tasing and pepper spraying individuals detained in police cars, as well as punching handcuffed individuals in the head.

Stops, detentions, and violence were followed in many cases by financial penalties. In 2011, more than 80 percent of all vehicles impounded in the valley were owned by Black and Latino drivers. It cost hundreds of dollars and substantial time to release them, compromising residents' ability to work, attend school, access healthcare, and more.

Finally, as the DOJ explained, incidents at all steps of this chain of police-resident interaction were hidden through various bureaucratic tactics—unconstitutional police activities were simply not recorded, violence against residents was justified as being in response to obstruction despite no evidence that there was any police work in progress that could be obstructed, and complaints were routed through administrative processes that precluded serious investigation or disciplinary action.[20]

Alongside this record of racist violence was a simultaneous record of disinterest in the well-being of residents of color in the valley. The report noted that LASD frequently ignored requests for police service, particularly from Latino residents and business owners, suggesting "a failure to provide basic law enforcement services" to an entire racial or ethnic group, and contrasted this absence with reports of unwarranted harassment of Latino day laborers in the valley, in violation of their First Amendment rights to seek employment. It further described a vast disparity in time to respond to calls for police service between the wealthier and whiter neighborhoods of the west side and the poorer and more heavily Black and Latino east side of Palmdale.

It is within the context of this widespread racist system of policing that the LASD also targeted Section 8 tenants for eviction. Here, the report was damning, showing that LASD took advantage of its powers to conduct or participate in searches of homes without cause, finding ways to humiliate tenants, criminalize them, and seize their property.

From 2008 through mid-2011, "LASD's Lancaster and Palmdale stations played a critical role in the campaign against voucher holders in the Antelope Valley, including by intimidating, harassing, and facilitating the termination of voucher holders from the program, both in conjunction with HACoLA investigators and independently." Their actions furthered racial discrimination in housing "by making housing unavailable, altering the terms and conditions of housing, and coercing, intimidating, and interfering with their housing rights, in violation of the Fair Housing Act." Deputies were allowed to run roughshod over tenants; they "received no training on the program, the elements that constitute a violation of the voucher holder's contract, or the difference between conducting administrative and criminal investigations, until May 2012."

With this freedom, the report stated that the LASD "sent numerous deputies on HACoLA compliance checks of the homes of voucher holders, often in the absence of any legitimate justification." The report added,

> More often than not, multiple deputy sheriffs, sometimes as many as nine, would accompany HACoLA investigators on their administrative housing checks. Deputies would routinely approach the voucher holder's home with guns drawn, occasionally in full SWAT armor, and conduct searches and questioning once inside. In over 40% of the cases in which LASD's files indicated the number of deputies involved, six or more deputies were present. The sheer numbers of armed, uniformed deputies who participated in many of the compliance checks call into question whether voucher holders were able to give meaningful consent to compliance inspections by HACoLA investigators.

Although the deputies were nominally there to protect HACoLA staff (a presumption of violence from tenants that was itself unwarranted), in reality, "LASD deputies often improperly co-mingled their law enforcement functions with the administrative process and participated in HACoLA investigations beyond the scope of securing investigator safety." This included directly questioning voucher tenants "about their compliance with the voucher program's rules" and referring them for "criminal prosecution for voucher program violations." Deputies used "probation/parole checks and arrest warrants to obtain information about voucher program violations," conducted searches and questioned tenants without issuing Miranda warnings, and provided "confidential information about voucher holders to third parties."[21] The report explained these practices as follows:

> LASD deputies were able to interview people and conduct searches before the individuals understood their rights, including that they might be incriminating themselves by participating in the housing contract compliance check. For example, deputies questioned voucher holders during compliance checks about information such as employment history and who resided in the home; these questions had no purpose other than to substantiate voucher program violations. LASD deputies would also use information gathered during these compliance checks to further criminal investigations based solely on the voucher holders' alleged voucher program violations. In some cases, LASD also used voucher program compliance checks as a vehicle to further unrelated criminal investigations, gaining access to voucher holders' homes and their residents without providing notice of their true purpose or administering necessary Miranda warnings.[22]

The report provided examples of deputies lying to tenants, using traffic stops as entry points for investigations of voucher status and possible violations, and entry into the home as a chance to search for opportunities to make criminal charges against tenants.

Finally, the report illustrated the lengths to which deputies and the local governments of the valley would go to punish voucher tenants. Palmdale had appointed a specific district attorney to prosecute voucher tenants criminally. LASD deputies would attempt not only to terminate tenants' vouchers on the basis of ineligibility, but then attempt to criminally prosecute those tenants for the issue they had been evicted over. The practice was generally not done by HACoLA in the rest of LA County. Despite the LASD's efforts to prosecute voucher tenants, the Department of Justice noted three sources of data disproving the accusation of voucher criminality. First, it reported that "The only crime-related analyses LASD provided [to the DOJ]. . . disprove the purported link between the voucher program and crime in the Antelope Valley." Second, it obtained a 2007 study ordered by a Lancaster sergeant which found that, "Section 8 housing did not change the crime statistics within their respective communities." Third, it noted that the City of Lancaster's own statistical analysis conducted in August of 2009 found "no link between crime and voucher holders in Lancaster." Rather, the Lancaster study found that "in certain neighborhoods, voucher program households might actually keep crime rates lower." Thus, rather than combating crime, the DOJ found that LASD's practices violated equal protection and fair housing law.

The result of all this was that "voucher holders in the Antelope Valley were subjected to far more intrusive and intimidating searches of their homes, and in some cases, harsher administrative or criminal consequences to those searches, than voucher holders elsewhere in the county." These practices led to disparate outcomes for tenants in the valley as compared to other parts of Los Angeles County, including termination of their voucher, criminal prosecution for administrative violation, and "relocation from the Antelope Valley for fear of further law enforcement harassment." Building on the findings letter, the DOJ Civil Rights Division, led by Charles Hart and Norrinda Brown, prepared litigation against the County, LASD, HACoLA, and cities of Palmdale and Lancaster, expanding on TCAL's initial case. In parallel to their litigation, the DOJ also negotiated settlement terms with the parties.

In 2015, the parties formally announced the settlement, registering both the DOJ's litigation and the settlement resolving it.[23] The suit asserted that police practices were violating the Fair Housing Act, a marked departure from the narrower vision of fair housing that focused, for example, on discriminatory landlords. The settlement included over one hundred specific items the LASD agreed to, spanning all the major areas covered in its findings report, as well as a monitoring program to ensure their implementation. It also included $700,000 in financial compensation to victims of LASD's unconstitutional treatment.

Jesse Smith summarized the DOJ's role: "The DOJ said, damn, this is really prevalent, and we're not happy with the settlement that you [TCAL] reached. They said there were people whose rights were violated by the LA County Sheriff's Department. Literally, not only were their Section 8 vouchers taken from them, but they were forcibly imprisoned. They were held in the back of police cars in handcuffs for hours without being charged. They were like, that's a violation of people's Fourth Amendment rights. Not having legal representation, and bringing false charges against them."

FIGURE 21. Front row from left: Emmett Murrell, Pharaoh Mitchell, V. Jesse Smith (at podium), and Darren Parker speak at a press conference about the Justice Department investigation of policing in the valley, July 2, 2013. Source: *Antelope Valley Times*.

Summarizing all the legal victories TCAL had achieved between 2011 and 2015, Smith said, "Nearly 2.4 million dollars was awarded to [voucher tenants], and to them alone, based on the work that we had done that was a supplement to that lawsuit. That's where that money came from. Like Pharaoh always said, that was a form of reparations for people of color in this community, and it worked out to their best interest." In addition to financial compensation, some voucher tenants got their vouchers back.

But as Smith explained, "If we went back into the archives and found how many people were abused by the LA County Sheriff's Department, throughout Palmdale, Lancaster, shoot, they'd be giving out a lot more money. That was only limited to a certain time period, and that was only limited to people who actually had the courage to file a complaint. I can't tell you how many people did not file a complaint, who were just scared and terrified."

Looking back, Smith describes the campaign as a victorious one.

Yeah, I see it as a victory. Not all of what we wanted, but it's better than what we could have gotten, so I'm happy. I was very happy with the settlements. Keep in mind there are two settlements that we're looking at. One is the one that Neighborhood Legal Services and County Counsel got for us. That's the one that stopped the money from coming in from the county Board of Supervisors to fund [inspections]. We got that cut off in its entirety. We also got the Los Angeles County Sheriff's Department . . .

there were more than 150 rules that were implemented that they had to follow, so they couldn't just pull people over anymore like they wanted to, they couldn't just put handcuffs on folks. Section 8, they couldn't show up at Section 8 homes anymore with six or seven police officers, without getting permission from a commanding officer, and then explaining why.

Then after we did that, the DOJ comes in and says, shoot, there are more remedies to be acquired here. In addition to the rules that you guys already have, we're implementing a whole set of additional rules from the federal level, and we're coming in and we're monitoring it now. In addition to that, each one of the entities that played a role in suppressing the rights of those who were victims of Section 8, and victims of the . . . LA County Sheriff's Department actions, now you got to pay. Now you got to pay, and it's got to come out of your pocket.

In broader terms, Emmett Murrell describes the symbolic achievement of the campaign: "I think we all wanted to say if we could stand up and meet it head on, others who watched how we handle our business would follow suit and our numbers would grow." In campaigning together, Murrell adds, "we became attached to one another and that's how we became a unified group."

But Smith also reflects on what the campaign could never undo, explaining, "You know what I think the real pain was, here where the story is? Hearing what people [went through]. . . . Hearing those stories was like, wow, that is just unbelievable that they experienced that. That to me was more painful, because that's something we couldn't eviscerate, we couldn't take that away, we couldn't even heal it, because it happened."

THE "COUNTER-REVOLUTION" OF BUREAUCRACY

In the years since TCAL's activism, the number of fraud hotline calls about voucher tenants, and the investigations and terminations that often follow, have dropped dramatically. The Housing Authority undid mechanisms of policing affecting thousands in the valley, and which might have spread more broadly through the county or to other jurisdictions in the country. But TCAL's victory was not complete. Some forms of the policing of housing were not addressed by TCAL's victories—namely the region's crime-free and nuisance ordinances. It would take until 2023 for California to adopt AB-1418, a law invalidating crime-free ordinances in its cities. More importantly, while federal settlements and consent decrees have been effective at creating institutional reform in a range of other policy areas, implementation of the settlement on LASD has failed.[24] This failure has played out through a process of democratic disconnection. Imagine, a cycle that connects a public claim of a rights violation to an official validation of that claim and mandate of redress and finally to a change in policy that eliminates the harm. In the valley, as in other places,[25] the connection to the last step has been cut, as the parties legally bound to implement reform do not do so, and the legal bodies tasked with enforcing implementation similarly fail.

A bureaucratic counter-revolution of sorts has effectively slowed down the implementation of the DOJ's settlement terms and covered up the original issues at hand for tenants in the valley. The result might be read as an example of what Teresa Rocha Beardall calls a "legal mirage" whereby rights and processes exist but are blocked by structural, human, financial, or other barriers.[26] In what follows, I trace two mechanisms of policing retrenchment: a public-facing production of normalcy in the valley and an internal slowdown in LASD's implementation of the settlement agreement. These operate within the larger toolbox that law enforcement agencies use to undermine, subvert, or otherwise resist public oversight and change.[27]

Producing Normalcy

Less than two months after the DOJ and the Los Angeles County Sheriff's Department signed their settlement agreement, the *Los Angeles Times* declared victory of sorts in a cover story of its California Section headlined, "Tensions Ease in High Desert."[28] The article opened with the story of Miguel Coronado, who became a community organizer and critic of the police after having been "handcuffed and shoved into a patrol car . . . for telling a girl that she could refuse to talk to a sheriff's deputy who was questioning her." Coronado now noted a decrease in the number of calls he had been receiving from other residents about police harassment. And he felt buoyed by the mayor appointing him to a city commission and high-ranking deputies giving him their phone numbers (and actually answering his calls).[29] Deputies also visited NAACP meetings to hold listening sessions and improve relations. For others, however, these acts were not enough to ease their concerns. Darren Parker told the paper that structural change was needed: "We have to put in checks and balances so that after we're gone, somebody doesn't suddenly forget where we are."

The article ended with a perhaps unintentional example of Parker's critique. A reporter and photographer had been invited to ride along with a sheriff's deputy. That morning, the officer "gunned the engine of his patrol car, jumping a curb to zoom across the lawn of an apartment complex" to pursue "two young black men who had eyed him suspiciously."[30] Presented to readers as totally normal, the stop (which the officer admitted had no legal basis), might be interpreted as part of the status quo ante to which the valley was reverting as tensions eased.

Academics also played a role in producing a sense of normalcy about the valley. The settlement agreement included a provision creating an office whose role was to monitor the implementation of the settlement's terms. One aspect of its work was to periodically re-engage the community to see how things were changing in terms of the LASD's treatment of the communities it had been caught discriminating against. The office contracted with Leap and Associates, a UCLA-affiliated research group led by UCLA faculty Jorja Leap and Todd Franke. In 2018, they administered a survey aimed at understanding perceptions of the LASD among people in the valley at large, rather than focused on the groups specifically targeted by the LASD's unconstitutional police practices. The survey was distributed through Antelope Valley organizations, including some community groups, as well as the Sheriff's Department itself.

Pharaoh Mitchell characterized the survey as biased from the start. He explained that its methods would ensure that the survey missed the very respondents at the center of the DOJ's settlement: Black residents in the valley, including older Black residents and voucher tenants. "What they were doing was wrong because they were doing all electronic surveys," he explained. "The people who really need to answer these surveys do not have access to these surveys. A lot of them don't have computers or anything so that's when they came up with the idea of the hard copy." Mitchell and others worked to distribute the surveys to Black residents who it otherwise would not have reached, but ultimately had little influence on the overall trajectory of the research.

Ultimately, only 10 percent of respondents were Black and only 6 percent of survey respondents were voucher renters.[31] Their perceptions of the LASD were considerably more negative than the general population's. For example, while two-thirds of the general population felt that LASD deputies treated everyone fairly, that figure dropped to less than half for respondents in the voucher program. Rather than describing this as clear evidence that the issues central to the litigation remained a serious concern, the report categorized it as variance from the overall population's satisfaction.[32] Only two other findings related to voucher tenants were included in the report: that tenants had unwanted police visits at higher rates than the general population, and that they expressed less confidence that police would respond to their safety needs or investigate on their behalf if they were the victim of a crime. As Mitchell summarized it, "They came out with the survey saying all in all the community said themselves it's doing great."

The survey was accompanied by a focus group, but this too marginalized voucher tenants.[33] The focus group's report only mentioned voucher tenants to note that the focus group was conducted as part of a settlement about discrimination against them. And the two key recommendations from the focus group were for LASD to continue community engagement, and for residents to "cultivate positive relationships with LASD in their neighborhoods."

Thus, the first major report focused on evaluating progress on the settlement buried the experiences of the groups who were central to the settlement under the views of valley residents who were not the target of racist policing, painting a picture of general satisfaction with policing in the valley that countered the urgency that had prompted the DOJ's initial intervention. Based on these findings it would be little surprise that, per settlement monitor David Muhammad, the department's most notable change had been to adopt a "Coffee with a Cop" program.[34]

Stonewalling Change

Meanwhile, at the national and county levels officials also found ways to stall progress. At the end of an interview in October 2016, one voucher tenant told me her fears of a Trump victory. "He's going to take everything that we barely have now," she worried, anticipating large cuts to the social safety net. "Housing, that's going to stop. AFDC, food stamps, GR [General Relief], all of that's gonna stop." Though his first term administration did seek cuts to the safety net, Democratic legislators successfully staved them off, securing increased voucher funding in budget negotiations. Where the Trump administration was successful was in changing the terms of local governance, including of vouchers in the valley. The administration shifted course from prior efforts to federally encourage local police reform, and Attorney General Jeff Sessions openly declared his disinterest in federal consent decrees as a tool of oversight and reform for local police departments. Departments currently in those oversight programs suddenly had little to fear from noncompliance. This environment may contextualize the near total refusal of the LA County Sheriff's Department to implement the settlement agreement, perhaps betting that even if it did not comply, the DOJ would not respond by resuming its litigation.[35]

Locally, Sheriff Alex Villanueva appeared to be the key figure responsible for the lack of implementation. Although his office declared his commitment to the agreement and intent to enforce it, one settlement monitor, Joseph Brann, pointed to Villanueva's election in 2018 as the moment when implementation momentum slowed.[36]

Over time, the non-implementation of the settlement became a significant and widely shared concern. A second survey of the valley, this time headed solely by Todd Franke (Leap and Associates was no longer listed on the report), was far more detailed and revealed significant and persistent problems in the valley.[37] In total, 65 percent of Black respondents and 65 percent of voucher-tenant respondents reported that they felt the LASD treated people unfairly, with race being the primary axis of disparate treatment. Just over a quarter of voucher tenants in the survey reported concern that the sheriffs might interfere with their ability to keep their housing, and 37 percent reported having had deputies enter their homes when they had not requested them. Their experiences were echoed by Black respondents, as 24 percent worried about police jeopardizing their housing and 26 percent reported unwanted police entry into their home. Respondents who were Hispanic or Latino reported somewhat similar numbers, at 29 and 16 percent, respectively.[38] In 2020, the settlement monitors wrote to Villanueva accusing his office of being a bottleneck in reform implementation.[39] In 2021, using data made newly available through California's Racial and Identity Profiling Act of 2015, Neighborhood Legal Services and California State University, Northridge found that Black residents of the valley were stopped 10,886 more times than would be expected given their share of the population, a fact that led them to conclude that there was "a near certainty that racial or ethnic animus is a determinative factor in how LASD conducts its stops."[40]

The cost of the LASD's "essentially stalemated implementation" of the settlement would soon become deadly. In June 2020, one day after the death of Robert Fuller in Palmdale, Los Angeles deputies entered the home of Michael Thomas, where Deputy Ty Shelton fatally shot him in the presence of his family and fiancée.

In a wrongful death lawsuit, his family claimed that the 911 call that police received and responded to was accidental, that noises they heard on the call did not constitute probable cause to enter the home, and that "within seconds, [deputies] began to assault Thomas, placing him in a headlock and twisting his arm when the shooting occurred."[41] Deputies did not substantiate their claim that Thomas was reaching for one of their weapons, and Thomas's hand disability further shed doubt on this claim. Thomas's daughter, Myesha Lopez, described the killing as a "senseless act of hate."

AV-NAACP President Pastor Jacob Johnson told *The Guardian* that "the deputies appeared to have violated at least several points of the consent decree," including sections on reforming use of force. The newspaper quoted Johnson: "'What's the penalty if they break a consent decree—the oversight committee stays on for two more years?' Johnson said. "To be honest, if I'm the sheriff's department, I could care less. Right now, there seems to be no repercussions. There seems to be no penalties."[42]

By 2022, the settlement monitors issued a report raising alarm about the non-implementation of mandated reforms. Although housing-related reforms had been consistently implemented, other key areas of the agreement were ignored. As the report stated, "the high number of individual provisions that have been found by our compliance assessments to have not met the Settlement Agreement (SA) requirements or have only partially done so are indicative of a crisis in the implementation of the SA."[43] Based on this assessment, the monitors made a public call for the re-involvement of the federal courts, writing, "If the Parties fail to act jointly or individually within a reasonable time to request intervention by the Court, the Monitors will contact the Court and ask for its active involvement in the enforcement of the SA."

By 2023, that call had gone unheeded. In March, Ty Shelton, who had earlier killed Michael Thomas, body-slammed custodian Eric Rios as he took out trash at a Palmdale school. That summer, one LASD deputy threw a Black woman to the ground outside a WinCo supermarket in Lancaster, and another deputy punched a Black woman twice in the face as she held her newborn. In December, Shelton shot and killed Niani Finlayson within seconds of entering her home unannounced, the very practice of unauthorized entry warned about in the settlement survey's fundings.[44]

TAKING STOCK

Notwithstanding the DOJ's slow and limited progress implementing its settlement with LASD, TCAL's work challenging the policing of housing in the valley has been far more successful, with implications for the valley, cities across the country, and the law.

At the local level, TCAL's success in breaking up the policing partnership and stopping larger agencies like the Housing Authority and county government from participating in local government's targeting of voucher tenants has resulted in a demonstrable shrinking of the policing of voucher tenants' homes in the Antelope Valley. Hundreds of calls to instigate inspections of voucher tenants every year are simply no longer happening (fraud hotline calls about tenants in the valley dropped from 446 in FY 08–09 to roughly 200 in FY 14–15) and evictions and terminations have dropped dramatically (from 278 in FY 08–09 to fewer than 10 in FY 14–15). Curbing the power of residents to police their neighbors is also a direct diminishment of the practices I theorized earlier as "policing as property." And to shrink the scope of policing without having to concede anything in return is a strong example of what abolitionist scholars have called "non-reformist reforms," those that make positive changes without further entrenching the carceral state (save perhaps the temporary increase in goodwill that accrued to the city and police after agreeing to the reforms).

Local organizers reflecting on their work had tempered views of their struggle. Smith expressed pride in what they were able to accomplish, and the power of the reports and monetary compensation as acknowledgements of the truth of what tenants went through. Murrell felt good that organizing made a difference, explaining, "For people who needed a place to stay, and they needed the assurances of the community to stand behind them, it wasn't until the community actually became involved that Section 8 was a battle worth fighting." Pharaoh Mitchell saw the work as resonant with other struggles around the country. "The Antelope Valley was a Ferguson before there was a Ferguson," he noted.[45] The two places are more than chronologically connected; in both, Black residents lived in a place whose economic station was determined by places external to it, and whose ability to change these circumstances was circumscribed by a pervasive system of policing. To shake that system somewhere was to shake it everywhere.

Blasi was clear-eyed as ever about the reality of change in the valley: "Ultimately, there's no set of cases that's going to change this." He explained, "This is about power, and who has it, and who doesn't. And the people who have it are really hanging on to it." But, he added, "You can slow them down. I mean, I felt really good about breaking the link between the sheriff, and the housing authorities, and the cities, because that threw a wrench in their system." The effects of that wrench in the system have reverberated beyond the valley.

At the regional and national level, in addition to their work in curbing the policing of housing locally, TCAL managed to prevent the rapid spread of Lancaster and Palmdale's programs. In the Los Angeles County Supervisors' public debates about the issue, Supervisor Antonovich not only supported the policing of voucher tenants but advocated strongly for the valley's policing regime to be replicated across the county. This advocacy suggests that such programs could have been turned into best practices or policy toolkits, able to spread quickly across jurisdictions and turned into a new normal. Thus, not only did TCAL squash the policing program targeting tenants in the valley, but their well-organized dissent also prevented it from being exported more broadly, especially as a similar effort to stop voucher policing in Antioch, California, had proved less successful. Had they too failed, we might today see the institutionalization of the valley's policing system in places all around the country. This is not to say that these practices will not appear elsewhere, but at minimum, TCAL bought people time and has created a template for how to fight these programs should they reappear.

In the years since their efforts, the work of TCAL organizers has been extended by other campaigns around the country, part of a broader movement to reduce the policing of housing. Although valley organizers had pointed to crime-free and nuisance housing ordinances as part of the broader structure of policing affecting tenants, it was not a main focus of their efforts. But their assertion that policing could violate the Fair Housing Act informed a template for organizations in other cities to use to challenge these kinds of ordinances. In Faribault, Minnesota, Selma Jones worked with the ACLU to sue the city government over its nuisance housing ordinance, which had allowed her neighbors to leverage police complaints about family birthday parties and her children's play into her legally mandated eviction. They obtained a settlement that significantly constrained the scope and application of Faribault's crime-free rental housing ordinance and the ability of police to order evictions.[46] In Bedford, Ohio, where similar nuisance law was being used to evict Section 8 tenants, tenants sued based on a claim that the law violated Fair Housing rights, and Bedford eventually struck the ordinance from its laws. In Peoria, Illinois, HOPE Fair Housing Center, Relman Colfax, and the Shriver Center on Poverty secured a settlement revising the city nuisance ordinances to curtail individuals' power to evict their neighbors through nuisance calls, and otherwise shrinking the nuisance ordinance.[47] In the largest step to date to de-police housing, California has recently banned crime-free housing ordinances.[48] And the Department of Justice issued notice to cities across the country that crime-free and nuisance housing ordinances may be unconstitutional.[49]

This unfolding effort to curtail or abolish crime-free and nuisance housing rules represents the hopeful future of organizing that builds on what TCAL began. In the area of housing, there is much more to do, including getting subsidized tenants robust Fourth Amendment protections from searches and seizures, ending the practice of home raids, scrapping one-strike eviction rules that use criminal legal system contact to separate families and evict tenants, and making tenant rights and due process more meaningful and practically able to be utilized.

Finally, TCAL's work against the policing of housing was not just a struggle over housing and policing, but also a struggle over the legal rights of people in poverty. The group's legal successes hearken back to some of the key victories of the welfare-rights movement of the late 1960s and early 1970s, and show the continued relevance of welfare-rights litigation today. In 1968, *King v. Smith* invalidated the policing of welfare recipients' homes to enforce the celibacy of women. Today, TCAL's efforts to stop neighbors from instigating home raids on the basis of suspected "unauthorized tenants" has protected the same rights to association and privacy. In 1969's *Shapiro v. Thompson*, the court invalidated state government attempts to block interstate mobility of welfare recipients. While not focused on state-to-state movement, TCAL's work extended Shapiro's legacy by stymieing the attempts of local governments to block the inmigration of subsidized housing tenants from other jurisdictions. Continuing to think about the policing of subsidized housing within a welfare rights framework may be productive. For example, in 1970, *Goldberg v. Kelley* ruled that recipients of government benefits could not be terminated without the opportunity for an administrative hearing. But in the context of subsidized housing, the right to due process is often underutilized, in part because tenants have so little of the access to legal representation that would allow them to take advantage of these rights. Although this issue was not part of TCAL's fight, it illustrates how continued subsidized-housing-rights work extends the legacy of the welfare-rights movement.

Back home, the valley's transformation has been limited. One bright spot occurred as part of the era of intense public organizing for a more just valley. In 2012, Juan Jauregui, Nigel Holly, and V. Jesse Smith realized that Palmdale's system of local elections violated the California Voting Rights Act (CVRA). Its use of at-large voting to allocate city council seats had allowed the city to maintain an almost entirely white city council despite decades of demographic change that had made it 54 percent Latino and 15 percent Black. They sued in 2012 (among their lawyers were California voting rights expert Robert Rubin and Lancaster Mayor R. Rex Parris), and a Los Angeles Superior Court judge found in their favor in 2013, noting that the CVRA applied to charter cities as well as those operating under general law.[50] The ruling prompted Palmdale to adopt a district-based system of voting for city council seats, which has changed the council's racial, if not political, makeup.

As important as these voting and housing accomplishments have been, some local organizers still expressed regret that their work could not spark the broader transformation of the valley that was needed. Emmett Murrell noted, "The thing that I think worked to the benefit of the powers that be was they didn't allow it to become an issue that involved more than just African Americans." He noted other community experiences of racism in the valley but explained that the framing of the issue as being about vouchers "kept us from galvanizing a whole other set of victims." Legal action, too, may have had an effect, as litigation imposed its own timeline of motions, rulings, and settlement negotiations on the movement, sapping some of its dynamism and urgency. Murrell said, "I think that we probably lost our chance at building something that would have had long-term positive consequences," but noted that their limited financial resources meant they were not equipped to organize at the scale of the valley's problems.

This somber tone would surely be justified were the story to have ended with the conclusion of the voucher struggle. But in this book's conclusion, I trace how local organizations in the valley have come to build and extend on TCAL's work, trying to achieve the broader transformation of the valley that Murrell and others hoped for.

Conclusion

Another Valley Is Possible

For nearly a century, people have visited the ruins of Llano del Rio to consider what lessons the socialist experiment offers to the present. For Aldous Huxley, its failure was a story of hubris and a lesson in realism; for Mike Davis, a place to consider the narrow and sprawl-crazed future of Los Angeles; for others, a place to imagine new utopias, or as Laura Nelson wrote, to simply "linger in the space between the dream and failure."[1] But at the opposite end of the Antelope Valley lies the remnant of a different early twentieth-century dream, which may also offer something to our understanding of the future.

In 1924, wealthy Los Angeles real estate developer Richard Peter Shea set out to build a castle in the desert. An Irish one, or at least a replica of a specific castle in Dublin. He built it in a location known at the time as Painted Rocks. It was called that because, according to local news accounts, Native activity was recorded on the area's granite rocks—markings, signs, and pictograms. Shea used the rocks for his castle. The *Los Angeles Times* described it as comprising 3,800 tons of granite, with walls three feet thick at their base and two feet wide at the height of the castle's turrets.[2] Inside was a maze of fourteen rooms. Shea spoke of plans to import kangaroos, deer, and most importantly, antelope to live on the grounds, perhaps so that the region could live up to its name. One of the reasons he commissioned the castle was in the hopes that the desert air would benefit his ailing wife. Other rumors suggested that he had grown up poor in the Antelope Valley and sought a triumphant return. Soon after completing the castle and grounds, Shea lost his wealth in the stock market crash of 1929. He and his wife returned to Los Angeles, where she died in 1932. Despondent, Shea walked into the Pacific Ocean with her ashes tied to him. The castle remains.

FIGURE 22. Shea's Castle after a snowfall. Source: Antelope Valley Rural Museum Collection/ Los Angeles County Library Digital Collections.

What does the valley look like from the vantage of Shea's Castle? A beautiful home for no one to live in, a ring for no finger, a crown for no head. It is Llano's antipode, void of sociality and belonging, providing no comfort to those who created it, fenced off even when there is nothing to protect. If Llano is a reminder of the difficulties of forging a socialist pathway, Shea's Castle is the opposite. To me, it symbolizes the terminus of the unequal, exclusionary, anti-social politics that have produced the events at the heart of this book.

In this conclusion, I try to recover an agenda for housing justice in the valley, focusing on this question at three scales. At the national level, I consider what this book contributes to debates about future housing policy; at the regional level, I suggest that the valley needs to remake its relationship to Los Angeles; and at the local level, I return to Sun Village to understand what it offers those seeking to chart a different future.

FEDERAL HOUSING POLICY AFTER "MOVING TO OPPORTUNITY"

Voucher movement into the Antelope Valley occurred as part of the long effort to promote the mobility of poor tenants in federally subsidized housing programs. As I described, reinvestment in public housing was forgone in favor of investments in mobility, though they largely failed to produce the economic progress that had been promised. Twenty years after the Moving to Opportunity Demonstration Project began, one of its most positive findings came out in print. While adults and older children saw no or even negative effects from moving out of public housing and into a lower-poverty neighborhood using a voucher, the youngest children in the experiment eventually grew up to have higher incomes and college attendance rates as adults compared to the adult children of public housing tenants who did not move.[3] The success, however, also demonstrated how paltry the social contract associated with MTO has come to be. That contract says to public housing tenants in the richest nation on earth that if they leave their homes and communities, their own economic fortunes might not change substantially and their older children may even suffer as a result, but in twenty years, their youngest children's incomes and educational attainment will improve. Perhaps because of these disappointments, MTO's architects and proponents have largely moved on.

In a 2010 lecture at the University of Chicago, Jens Ludwig, the former project director of the Moving to Opportunity Demonstration Project evaluation, reflected on what he had learned from the study. "MTO has convinced me that one of the most important things that we can do to improve the quality of life of poor families is improve public safety."[4] This might sound like a call for violence prevention, social services, or more responsive emergency services. But as Ludwig would explain, he saw HUD's rental assistance programs for poor families, both public housing and vouchers, as being better scrapped altogether, with the funds being used to increase the policing of poor neighborhoods.

Indeed, the prison bookended his vision of and for poor Black tenants in public housing. When he saw Chicago's projects, he could only interpret them as carceral. He saw the cinderblocks, boarded-up windows, fenced breezeways, and other grim characteristics of late-twentieth century structures as easily mistaken for a "supermax prison," rather than as the product of generations of racist disinvestment (that itself is part of the story of the expansion of imprisonment). Intentionally or not, he omitted the question of whether the way public housing is policed might *make* it carceral. But he offered no vision of it beyond that: no sense of what it once was, what promises it represented, what happened to it, what it could be. To see it as a prison suggests that demolishing it and moving its tenants away is liberation.

As the lecture proceeded, Ludwig would go on to cheerfully explain the methodological details of the MTO experiment, its place in the long trajectory of Chicago School neighborhood effects and mobility theory, and the disappointing results of the evaluation. As state of the art as the research methods were, however, Ludwig's conclusions followed the narrow path first set out by Park and Burgess. Federal housing policy, he concluded, "is not very good at changing neighborhood environments." From this conclusion, one might consider it a priority to figure out how federal policy could improve tenants' lives. But this line of thinking lies outside a narrow framework that sees federal policy as only able to produce prison-like public housing or ineffectual moves away from it.

Thus, Ludwig advocated for abolishing the Department of Housing and Urban Development, whose $40 billion budget he believed should be eliminated so that it could be spent elsewhere. Ludwig argued that the economic return on investments in policing was greater than on investments in housing assistance. "I think the U.S. is way underpoliced right now," he concluded. "We spend about a hundred billion dollars a year on policing; [HUD's] 40 billion dollars would represent a huge proportional change in policing intensity in some of the most dangerous inner-city neighborhoods in the United States."

This goal has been partly fulfilled. Although HUD's budget has not been eliminated, since 2010 federal, state, and local spending on policing has grown by an amount that rivals the nation's public housing and voucher program budgets. But these dollars have not delivered on the promise of safer environments in which low-income families can thrive. Indeed, as the Crime Lab that Ludwig now heads states on its homepage, in far too many communities, policing is neither fair nor effective.

Alongside continued public investment in policing has flourished the private policing of housing. It once seemed quaint to me that the harassment of Michelle Ross was coordinated through a Facebook page, but today, the use of digital platforms to police neighborhoods has become institutionalized through technologies and social media applications such as Nextdoor, Ring, and Citizen, which empower and profit from the collective policing and harassment of Black and brown people in neighborhoods across the country.[5] This deepened entanglement of the public and policing illustrates the growth of policing as a form of social status and a marker of personhood or citizenship. It operates alongside other efforts to put policing power into the hands of citizens, at times for the political ends of the state.[6] Jon Michaels and David Noll refer to this as "vigilante federalism," a trend by which governments empower private individuals to carry out their political ends.[7] Examples have appeared in state legislation empowering citizens to personally enforce abortion bans and censor the content taught in schools. Policing, in these instances, is becoming an essential ingredient in inflating the citizenship of those who seek to abrogate abortion and speech rights. It creates, as Aziz Huq notes, the private suppression of the constitutional rights of others.[8]

Meanwhile, the national turn away from public housing and toward vouchers has subordinated poor tenants in the housing market and exposed them to multiple forms of policing and risks of eviction. It's clear that we need a different way forward. Indeed, a decade after his comments favoring investment in police over housing, Ludwig now calls for increased federal spending on schools and jobs to combat crime, and an emphasis on social interventions rather than police to reduce conflict and prevent gun violence. It is among the many signs that the consensus is shifting. To reverse the trends that have produced the pain at the core of this book, we might work towards what Hilary Malson calls "abolitionist housing justice"—an agenda of tearing down oppressive housing policies and building up alternatives that further housing justice.[9] In this book's case, we need to both reduce the policing of housing and build up a more just system of public housing. This combination may produce the kinds of homes in which people and communities can flourish.

Abolition and housing justice have important continuities. The forces they respond to—imprisonment and eviction (or any process that produces homelessness)—are punitive responses to social problems rather than ameliorative solutions to them. Imprisonment and eviction are often justified by discourses of fear and demonization, as well as a belief that there are no alternatives. In contrast, abolitionist politics is premised on the idea that no one is disposable, and housing justice is premised on a universal right to housing, in other words, that no one should be unhoused. Where abolitionists seek to build a society that responds to social problems through nonpunitive solutions and thus obviates the prison, housing justice seeks a reorganization of the housing system such that eviction and homelessness are eliminated.

A key step towards abolitionist housing is de-policing housing. The miasma of ways that home is policed today represent a laundry list of targets: crime-free housing policies that exclude tenants based on criminal legal system involvement, nuisance ordinances that allow neighbors to harass and evict each other, home raids, crime initiatives that weaponize code enforcement, one-strike eviction rules in subsidized housing, and the rising suite of technologies and digital platforms that empower neighborhood policing and eviction.[10]

As daunting as that list is, there are reasons to be hopeful. Cases of de-policing housing exist throughout history—consider *Shelley v. Kraemer* in 1948, which ended the state's ability to enforce (using police) racially restrictive covenants, or 1961's *Mapp v. Ohio*, in which Dollree Mapp successfully contested the warrantless raid of her home by Cleveland police, expanding protections for subjects of police searches nationwide, and most recently, California's legislation nullifying crime-free housing ordinances throughout the state. In this vein, the idea of ending eviction, or what Larissa Bowman has called "eviction abolition," has increasingly become a horizon for housing justice work, one spurred by the success of the eviction moratorium during the COVID-19 pandemic.[11] Tenant and social movement organizing against eviction has continued to grow in the years since the expiration of the moratorium. It has included both expanding legal representation and procedural protections for tenants, and the more radical effort to reduce their evictability in the first place, by constraining the reasons tenants can be evicted. This work is often targeted at the private market, but it would dramatically improve the lives of tenants in voucher and public housing programs too.

In addition to reducing the policing of housing and the evictions it produces, abolitionist housing might entail building up better housing supports than current housing policies have to offer. Overall, there is little doubt that budgets for housing assistance must be dramatically increased (for example, only a quarter of tenants eligible for vouchers receive them). But the experiences of voucher tenants in the valley show that we must do so absent the dispersal and mobility imperatives that helped engineer this conflict and provided tenants little more than physical shelter. Instead, we might return to John O. Calmore's call for "spatial equality," a perspective on housing policy that, rather than relying entirely on mobility also emphasizes investment in programs like public housing, so that low-income households have good homes wherever they wish to live.[12] In the valley, this might include converting currently vacant housing to public ownership. This would be superior to vouchers because the dollars that flow through the voucher program into the valley are temporary—they will disappear if and when the geography of voucher usage shifts. Public housing funded with these dollars would be resilient to the valley's economic fortunes.[13] The idea of public housing in the valley might sound fantastical, but much of the valley's original single-family housing stock originated as a sort of public housing, the direct result of massive federal housing investments for aerospace workers who otherwise could not afford them. And had the 1948 Proposition 14 described in chapter 2 passed, the state would have a long-standing and robust public housing sector continuing to invest in just such places.

A STRUGGLE OVER SUBORDINATION

At the regional level, the key force shaping the valley remains its relationship to Los Angeles. It has been a site of repeated spatial fixes for Los Angeles, absorbing the surpluses of the metropolitan core repeatedly through the twentieth century. But as this relationship evolves into the twenty-first century, the contest over its status remains central to the valley's future. Though no cities are truly their own masters, parties across the valley seem to sense that the valley must change its relationship to Los Angeles in order to gain autonomy.

Today's Struggle over the Safety Valve

Today, Los Angeles still sees the valley as a possible solution to its crises, namely the metropolis's acute housing shortage. In 2019, as mandated by state law, the Southern California Association of Governments (SCAG), encompassing Imperial, Los Angeles, Orange, Riverside, San Bernardino, and Ventura counties, began its Regional Housing Needs Assessment in order to determine how to allocate responsibility to construct the 1.3 million units of housing that the region will need in order to meet housing demand by the end of the decade.

In the first iteration of the group's plan for the Southern California region, it created a formula that would allow wealthy coastal areas to escape new building mandates, shifting the responsibility to build to further inland areas, including the Antelope Valley. The draft allocation plan sparked resistance from regional planners who warned that the plan would deepen urban sprawl and worsen commutes by putting housing far from jobs, and in so doing, conflict with the region's climate goals by structuring housing production to create more emissions.[14]

Their political pressure pushed SCAG to revise its plan. As a result, Lancaster and Palmdale went from being required to build over 28,000 units to just 15,000 units over the 2020s. Many celebrated the revisions as holding back urban sprawl and forcing wealthy coastal regions to build their fair share of the region's housing. However, although this specific idea to solve the housing crisis through dispersal to the desert was batted back, Los Angeles has continued to think about the valley within this narrow paradigm.

Two years after the regional plan controversy, in an interview with Steve Lopez of the *Los Angeles Times*, then-mayoral candidate Karen Bass discussed ideas for solving the crisis of houselessness for people with mental illnesses. Bass suggested, "There's a big chunk of land in Palmdale and maybe we could create a village out there."[15] Bass had been referring to building clinics, but her phrasing caused an instant panic in the valley. Lancaster Mayor Rex Parris, who had previously attempted to pay unhoused people to take buses out of the valley, then tried to make it more difficult for service groups to provide food for homeless people, and finally suggested shooting homeless criminals, used the comments to declare a state of emergency, and issued a press release printed verbatim in the local paper denouncing the remarks.[16] Palmdale's city council took similar measures, unanimously approving a resolution opposing what it called Bass's "homeless village."[17]

The following year, Palmdale recorded the nation's tenth-largest increase in high-income households—adding 3,306 families with incomes over $200,000 and lifting the share of high income households in the city to 13.6 percent.[18] The possibility of people in poverty arriving in the city threatened its increasing wealth.

Soon, news reports emerged that Palmdale City Council member Ronda Perez was in talks with the City of Santa Monica about a proposal that would stoke those fears. To avoid fulfilling its legally obligated requirement to build housing per the Southern California Association of Governments' Regional Housing Needs Assessment, Santa Monica could pay Palmdale to take on its housing development obligations. It would be another form of exclusion, banishment, and enactment of a spatial fix, extending the valley's role as the core's safety valve. Perez broke it down simply: "They are land-poor and we are land-rich."[19] But as news broke, her colleagues turned against the plan. The same themes of opposition to unhoused residents arose. The *Antelope Valley Press* reported Palmdale Mayor Laura Bettencourt's belief "that Santa Monica would use it to transfer its unhoused population." Bettencourt declared, "I am wholeheartedly, 100% against this and I would probably fight this with every breath in my body."[20] Reports suggested that, when floating the plan, a Santa Monica official had intimated that if Palmdale didn't get on board, Lancaster would.

These developments suggest that the unequal relationship between Los Angeles and the valley that undergirds the conflict remains in place. It suggests that Los Angeles will continue attempting to offload its crises onto the valley, in a manner that engineers conflict. To break this pattern is to perhaps search for a different path forward for the valley.

Contesting the Safety Valve

The valley's political leaders have tried to change their relationship to Los Angeles not just by fruitless attempts to stop unhoused and poor people from moving up, but also by searching for new sources of economic growth. The valley has diversified its economy, and secured stops on on Brightline West and the California High Speed Rail Line, ensuring its connection to the rest of the region when the projects are completed. It still remains home to key military weapons manufacturers, including Lockheed Martin, BAE systems, and Northrup Grumman. But as has been the case throughout the valley's history, its reliance on a military economy has never provided it with stable and widespread prosperity. The companies have recently enjoyed record profits from conflicts around the world, including contracts to supply arms used in Israel's genocidal war on Gaza.[21] Just as George Prioleau, Ed Dwight, and Black workers throughout the valley benefited little from participation in the military, participation in the arms industry has not brought sustainable or widespread prosperity to the valley. Even the youthful excitement of seeing fighter jets fly overhead during testing, as Alexandro Ochoa writes in "Querida Palmdale," eventually gives way to a somber understanding of what and why they are.[22]

Meanwhile, the valley has also built new industries. One is in the green sector. Lancaster has become a major construction home for BYD, producing electric buses and batteries.[23] These efforts helped make the Antelope Valley Transit Authority the first in the nation to go fully electric.[24] In parallel, the valley has dramatically expanded its solar farms; just outside Lancaster, the Antelope Valley Solar Ranch, with 3.8 million solar panels, stands as one of the nation's largest solar facilities.[25] A second major economic transformation has been the growth of warehouse and distribution facilities in the valley, as major retailers seek staging grounds in proximity to the Los Angeles core and as part of the broader expansion of the logistics economy in Southern California.[26] Trader Joe's is building a food assembly and distribution center there, Amazon has located a major packing and shipping center in Palmdale, and Rite Aid operates a 1-million-square-foot warehouse in Lancaster.[27]

While these efforts reflect a newly diversifying economy, they represent the continuation of the safety valve dynamic rather than an attempt to overcome it. The construction of the solar farm and local wind power turbines has cut down Joshua trees and been linked to the spread of "valley fever," a potentially debilitating respiratory infection caused by fungal spores in dry soil in the valley and throughout Arizona and California.[28] And the presence of big-box industries in the valley is happening on desperately unequal terms for the people of the valley. Workers at these warehouses report extreme heat and poor working conditions. Drivers working for an Amazon subcontractor have led a unionization campaign aiming to force recognition that Amazon is their joint employer, a key step towards unionizing delivery workers at the retail giant.[29] In these ways, the limits of the valley's new economy suggest that a broader transformation is necessary to escape the boundaries of the safety valve relationship. Others are attempting just such a transformation.

FIGURE 23. Antelope Valley Solar Farm, 2016. Source: Adam Reeder.

In a March 2021 op-ed in the *Antelope Valley Times*, Waunette Cullors, a long-time activist involved in civil rights and education activism in the Antelope Valley, called for Lancaster and Palmdale to end their contracts with the Los Angeles County Sheriff's Department.[30] This marked a shift in the trajectory of struggle: whereas TCAL's work had been to stop the policing of voucher tenants' homes, Cullors's call recognized the larger structural change that needed to occur in order for the valley to exercise control both over its public safety and over its broader economic and social fortunes. Cullors noted that Lancaster and Palmdale spent 39 and 35 percent of their general funds, respectively, on contracts with the LASD for policing services. "Why," she asked, "do our local elected mayors and city council members continue to approve these kinds of expenditures to bring in outsiders to inflict daily harm on the very people who they represent?" It was a reminder that, as long as the valley contracts with the county for law enforcement services, its people will remain at the mercy of a department that has treated them with discrimination and violence.

This was the opening bell of a campaign called "Cancel the Contract." Founded by a coalition of community organizations and leaders in the valley, the campaign is a product of long-term frustration with the department's abusive treatment of children in the valley's schools and stonewalling of reforms as mandated by its settlement with the Department of Justice. Cancel the Contract aims to end the cities of the Antelope Valley's relationships with the LASD.[31] Canceling the LASD contract would open millions of dollars to build new systems of public safety in the valley. The demand reflects the realities of organizers facing a totally intransigent department unwilling and perhaps even unable to implement the reforms it agreed to in its settlement with the Department of Justice.

One of the key campaign areas of the Cancel the Contract campaign is around policing in the Antelope Valley's schools, which extends criticism of the LASD from its policing of Black homes to its policing of Black students. Springing from teacher organizing, researchers found that deputies have been stopping Black teens at rates ranging from 1.5 to 4 times higher than white students. ProPublica found that stops of high school students accounted for 7 percent, of the deputies' four thousand stops of civilians in Lancaster.[32] These stops are also accompanied by violence toward students; one deputy serving as a school resource officer body-slammed a sixteen-year-old Black girl at Lancaster High School in August 2021.[33] The student had asked the deputy why he was staring at her; he attacked her as she was walking away from him. If unbound from the costly LASD contracts that have resulted in this type of violence, Cancel the Contract and its partners envision a menu of programs that could keep students safe in schools without being rooted in criminalization of children and the reliance on police.[34] As Cancel the Contract co-chair Raquel Derfler explained, "we push every lever to try to make change."

Viewing the organization in historical context, Cancel the Contract extends the work of Charles Graves and Cordia Anita Roberts to establish schools Black children could attend, the work of the South Antelope Valley NAACP when it organized against racially segregated schooling, and the Antelope Valley NAACP in the decades since, as it challenged local schools' adoption of Confederate mascots. Despite the dramatic changes in the valley's economy, relationship to Los Angeles, and demography, Black organizing in the valley has been a constant. Though it has not made the valley a just place, it has shown what the valley must do to become a more just place.

But Cancel the Contract also represents a more fundamental possibility. Its strategy represents not just a way out of the racist structure of policing that has dominated the valley for generations, but also the most serious and clear-eyed attempt to transform the valley's relationship to Los Angeles, a prerequisite to meaningful transformation of the valley. To question the LASD contract is to open the entirety of the valley's unequal relationship to Los Angeles up to question. In changing these terms, the valley would gain a measure of autonomy it has never had in its modern history.

Certainly, the relationship whereby the valley is Los Angeles's safety valve must be broken. But that alone is not enough. The corollary question is what an alternate version of the valley might be like. Here, Katherine McKittrick has suggested a future in which "the comfortable lens of insides/outsides" must be abandoned, perhaps in favor of a vision of these places as "sites through which 'co-operative human efforts' can take place."[35] To explore these possibilities, I close this book by returning to Sun Village, following its post-1960s history to try to see how the town might be fulfilling this vision.

SUN VILLAGE

In the years since the passage of the Fair Housing Act, Sun Village experienced the paradoxical but common post–Civil Rights Act phenomenon of winning rights but losing land. The Black town suffered from the opening of the valley to Black residency.

In 1989, the *Los Angeles Times* reviewed the fate of Sun Village in an article titled "Black Enclave Withers Amid Antelope Bloom."[36] The article described Palmdale and Lancaster as 1980s boomtowns, while Sun Village's population had dropped from two thousand to five hundred and its bustling downtown had been largely boarded up. Meanwhile, the Black population of the Antelope Valley had grown from 3 to 5 percent, the beginning of a trend that today sees the Black population of the valley stand at roughly 17.5 percent.[37]

Newspaper accounts in the early 1990s suggested significant Black migration from Los Angeles to the Antelope Valley, and framed it as an escape from the city's violence.[38] Despite everything its residents had done in the prior decades, Sun Village could not compete with the resources and amenities of Lancaster and Palmdale, and Black residents moving to the valley had many reasons to choose to move to these cities rather than Sun Village, despite the likelihood that they would be met with racism within them.

As Sun Village shrank, the white neighborhood to its south, Littlerock, encroached. Its acts are legible through what Louise Seamster and Danielle Purifoy call "creative extraction," the development of white places through their predation of Black places.[39] First, in the 1940s, the valley's "white urban regime" had excluded Black residents and necessitated their creation of Sun Village.[40] Then, in the 1950s and 60s, it exploited Sun Village, employing its residents in the valley's low-wage positions and sustaining the valley's segregated schools by building parallel ones in Sun Village. Now, it sought to consume Sun Village. In 1992, the Antelope Valley Union High School District established a high school in Sun Village but named it Littlerock High, alarming local residents. They petitioned to change the name to Sun Village High but were denied, with some Littlerock residents claiming that Sun Village no longer existed or would cease to exist soon.[41]

Attempts to submerge Sun Village mounted. The Littlerock town council began holding meetings in Sun Village, in another attempt to claim that the village was not a unique place but rather just a portion of Littlerock. Despite campaigns for signage dating back to the mid-1960s, Littlerock was listed on freeway signs, but Sun Village was not. And when the postal system consolidated, it closed Sun Village's branch but left Littlerock's open. In 1992, residents tried to make a separate

FIGURE 24. Peg Lee, supervisor at Jackie Robinson Park, points to Jackie Robinson in a photo from the park's establishment. Source: Photo by Anne Cusack/*Los Angeles Times* via Getty Images.

town council in the Antelope Valley to represent their interests but were unsuccessful. One resident, Eugene Washington, noted how the shift in the towns' relationship was always driven by Littlerock's interests. A reporter recorded that he "remembers when Littlerock didn't want anything to do with Sun Village—when a black person 'wouldn't dare say you lived in Littlerock,' for fear of angering whites. 'It's all right for Sun Village to be Littlerock now?,'" he fumed.[42]

Efforts to erase Sun Village might be read as an echo of the effort to erase Bruce's Beach. Even now, as the City of Manhattan Beach has apologized for its dispossession of the community, the descendants of George and Ethel Prioleau have struggled to get their family's experience recognized and repaired.[43]

In Sun Village, however, erasure was not possible, in part because people kept the community institutions that Sun Village residents built in the 1950s and '60s strong. Peg Lee, administrator of the Jackie Robinson Park, explained that the work of maintaining the park was deeply political. Reflecting on the instructions she received from the park's founders, she recalled, "Now, when I came in, I started a lot of programs, because those ladies asked me not to give away the park. They saw I was new, and I was a professional woman. And they told me that I must remember that the Blacks had to give up land just to get a park out there."

Lee added that this work was not just about physical places like the park but also about recognition of the place as one with Black origins. "It's about trying to keep the Sun Village name alive. All the new people coming in, we're trying to educate them to say Sun Village. . . . Hopefully, one day [the signs] will say Sun Village. So, that's just how it is all over the area."

Lee's work succeeded, and the park has remained an important center for recreation, historical memory, community events, and the distribution of resources and assistance. It hosts Juneteenth celebrations, serves as a cooling center on the hottest days of the summer, and was a hub for resource distribution during the COVID-19 pandemic. The persistence of Sun Village and its institutions contrasts the valley's vicissitudes and exceeds the narrow framework of racism and resistance to it that often bounds public and scholarly interest.[44]

As Bishop Hearns put it to me, "We were not permitted in the contiguous areas [of the Antelope Valley] in the early part, but that didn't stop us. We were not given a good opportunity to get into the best of the schools, but that didn't stop us. Nothing has stopped Sun Village. We . . . built ourselves up to a point to where we can make a statement that we are part of the Antelope Valley. From nothing to something."

Sun Village's persistence in struggling for justice has echoes across the valley. One can see it in the ongoing work of the Antelope Valley NAACP, which organized for decades to remove Confederate mascots from schools. One can see it in the blossoming of other struggles in the valley, such as Latinos for Social Justice in the 1990s. And perhaps most importantly, Sun Village's legacy is also embodied in TCAL's work to stop the policing and eviction of voucher tenants in the valley, and Cancel the Contract's work to make schools police-free. In this way, although the valley is characterized by constant flows of people in and out, Sun Village's institutions, memory, and politics have persisted.

Rather than to establish the valley through being valuable to Los Angeles, Sun Village illustrates the lasting value of land, institutions, and material resources, things the valley can exercise control of for the benefit of its residents. Elsewhere in the state are attempts to re-orient around these more grounded issues. Work to repatriate land to Native nations has increased across the state, and a new statewide push for reparations has recognized that land theft is a crucial component of the harm that could be repaired.[45]

Yet historian David Ponton warns of the pitfalls of allowing the hope of a different future to excuse or overshadow material realities of anti-Blackness past and present.[46] That people are working to remake the valley does not redeem it and should not discount its violence. The valley may continue striving for its past glory as a wealthy and segregated suburb, but that past was a mirage. Achieving it requires the valley to continue repressing and excluding for the foreseeable future all those who fall outside that narrow and false memory.

Unlikely as it is, a different possibility remains. As Pharaoh Mitchell explained, "In this community, we have so much opportunity, you know? If people wanted to treat each other with respect and dignity, we have so much potential. I mean we got room everywhere. I mean literally, we got deserts all around us. So we got more than enough to build." His words offer a different opportunity. To treat the valley as an oasis, as Mitchell and others have striven so hard to do, is to create conditions that might allow it to finally flourish.

ACKNOWLEDGMENTS

In writing this book, I have benefited from the support and insights of friends, colleagues, teachers, and institutions.

Most importantly, thank you, Gary Blasi, for inviting me into this work in the early 2010s, and nurturing my interest in it.

Thank you to everyone who agreed to participate in the interviews and other research activities that substantiate this book; without your kindness it would not have been possible to write. Thank you to my writing group and check-in partners—Phi Su, Theresa Rocha Beardall, Demar Lewis IV, and Preeti Sharma—for all your advice, editing of drafts, and commiseration.

Thank you to my departmental and UIC colleagues, including A. Naomi Paik, Adam Goodman, Alana Gunn, Amanda Lewis, Amie Shuck, Andy Clarno, Ash Stephens, Ashley Muchow, Atef Said, Bill McCarty, Chris Maggio, Danielle Beaujon, Danielle Smith, David Stovall, Dean Adams, Gayatri Reddy, Greg Matoesian, Jennifer Jones, Jessica Bird, Julian Thompson, Kareem Rabie, Kasey Henricks, Liat Ben-Moshe, Lisa Frohmann, Lynn Hudson, Mahesh Somashekhar, Maria Krysan, Mark Canuel, Nadine Naber, Nicole Nguyen, Patrisia Macias-Rojas, Peter Ibarra, Renee Cross, Ronak Kapadia, Sarah Ullman, Sharon Casillas, Susila Gurusami, and especially Beth Richie. You have read drafts, helped me navigate the academy, taught me so much, and made the early years of this job so rewarding.

To my manuscript workshop participants: thank you, Ananya Roy, for your years of intellectual and political support for this project. I am so grateful for your generosity. Thank you, Karida Brown, for your long encouragement of my work and for pushing me to go further. Thank you, Alex Vitale, for your infusion of ideas, connections, and excitement into this project. Thank you, Craig Willse, for your decade of friendship, mentorship, and feedback.

Thank you to Norrinda Brown for your generous advice from early on in this work, and for the ways your work has set the cornerstone for what I attempted. I remain deeply indebted to you. I thank Adi Alsaid, Amanda Ufheil-Somers, Andrew Kadi, Angélica Becerra, Brenden Beck, Brian McCabe, Elizabeth Korver-Glenn, Eva Rosen, Jessica Simes, Monica Bell, Nour Joudah, Randa May Wahbe, and Robin Bartram for your thoughtful and generative support, advice, ideas, invitations, and feedback on drafts and presentations. I also thank the anonymous readers who reviewed this work for UC Press. Thank you to the amazing community of the American Bar Foundation, especially Anna Reosti, Hardeep Dhillon, James Gathii, and Ajay K. Mehrotra, for your feedback and support. Thank you, Nashiha Alam, Fatima Basharet, Jacob Reed, Victoria Shepp, Celia Magnone, and Katherine Eames for research support. Thank you to Christopher Galeano for your work chronicling the legal struggle against voucher policing. Thank you to Breanna Chico for support with archival research in the valley, Hilary Malson for your collaboration over the years in studying this place, and Anishah and Karim for letting me crash and work-shopping my presentations. And thank you, Anna Gonzales and the Patton family, for your gracious feedback and assistance.

I thank the institutions at UIC who graciously funded and supported this work, including the Institute for Research on Race and Public Policy and the Institute for the Humanities. I also thank the academic institutions and departments that have kindly hosted me for talks and helped me develop this work, including the American Bar Foundation; the Duke University Race Working Group; the NYU Urban Initiative; the UC Irvine Department of Criminology, Law and Society; Will Garriot and the Drake University Department of Law, Politics, and Society; and the University of Wisconsin Madison Institute for Research on Poverty.

This book began as my dissertation in the sociology department at UCLA. I remain thankful to my committee, and particularly Darnell Hunt, for continued support over the years.

While conducting the research that appears in this book, I published findings and ideas in several journals. The introduction contains material from "Mended Windows, Not Broken Windows: A Du Boisian Analysis of Urban Policing," *City and Community* 23, no.4 (2024): 320–40, coauthored with Theresa Rocha Beardall and Demar F. Lewis IV. Chapter 3 contains findings published in "Opposing and Policing Racial Integration: Evidence from the Housing Choice Voucher Program," *Du Bois Review: Social Science Research on Race* 17, no. 2 (2020): 363–87, as well as theory first explored in "Policing, Property, and the Production of Racial Segregation" in *The Sociology of Housing: How Homes Shape Our Social Lives*, edited by Brian J. McCabe and Eva Rosen (Chicago: University of Chicago Press, 2023), 291–304. Chapter 4 contains findings published in "Deconcentration without Integration: Examining the Social Outcomes of Housing Choice Voucher Movement in Los Angeles County," *City and Community* 14, no. 4 (2015): 364–3=91, "The New Man in the House Rules: How the Regulation of Housing Vouchers Turns Personal Bonds into Eviction Liabilities," *Housing Policy Debate* 30, no. 6 (2020): 926–49, and "From Broken Windows to Broken Homes: Homebreaking as Racialized and Gendered Poverty Governance," *Feminist Formations* 33, no. 1 (2021): 1–32, co-authored with Susila Gurusami.

To Maura Roessner and the staff at UC Press, thank you for your vision for this project, and your consistent support and patience with me.

Thank you to my family—Mom, Dad, Shazia—whom I love so dearly.

To all, I ask forgiveness for this book's errors of ignorance or misinterpretation.

METHODOLOGICAL APPENDIX

My first encounter with this case came in 2010, through UCLA law professor Gary Blasi, a towering figure in Los Angeles's legal aid and housing rights community who had been contacted for help responding to the eviction crisis among voucher tenants. I had been helping him put together some demographic data about the valley, to contextualize the eviction crisis among voucher tenants. One day in the spring of 2010 I tagged along as he drove up to the valley to join a community forum and talk to people about the issue. As I describe in the book, Blasi was laying the groundwork for Ross's lawsuit.

My work with Blasi was brief; he only needed my assistance with some census demographic data and mapping. While assisting him, I was also taking my first year of classes in the sociology department at UCLA, including a class on racial residential segregation. There, I found that what I was learning about the experiences of voucher tenants in the valley had nothing in common with the literature I was reading. It was an eye-opening and upsetting experience that motivated me to develop a research project based on interviewing voucher tenants about their social and economic experiences in the valley. I began interviewing tenants in the summer of 2011, driving to the Palmdale office of the Housing Authority of the County of Los Angeles on weekday mornings in the summer to set up a folding table and my recruitment materials. I'd spend the day recruiting participants into the project, then return home and spend the next day or two calling them to conduct the interviews by phone. In the summer of 2011, I interviewed eighteen respondents.

Tenants were wary of speaking to me, and rightly so. Some feared being seen interacting with me outside the office, or some form of retaliation should their participation ever come to light. Others simply didn't trust me, a South Asian twenty-something from "down below" who stuck out in so many ways. My interview plan did me no favors with those who did participate—it was structured in a stilted, almost census-like format, that may have been off-putting.

Nevertheless, many were patient or forgiving and answered my questions. My interview plan included questions about tenant demography, economic outcomes, and social integration. Tenants spoke of those things but much more as well. They spoke of social exclusion, harassment, and racism that prevented any semblance of normal life, let alone social or economic progress. They also described being surveilled and policed not just by local government, but by their neighbors as well. I learned to adapt and let my interview guide fall by the wayside as they took our conversations where they needed to go. Their testimonies changed my understanding of what was happening—the story wasn't just about social rejection but about the dangerous implementation of that hostility through action. Because these data didn't come through systematic and consistent questions on my part, the data was more uneven and inconsistent than ideal. Had I gone to the valley better prepared, I could have asked better questions and perhaps obtained richer and more complete data.

My original plan was to compare what tenants were experiencing in the valley to what public housing tenants experienced in Los Angeles proper. I visited public housing developments in the Westmont area of Los Angeles to conduct interviews that would serve as that basis of comparison. In total during the late summer and early fall I interviewed nine residents of public housing in the Westmont area. The work helped me better grasp the sinews between public housing and Section 8 and between core and periphery, as many LA public housing tenants spoke of thinking about moving to the valley, or family they knew who had made the move.

In the following years, I worked to analyze and publish the data. I returned to fieldwork in 2015, now focused solely on the Antelope Valley. My dissertation chairs encouraged me to interview private residents in the valley to get a second perspective on vouchers. So, on weekends in summer 2015 and 2016, I went door to door in neighborhoods with high rates of voucher tenant residency to ask private renters and homeowners about their views and actions. I encountered similar problems of distrust, with many door knocks resulting in residents declining to participate. But among those who participated, it quickly became clear that not only did private renters and homeowners deeply resent voucher tenants but that they were eager to use surveillance and policing as tools to evict them from the neighborhoods. In total I interviewed forty-three local residents. During that period, I also returned to the Housing Authority to continue interviewing voucher tenants. I wanted to keep continuity with interviews from 2011, and maintained some questions to do so, but also allowed the interview guide to evolve to ask questions about surveillance and policing experiences to better reflect what I had learned during my first wave of fieldwork.

By the end of 2016, I had amassed interviews with thirty-nine voucher tenants, and forty-three valley residents. (One additional voucher interview would be completed much later). I had also lucked into interviews with two landlords, and made connections with housing authority staff and local figures on whom I would later rely for historical and other context.

During my interviews with private renters and homeowners, they often referenced a past Antelope Valley that they were trying to protect—a time when it was a happy middle-class region with few problems and few outsiders. They made it clear that while policing was a new technique of segregation in the valley, it was part of a long struggle over the valley's social hierarchies and distribution of power. Their invocation of the past suggested to me that I needed to explore that past too.

After I completed my dissertation and decided to continue the research as a book project, I began to expand the project to fill in that history. I returned to the Antelope Valley in the summer of 2019 to begin writing a history of Sun Village, interviewing local activists, important figures like Bishop Hearns, and lawyers like Professor Blasi, and collecting other information that would fill in the gaps in my research. Most importantly, news archives from the Antelope Valley are not digitized, existing only on microfilm at the Palmdale Library. In person, I worked through as much of this history as I could during my fieldwork, reading news archives from the *South Antelope Valley Press* from the early 1900s to the early 1970s. The pandemic intervened and I could not return to the valley to complete reading those news archives. This is a major gap in the project, as my history of Sun Village can't fully capture the post-'60s era. It is a limitation of this project that I hope is filled by others.

Later in 2019, I was asked to serve as an expert witness in a police practices fair housing case in Peoria, Illinois. The case had essentially built on the earlier work of The Community Action League's lawsuit, assessing that discriminatory enforcement of crime-free and nuisance housing ordinances could violate the Fair Housing Act. For me, the case illustrated that what happened in the valley was also happening in cities around the country, and that TCAL's work had something to offer to those experiencing the policing of housing elsewhere. The experience helped frame the book and shape what would come to be its last chapter.

In the summer of 2020, protest over police and vigilante killings of George Floyd, Ahmaud Arbery, and Breonna Taylor reverberated in the valley, and grew after the death of Robert Fuller. As people organized protests, I received a text from an acquaintance in the valley who I had worked with, about widespread rumors of a Klan counter-protest. They asked if I had heard of Richard Butler. I hadn't. But I built chapter 2 around trying to answer this question, following Butler to his mentor Wesley Swift, and attempting to trace the history of right-wing politics in the valley from Swift's era to the present.

Working from afar in 2020 and 2021, I also reviewed the Bancroft Library's digital archives of the West Coast Regional office of the NAACP, which contained records of chapter activism. I also read digitized archives of the California Women's Club, of which there was a Sun Village branch. Finally, I conducted some interviews by phone, including with Lancaster Mayor Rex Parris and several local activists who challenged his policies. I was not able to complete interviews with all the activists who were central to TCAL's work. Darren Parker, a key figure, passed away before a scheduled interview in 2019. Others were difficult to find contact information for, or we couldn't manage to connect while I was in town.

There were other sources of information I could not pursue as well. I attempted interviews with the DOJ's personnel overseeing the consent decree but was unsuccessful. I gained IRB permission to interview landlords in the valley but ran into a series of dead ends in my attempts to reach them, and then was unable to continue the work once the pandemic began. Important questions about the economy of landlords and corporate investors in the valley remain unanswered but deserve further research and scrutiny.

Finally, and most importantly, my interviews with voucher tenants are largely with people who managed not to be evicted, or who may have been evicted once but kept their vouchers and found other housing in the valley. Those who were evicted from their homes, forced out of the valley altogether, or had their lives shortened by the violence of the process and its aftermath—my study could not reach them. Voucher tenants I spoke to sometimes relayed the stories of their family and friends who had been evicted and left the voucher program or the valley, but for the most part, this book conveys the experiences of those who survived the valley's policing. What is not on these pages, then, was surely worse.

NOTES

Throughout the book, otherwise unattributed quotations are from interview transcripts.

PREFACE

1. Per signage in the museum.

2. Accounts of Indigenous presence in and around the valley are inconsistent across texts and sources. Friends of the Antelope Valley Indian Museum and the Native American Advisory Council of the Museum of Art and History in Lancaster produced the map "Tribes without Borders," which attempts to illustrate tribal presence without strict boundary lines that had been contested or rendered inconsistently in prior texts. For more, see https://www.lancastermoah.org/this-valley-is-sacred.

3. David Colker, "Museum of an Unreal World | Antelope Valley: This Ethnocentric Showcase of American Indian Artifacts Displays More Artistic License than Historical Verity," *Los Angeles Times*, March 15, 1991, https://www.latimes.com/archives/la-xpm-1991 -03-15-ca-253-story.html.

4. See, for example, Patrick Wolfe, "Settler Colonialism and the Elimination of the Native," *Journal of Genocide Research* 8, no. 4 (2006): 387–409.

5. Katherine McKittrick, *Demonic Grounds: Black Women and the Cartographies of Struggle* (Minneapolis: University of Minnesota Press, 2006), x.

6. See "Charles Graves," Local History, The Unofficial Website of Rosamond, CA 93560, accessed July 19, 2023, http://www.rosamondca.us/history/Graves.htm.

7. Lauren Lien, "Yoshio Ekimoto," *Lancaster Museum of Art and History News* (blog), July 12, 2018, https://www.lancastermoah.org/single-post/yoshio-ekimoto.

8. Dayle DeBry, "Japanese Farmers in the Antelope Valley," *Antelope Valley Rural Museum Newsletter*, June 2018, 4–6.

9. Mike Davis, *City of Quartz: Excavating the Future in Los Angeles*, new ed. (New York: Verso, 2006).

10. Hannah Rogers, "The Llano del Rio Cooperative Colony," *Lancaster Museum of Art and History News* (blog), September 27, 2021, https://www.lancastermoah.org/single-post /the-llano-del-rio-cooperative-colony.

11. Paul Greenstein, Lionel Rolfe, and Nigey Lennon, *Bread and Hyacinths: The Rise and Fall of Utopian Los Angeles* (Los Angeles: California Classic Books, 1992).

12. Jennifer C. Mueller, "'Imagine an Ignorance That Fights Back': Honoring Charles Mills, Our Inheritance and Charge," *Sociology of Race and Ethnicity* 8, no. 4 (2022): 443–50.

13. See Henri Lefebvre, *The Production of Space*, trans. Donald Nicholson-Smith (Oxford: Blackwell, 1991).

14. See "Map Room," Million Dollar Hoods (research team website), last modified August 3, 2021, http://milliondollarhoods.org, for a breakdown of incarceration spending by neighborhood in Los Angeles. Lancaster and Palmdale routinely rise to the top of rankings of LASD spending.

15. American Civil Liberties Union of Southern California, *Banished and Abandoned: Criminalization and Displacement of Unhoused People in Lancaster*, February 2021, https://www.aclusocal.org/en/publications/banished-and-abandoned-lancaster. See also PolicyLink and USC Program for Environmental and Regional Equity, *An Equity Profile of the Los Angeles Region*, 2017, https://dornsife.usc.edu/eri/publications/equity-profile-los-angeles -region.

16. See Los Angeles County Department of Public Health, Office of Health Assessment and Epidemiology, *Life Expectancy in Los Angeles County: How Long Do We Live and Why? A Cities and Communities Report*, July 2010. http://publichealth.lacounty.gov/epi/docs /Life%20Expectancy%20Final_web.pdf.

17. As Danielle Purifoy notes, the term "Black town" means something different than what a "White town" might connote, "not only because of the persistent forms of violence leveled at them, but also because Black towns do not develop from the same experiences and purposes as White towns." See "Black Towns and (Legal) Marronage," *Annals of the American Association of Geographers* 113, no. 7 (2023): 1600.

18. "Museum of the New Llano Colony, Louisiana," accessed July 22, 2023, http://newl lanocolony.com.

19. See "Five Residents of Poston File Exclusion Test Case," *The Poston Chronicle* (Poston Internment Camp, AZ), September 16, 1944.

20. For more on these solidarities, see Scott Kurashige, *The Shifting Grounds of Race: Black and Japanese Americans in the Making of Multiethnic Los Angeles* (Princeton: Princeton University Press, 2008).

21. U.S. Congress, Senate, Committee on Governmental Affairs, Subcommittee on Civil Service, Post Office, and General Services, Recommendations of the Commission on Wartime Internment and Relocation of Citizens: Hearings before the Subcommittee on Civil Service, Post Office, and General Services of the Committee on Governmental Affairs, United States Senate, on S. 2116 . . . August 16, 1984, Los Angeles, CA, August 29, 1984, Anchorage, AK., 98th Cong., 2nd sess., 1984, 182–83.

22. Ann Simmons, "A Monument to Japanese Americans in the Antelope Valley is Restored," *Los Angeles Times*, May 17, 2008, https://www.latimes.com/local/la-me-japanese17 -2008may17-story.html.

23. See, for example, "Indian News Via California," *Navajo Times* (Window Rock, AZ), October 12, 1967. More on this topic appears in chapter 2.

INTRODUCTION

The epigraph is from Thom Andersen, dir., *Los Angeles Plays Itself* (New York: The Cinema Guild, 2014).

1. Tracy Rosenthal and Leonardo Vichlis, *Abolish Rent: How Tenants Can End the Housing Crisis* (Chicago: Haymarket Books, 2024), 35.

2. Norrinda Brown, "Section 8 is the New N-Word: Policing Integration in the Age of Black Mobility," *Washington University Journal of Law and Policy* 51, no. 1 (2016): 61–93.

3. Jennifer Santos, "Sec. 8 hate on social net," *Antelope Valley Press*, January 6, 2011.

4. Today, the agency has changed its name and is known as the Los Angeles County Development Authority.

5. Priscilla Ocen, "The New Racially Restrictive Covenant: Race, Welfare, and the Policing of Black Women in Subsidized Housing," *UCLA Law Review* 59, no. 6 (2012): 1540–82.

6. David Harvey, *Spaces of Capital: Towards a Critical Geography* (New York: Routledge, 2001).

7. Ruth Wilson Gilmore, *Golden Gulag: Prisons, Surplus, Crisis, and Opposition in Globalizing California* (Berkeley: University of California Press, 2007).

8. Greg Grandin, *The End of the Myth: From the Frontier to the Border Wall in the Mind of America* (New York: Metropolitan Books, 2019).

9. Neil Smith, "Gentrification and Uneven Development," *Economic Geography* 58, no. 2 (1982): 139–55, cited in Tom Slater, *Shaking up the City: Ignorance, Inequality, and the Urban Question* (Oakland: University of California Press, 2021).

10. Seeing the valley as a permanent, if distended, element of Los Angeles fits Neil Brenner's critique of urban studies' false dichotomies about what is and is not "urban." See "Theses on Urbanization," *Public Culture* 25, no. 1 (January 2013): 85–114.

11. Roger W. Lotchin, *Fortress California, 1910–1962: From Warfare to Welfare* (New York: Oxford University Press, 1992).

12. Prentiss A. Dantzler, "The Urban Process under Racial Capitalism: Race, Anti-Blackness, and Capital Accumulation," *Journal of Race, Ethnicity and the City* 2, no. 2 (2021): 113–34.

13. Ananya Roy, "Racial Banishment," in *Keywords in Radical Geography: Antipode at 50*, ed. Antipode Editorial Collective (Hoboken, NJ: Wiley, 2019), 227–30. See also Katherine Beckett and Steve Herbert, *Banished: The New Social Control in America* (New York: Oxford University Press, 2009).

14. Alex Schafran, "Race and Foreclosure on the Edge of the Bay Area," *Polis*, December 1, 2011, https://www.thepolisblog.org/2009/08/introducing-polis_9535.html. See also Alex Schafran. *The Road to Resegregation: Northern California and the Failure of Politics* (Berkeley: University of California Press, 2018).

15. McKittrick, *Demonic Grounds*, 6.

16. McKittrick, *Demonic Grounds*, xv.

17. Nancy MacLean, *Democracy in Chains: The Deep History of the Radical Right's Stealth Plan for America* (New York: Penguin Press, 2017).

18. See lineages of public housing tenant activism in works such as Akira Drake Rodriguez, *Diverging Space for Deviants: The Politics of Atlanta's Public Housing* (Athens:

University of Georgia Press, 2021); Jacqueline Leavitt, "Women under Fire: Public Housing Activism in Los Angeles," *Frontiers: A Journal of Women Studies* 13, no. 2 (1993): 109–30; Michael Karp, "The St. Louis Rent Strike of 1969: Transforming Black Activism and American Low-Income Housing," *Journal of Urban History* 40, no. 4 (July 2014): 648–70; Rhonda Y. Williams, *The Politics of Public Housing: Black Women's Struggles Against Urban Inequality* (New York: Oxford University Press, 2004); Roberta M. Feldman and Susan Stall, *The Dignity of Resistance: Women Residents' Activism in Chicago Public Housing* (Cambridge: Cambridge University Press, 2004).

19. Alexander Polikoff, *Waiting for Gautreaux: A Story of Segregation, Housing, and the Black Ghetto* (Chicago: Northwestern University Press, 2007).

20. Robert Park and Ernest Burgess, eds., *The City* (Chicago: University of Chicago Press, 1925).

21. See Prentiss Dantzler, Elizabeth Korver-Glenn, and Junia Howell, "Introduction: What Does Racial Capitalism Have to Do with Cities and Communities?," *City & Community* 21, no. 3 (2022): 163–72. The authors also note Joyce Ladner's critique of this type of research as situating the Black experience as an exception to supposedly universal rules of urban sociological research.

22. "Public housing programs should emphasize scattered site construction, rent supplements should, wherever possible, be used in nonghetto areas, and an intensive effort should be made to recruit below-market interest rate sponsors willing to build outside the ghettos" (Kerner Commission, *Report of the National Advisory Commission on Civil Disorders* [Washington, DC: US Government Printing Office, 1968], 263.)

23. Keeanga-Yamahtta Taylor, *Race for Profit: How Banks and the Real Estate Industry Undermined Black Homeownership* (Chapel Hill: University of North Carolina Press, 2019).

24. Melanie Kayser Schmidt Arias, "Experimental Citizens: The Experimental Housing Allowance Program and Housing Vouchers as American Social Policy in the 1970s and 1980s" (PhD diss., University of California, Los Angeles, 2013).

25. Lee Rainwater, *Behind Ghetto Walls: Black Families in a Federal Slum* (Chicago: Aldine, 1970), 408.

26. Loïc Wacquant, *The Invention of the "Underclass": A Study in the Politics of Knowledge* (Newark: Polity, 2022).

27. William J. Wilson, *The Truly Disadvantaged: The Inner City, the Underclass, and Public Policy* (Chicago: University of Chicago Press, 1987).

28. Edward G. Goetz, *New Deal Ruins: Race, Economic Justice, and Public Housing Policy* (Ithaca: Cornell University Press, 2013).

29. Susan J. Popkin, et al., *The Hidden War: Crime and the Tragedy of Public Housing in Chicago* (New Brunswick: Rutgers University Press, 2000).

30. Goetz, *New Deal Ruins*, 62.

31. Edward G. Goetz, "The Audacity of HOPE VI: Discourse and the Dismantling of Public Housing," *Cities* 35 (December 2013): 342–48.

32. Goetz, *New Deal Ruins*, 71.

33. Digital Scholarship Lab, "Renewing Inequality," *American Panorama*, ed. Robert K. Nelson and Edward L. Ayers, accessed July 10, 2023, https://dsl.richmond.edu/panorama/renewal/#view=0/0/1&viz=map&text=about.

34. Derrick A. Bell, "Brown v. Board of Education and the Interest-Convergence Dilemma," *Harvard Law Review* 93, no. 3 (1980): 518–33.

35. See, for example, accounts of left-leaning political and intellectual elites' embrace of vouchers in John Arena, *Driven from New Orleans: How Nonprofits Betray Public Housing and Promote Privatization* (Minneapolis: University of Minnesota Press, 2012); Lily Geismer, *Left Behind: The Democrats' Failed Attempt to Solve Inequality* (New York: Public Affairs, 2022); and Elizabeth Popp Berman, *Thinking Like an Economist: How Efficiency Replaced Equality in US Public Policy* (Princeton: Princeton University Press, 2022). The following accounts trace these broad changes in more detail regarding vouchers: Lous Winnick, "The Triumph of Housing Allowance Programs: How a Fundamental Policy Conflict Was Resolved," *Cityscape* 1, no. 3 (1995): 95–121; Charles J. Orlebeke, "The Evolution of Low-Income Housing Policy, 1949 to 1999," *Housing Policy Debate* 11, no. 2: 489–520; and Larry Bennett, Janet L. Smith, and Patricia A. Wright, *Where Are Poor People to Live? Transforming Public Housing Communities* (Armonk, NY: M. E. Sharpe, 2006).

36. For an extended and thorough critique of neighborhood effects, see Tom Slater, "Neighborhood Effects as Tautological Urbanism," in *Shaking up the City: Ignorance, Inequality, and the Urban Question* (Oakland: University of California Press, 2021).

37. Xavier de Souza Briggs, Susan J. Popkin, and John Goering. *Moving to Opportunity: The Story of an American Experiment to Fight Ghetto Poverty* (New York: Oxford University Press, 2010).

38. See, for example, Henry G. Cisneros and Lora Engdahl, eds., *From Despair to Hope: Hope VI and the New Promise of Public Housing in America's Cities* (Washington, DC: Brookings Institution Press, 2010).

39. Susan Clampet-Lundquist and Douglas Massey, "Neighborhood Effects on Economic Self-Sufficiency: A Reconsideration of the Moving to Opportunity Experiment," *American Journal of Sociology* 114, no. 1 (2008): 107–43; Robert J. Sampson, "Moving to Inequality: Neighborhood Effects and Experiments Meet Social Structure," *American Journal of Sociology* 114, no.1 (2008): 189–231; Molly W. Metzger, "The Reconcentration of Poverty: Patterns of Housing Voucher Use, 2000 to 2008," *Housing Policy Debate* 24 no. 3 (2014): 544–67.

40. Lawrence F. Katz, Jeffrey R. Kling, and Jeffrey B. Liebman, "Moving to Opportunity in Boston: Early Results of a Randomized Mobility Experiment," *The Quarterly Journal of Economics* 116, no. 2 (2001): 607–54; Jeffrey R. Kling, Jeffrey B. Liebman, and Lawrence F. Katz, "Experimental Analysis of Neighborhood Effects," *Econometrica* 75, no. 1 (2007): 83–119; Tama Leventhal and Jeanne Brooks-Gunn, "Moving to Opportunity: An Experimental Study of Neighborhood Effects on Mental Health," *American Journal of Public Health* 93, no. 9 (2003): 1576–82.

41. J. Rosie Tighe, Megan E. Hatch, and Joseph Mead, "Source of Income Discrimination and Fair Housing Policy," *Journal of Planning Literature* 32, no. 1 (2017): 3–15.

42. Poverty and Race Research Action Council and National Housing Law Project, "Expanding Federal Support for Tenant Organizing in Federally Assisted Housing and the Housing Choice Voucher Program," February 15, 2022, https://www.prrac.org/expanding -federal-support-for-tenant-organizing-in-federally-assisted-housing-and-the-housing -choice-voucher-program-february-2022.

43. Eva Rosen, *The Voucher Promise: "Section 8" and the Fate of an American Neighborhood* (Princeton: Princeton University Press, 2020).

44. Ingrid Gould Ellen, Katherine O'Regan, and Sarah Strochak, *Using HUD Administrative Data to Estimate Success Rates and Search Durations for New Voucher Recipients* (U.S. Department of Housing and Urban Development, Office of Policy Development and Research, December 2021), https://www.huduser.gov/portal/portal/sites/default/files/pdf/Voucher-Success_Rates.pdf.

45. Jane Rongerude and Mônica Haddad, "Cores and Peripheries: Spatial Analysis of Housing Choice Voucher Distribution in the San Francisco Bay Area Region, 2000–2010," *Housing Policy Debate* 26, no. 3 (2016): 417–36.

46. Junia Howell, Ellen Whitehead, and Elizabeth Korver-Glenn, "Still Separate and Unequal: Persistent Racial Segregation and Inequality in Subsidized Housing," *Socius* 9 (2023): 1–16.

47. Howell, Whitehead, and Korver-Glenn, "Still Separate and Unequal."

48. Henry O. Pollakowski, et al., "Childhood Housing and Adult Outcomes: A Between-Siblings Analysis of Housing Vouchers and Public Housing," *American Economic Journal: Economic Policy* 14, no. 3 (2022): 235–72.

49. Anne Bonds, "Race and Ethnicity I: Property, Race, and the Carceral State," *Progress in Human Geography* 43, no. 3 (2019): 574–83.

50. Rachel D. Godsil, "Race Nuisance: The Politics of Law in the Jim Crow Era," *Michigan Law Review* 105, no. 3 (2006): 505–58.

51. Simone Browne, *Dark Matters: On the Surveillance of Blackness* (Durham: Duke University Press, 2015).

52. Quintard Taylor, "Slaves and Free Men: Blacks in the Oregon Country, 1840–1860," *Oregon Historical Quarterly* 83, no. 2 (1982): 153–70.

53. Kate Masur, *Until Justice Be Done: America's First Civil Rights Movement, from the Revolution to Reconstruction* (New York: W. W. Norton, 2021), 225–66.

54. Andrew Delbanco, *The War Before the War: Fugitive Slaves and the Struggle for America's Soul from the Revolution to the Civil War* (New York: Penguin Press, 2019).

55. James W. Loewen, *Sundown Towns: A Hidden Dimension of American Racism* (New York: New Press, 2005). Loewen identifies Palmdale as a possible sundown town.

56. For an early historical example of police abetting racial violence intended to segregate, see Simon Balto, *Occupied Territory: Policing Black Chicago from Red Summer to Black Power* (Chapel Hill: University of North Carolina Press, 2019), 91–122.

57. Henry Freedman, "Sylvester Smith, Unlikely Heroine: *King v. Smith* (1968)," in *The Poverty Law Canon: Exploring the Major Cases*, ed. Marie A. Failinger and Ezra Rosser (Ann Arbor: University of Michigan Press, 2016), 51–71.

58. Ellora Derenoncourt, "Can You Move to Opportunity? Evidence from the Great Migration," *The American Economic Review* 112, no. 2 (2022): 369–408.

59. See Monica C. Bell, "Anti-Segregation Policing," *New York University Law Review* 95, no. 3 (2020): 650–765; Daanika Gordon, *Policing the Racial Divide: Urban Growth Politics and the Remaking of Segregation* (New York: New York University Press, 2022).

60. These formulations emerged from the wartime mothers' pensions administered by some states. See Mimi Abramovitz, *Regulating the Lives of Women: Social Welfare Policy from Colonial Times to the Present* (Boston: South End Press, 1996); Dorothy Roberts, "Welfare and the Problem of Black Citizenship," *The Yale Law Journal* 105, no. 6 (1996): 1563–1602; Richard A. Chikota, "Pre-Dawn Welfare Inspections and the Right of Privacy," *Journal of Urban Law* 44, no. 1 (1966): 119–35.

61. Chad Freidrichs, dir., *The Pruitt-Igoe Myth: An Urban History* (Unicorn Stencil, 2011).

62. Freidrichs, dir., *The Pruitt-Igoe Myth*.

63. Freedman, "Sylvester Smith."

64. Davis, *City of Quartz*.

65. W. E. B. Du Bois, *Black Reconstruction in America: An Essay Toward a History of the Part which Black Folk Played in the Attempt to Reconstruct Democracy in America, 1860–1880* (New York: The Free Press, 1998 [1935]).

66. Cheryl I. Harris, "Whiteness as Property," *Harvard Law Review* 106, no. 8 (1993): 1707–91.

67. See Martin Legassick and David Hemson, *Foreign Investment and the Reproduction of Racial Capitalism in South Africa* (London: Anti-Apartheid Movement, 1976). These accounts are compatible with work on internal colonialism, such as Robert Blauner, *Racial Oppression in America* (New York: Harper and Row, 1972).

68. Cedric J. Robinson, *Black Marxism: The Making of the Black Radical Tradition*, 3rd ed (Chapel Hill: University of North Carolina Press, 2020).

69. Julian Go, "Three Tensions in the Theory of Racial Capitalism," *Sociological Theory* 39, no. 1 (2021): 38–47.

70. Prentiss A. Dantzler, "The Urban Process under Racial Capitalism: Race, Anti-Blackness, and Capital Accumulation," *Journal of Race, Ethnicity and the City* 2, no. 2 (2021): 113–34.

71. Walter Johnson offers such an in-depth reading of Du Bois as a theorist of what would come to be known as racial capitalism. Prominent in his analysis is the case of East St. Louis. See *The Broken Heart of America: St. Louis and the Violent History of the United States* (New York: Basic Books, 2020).

72. W. E. B. Du Bois, *Darkwater: Voices from within the Veil* (New York: Harcourt, Brace and Howe, 1920); Ida B. Wells-Barnett, *The East St. Louis Massacre: The Greatest Outrage of the Century* (Chicago: The Negro Fellowship Herald Press, 1917).

73. Du Bois, *Darkwater*, 84–85.

74. Du Bois, *Darkwater*, 90, 94, 84.

75. Robert Vargas, "Four Ways Race and Capitalism Can Advance Urban Sociology," *City & Community* 21, no. 3 (2022): 256–62. See David Hugill, *Settler Colonial City: Racism and Inequality in Postwar Minneapolis* (Minneapolis, University of Minnesota Press, 2021); Camille Petersen, "Capitalizing on Heritage: St. Augustine, Florida, and the Landscape of American Racial Ideology," *City & Community* 21, no. 3 (2022): 193–213; and Brian Jordan Jefferson, "Cities, Crime, and Carcerality: Beyond the Ecological Perspective," *Journal of Planning Literature* 32, no. 2 (2017): 103–16.

76. See Sarah Haley, *No Mercy Here: Gender, Punishment, and the Making of Jim Crow Modernity*, (Chapel Hill: University of North Carolina Press, 2016); and Shauna J. Sweeney. "Gendering Racial Capitalism and the Black Heretical Tradition," in *Histories of Racial Capitalism*, ed. Justin Leroy and Destin Jenkins (New York: Columbia University Press, 2021), 53–84.

77. Du Bois, *Darkwater*, 98.

78. Aldon D. Morris, *The Scholar Denied: W. E. B. Du Bois and the Birth of Modern Sociology* (Oakland: University of California Press, 2017).

79. Hilary Malson, "Tearing Down and Building Up': A History, Theory and Practice of Abolitionist Housing Justice in the US," in *Handbook on Planning and Power*, ed. Michael

Gunder, Kristina Grange, and Tanja Winkler (Cheltenham, UK: Edward Elgar Publishing, 2023), 211–27.

80. Ruth Wilson Gilmore, "Abolition Geography and the Problem of Innocence," in *Futures of Black Radicalism*, ed. Gaye Theresa Johnson and Alex Lubin (New York: Verso, 2017), 225–40.

81. bell hooks, *Yearning: Race, Gender, and Cultural Politics* (Boston: South End Press, 1990), 77.

1. SUN VILLAGE

The epigraph is from Ann Simmons, "Feeling Burned in Sun Village," *Los Angeles Times*, September 24, 2012, A.1.

1. Karla Slocum, *Black Towns, Black Futures: The Enduring Allure of a Black Place in the American West* (Chapel Hill: University of North Carolina Press, 2019).

2. Russell M. Smith and Leora Waldner, "Why Majority-Minority Cities Form: Non-White Municipal Incorporation in the United States, 1990–2010," *Urban Geography* 39, no. 1 (2018): 149–66; Slocum, *Black Towns, Black Futures*.

3. I see these twin forces, segregation and scarcity, as manifestations of the mutually constitutive nature of capitalism and racism that is cohered in Cedric Robinson's theory of racial capitalism; see *Black Marxism*. For a closer examination of the applicability of racial capitalism to urban scholarship, see: Dantzler, Korver-Glenn, and Howell, "Introduction: What Does Racial Capitalism Have to Do with Cities and Communities?" *City & Community* 21, no. 3 (2022): 163–72.

4. Allensworth: Robert Mikell, "The History of Allensworth, California (1908-)," BlackPast.org, September 27, 2017, https://www.blackpast.org/african-american-history /history-allensworth-california-1908; Morgan P. Vickers, "Finding History, Hope, and Humanity in Allensworth, the First Black Town in California," *Roadtrippers*, January 26, 2021, https://roadtrippers.com/magazine/colonel-allensworth-state-park. San Bernardino: Nick Cataldo, "Cajon Pass Brought First Black Pioneers to San Bernardino Valley," *San Bernardino Sun*, February 22, 2016, https://www.sbsun.com/2016/02/22/cajon-pass-brought -first-black-pioneers-to-san-bernardino-valley. Indio: Chris Clarke, "African-Americans Shaping the California Desert: Coachella Valley," SoCal Focus, KCET, February 9, 2012, https://www.kcet.org/socal-focus/african-americans-shaping-the-california-desert-coach ella-valley. Palm Springs: Nathan Solis, "Palm Springs promises to 'right that wrong' for Black, Latino community destroyed in 1960s," *Los Angeles Times*, April, 12, 2024, https:// www.latimes.com/california/story/2024–04–12/palm-spring-promises-to-right-wrongs -done-to-section-14.

Charles Graves (see preface) was by no means alone; journalist Delilah L. Beasley documented Black homesteaders creating communities across the Mojave Desert and Victorville during the early 1900s. As she wrote in her 1919 *The Negro Trailblazers of California*, "The deserts of California, namely the Mojave and at Victorville, are government lands, and quite a few colored people have taken up homesteads on this land and are improving them." See Chris Clarke, "African-Americans Shaping the California Desert: Homesteading in the Mojave," SoCal Focus, *KCET*, February 1, 2012, https://www.kcet.org/socal-focus/african -americans-shaping-the-california-desert-homesteading-in-the-mojave.

5. The Prioleaus purchased the southern half of Lot 4, Block 12, in 1919, for $10. See City of Manhattan Beach California, "History Advisory Board Report," October 25, 2021, https://www.manhattanbeach.gov/home/showpublisheddocument/50404/637916667376600000; Mark McDermott, "History—Prioleau Family Objects to Bruce's Beach Plaque Language," *Easy Reader and Peninsula Magazine*, March 16, 2023, https://easyreadernews.com/history-prioleau-family-objects-to-bruces-beach-plaque-language.

6. Trevor Goodloe, "George Prioleau (1856–1928)," BlackPast.org, March 17, 2010, https://www.blackpast.org/african-american-history/chaplain-george-prioleau-1856-1927.

7. Goodloe, "George Prioleau (1856–1928).

8. Paul Robinson, "Race, Space, and the Evolution of Black Los Angeles," in *Black Los Angeles: American Dreams and Racial Realities*, ed. Darnell Hunt and Ana-Christina Ramon (New York: New York University Press, 2010), 34.

9. See Andrea Gibbons, *City of Segregation: One Hundred Years of Struggle For Housing in Los Angeles* (New York: Verso, 2018); Douglas Flamming, *Bound for Freedom: Black Los Angeles in Jim Crow America* (Berkeley: University of California Press, 2005); Josh Sides, *L.A. City Limits: African American Los Angeles from the Great Depression to the Present* (Berkeley: University of California Press, 2006); Marne Campbell, *Making Black Los Angeles: Class, Gender, and Community, 1850–1917* (Chapel Hill: University of North Carolina Press, 2016).

10. City of Manhattan Beach, "Bruce's Beach."

11. City of Manhattan Beach, "History Advisory Board Report."

12. City of Manhattan Beach, "History Advisory Board Report."

13. "The History of Bethel African Methodist Episcopal Church of Los Angeles," Bethel African Methodist Episcopal Church of Los Angeles, accessed August 10, 2022, https://img1.wsimg.com/blobby/go/761b851e-08ef-4475-ac8d-bbbac2c945d7/downloads/The%20History%20of%20Bethel%20African%20%20%20Methodist%20Epis.pdf.

14. The Bruces received $14,500 for Lots 8 and 9 on Block 5, and the Prioleau family received $1,874.37 for their portion of Lot 4, Block 12.

15. Flamming, *Bound for Freedom*, 290–91.

16. Today a senior center in Betty Hill's name is located on the former site of the Bethel A.M.E. Church the Prioleaus built.

17. See United States Housing Act of 1937, Pub. L. No. 93–383, 88 Stat. 653 (1937) as well as Alex F. Schwartz, *Housing Policy in the United States*, 3rd ed. (New York: Routledge, 2014).

18. Donald Craig Parson, *Making a Better World: Public Housing, the Red Scare, and the Direction of Modern Los Angeles* (Minneapolis: University of Minnesota Press, 2005), 18.

19. Parson, *Making a Better World*, 33. It would go on to build ten projects under the 1937 Housing Act, including Pico Gardens, Pueblo Del Rio, Estrada Courts, Aliso Village, and others along the city's east and south side corridors. Paul R. Williams was the architect of Pueblo Del Rio. Williams, the first Black member and fellow of the American Institute of Architects, designed timeless homes, public buildings, and churches throughout the city. During this period, Jesse L. Terry became the first Black appointee to the housing commission. Jesse L. Terry Manor is named in her honor.

20. Parson, *Making a Better World*, 66.

21. For example, see Parson, *Making a Better World*, 92–93.

22. Andrew Deener, *Venice: A Contested Bohemia in Los Angeles* (Chicago: University of Chicago Press, 2012).

23. Parson, *Making a Better World*, 91.

24. Ca. Const. art. XXXIV, § 1–4. https://leginfo.legislature.ca.gov/faces/codes_display Text.xhtml?lawCode = CONS&division = &title = &part = &chapter = &article = XXXIV.

25. Incidents of veterans denied housing due to their political activity, the dashed promise of the Elysian Park Heights Project and subsequent razing of Chavez Ravine to build Dodger Stadium, and a range of other reactionary moves against public housing had decimated its support within the city's political class.

26. Parson, *Making a Better World*, 47.

27. Civilian Conservation Corps (U.S.). Company 604, *Valyermo News* (Palmdale, Calif.: Company 604), Center for Research Libraries, https://catalog.crl.edu/Record /c244668d-0d00-5bb7-a476-20d5bf3c4fb3#details. After the CCC program ended, the site was used as an LAPD Recreation camp for young boys. See "Police Open Boys' Camp," *The Los Angeles Times*, June 27, 1939.

28. On the history of tuberculosis treatment and recovery in the valley, see "Healthcare in the Early Antelope Valley," Lancaster Museum of Art and History, August 4, 2021, https://www.lancastermoah.org/single-post/healthcare-in-the-early-antelope-valley. On forcible removals from L.A. hospitals to the valley by sheriffs, see Jill Leovy. "Breathing New Life: Olive View: Opened as a TB Sanitarium in 1920, the Hospital, Now a Modern Facility, Turned 75 This Week," *Los Angeles Times*, October 28, 1995.

29. Kelly Lytle Hernández, *City of Inmates: Conquest, Rebellion, and the Rise of Human Caging in Los Angeles, 1771–1965* (Chapel Hill: University of North Carolina Press, 2017), 51–63.

30. Abraham Hoffman, "Angeles Crest: The Creation of a Forest Highway System in the San Gabriel Mountains," *Southern California Quarterly*, 50, no. 3 (September 1968): 309–45.

31. Because the highway was also a route to mountain recreation, it was in high demand even before construction was finished. Abraham Hoffman reports that the forest highway had more users than the entire California National Parks system combined.

32. Lotchin, *Fortress California*, 196–97.

33. It was given that name in 1949, in honor of Captain Glen Edwards who had died in a crash there in 1948.

34. *South Antelope Valley (CA) Press*, February 11, 1943. Unlike in the metropolis, Lancaster Homes was not repurposed into public housing after the war.

35. *South Antelope Valley (CA) Press*, August 1, 1946.

36. *South Antelope Valley (CA) Press*, September 26, 1946.

37. Lauren Kessler, *The Happy Bottom Riding Club: The Life and Times of Pancho Barnes* (New York: Random House 2000).

38. Tom Wolfe, *The Right Stuff* (New York: Farrar, Straus and Giroux, 1978).

39. *South Antelope Valley (CA) Press*, June 5, 1952.

40. *South Antelope Valley (CA) Press*, March 27, 1952.

41. *South Antelope Valley (CA) Press*, August 14, 1952.

42. *South Antelope Valley (CA) Press*, September 11, 1952.

43. *South Antelope Valley (CA) Press*, July 30, 1953.

44. *South Antelope Valley (CA) Press*, November 19, 1953.

45. *South Antelope Valley (CA) Press*, March 25, 1954.

46. Sebastian Rotella, "Sun Village: Black Enclave Withers Amid Antelope Boom," *Los Angeles Times*, August 27, 1989, https://www.latimes.com/archives/la-xpm-1989–08–27-me-1851-story.html.

47. Emily Ludolph, "Ed Dwight Was Set to Be the First Black Astronaut. Here's Why That Never Happened," *New York Times*, July 16, 2019, https://www.nytimes.com/2019/07/16/us/ed-dwight-was-set-to-be-the-first-black-atronaut-heres-why-that-never-happened.html.

48. Amanda Holpuch, "63 Years Later, First Black Man Trained as Astronaut Goes to Space," *New York Times*, May 19, 2024, https://www.nytimes.com/2024/05/19/science/space/ed-dwight-black-astronaut-space-flight-blue-origin.html.

49. The U.S. Geological Survey, "Feature Details: Feature ID 272117," updated January 19, 1981, https://edits.nationalmap.gov/apps/gaz-domestic/public/summary/272117.

50. Grubbs remained active in the community later, sponsoring high school graduates' educations at Antelope Valley Junior College, and supporting little league players in the area.

51. Simmons, "Feeling Burned in Sun Village."

52. *South Antelope Valley (CA) Press*, February 13, 1947.

53. Valle Verde and Sun Village represent two moments of inter-racial solidarity when white landowners sold land to Black developers so that Black families could rent or purchase it without being bound by restrictive covenants.

54. Rotella, "Sun Village"; *Los Angeles Times*, February 6, 1950.

55. *Los Angeles Sentinel*, October 28, 1954.

56. The Patton family, for example, "raised pigs, chickens, rabbits, goats, [and] a garden"; see Chapel of the Valley Mortuary, "Obituary of Lois Emma Patton," June 2014, https://web.archive.org/web/20230706215354/https://www.tributearchive.com/obituaries/22859218/lois-emma-patton.

57. Ann M. Simmons, "For Sun Village and Littlerock, Historic Distrust Persists," *Los Angeles Times*, September 23, 2012, https://www.latimes.com/local/la-xpm-2012-sep-23-la-me-sun-village-20120924-story.html.

58. Rotella, "Sun Village."

59. Daniel Martinez HoSang, *Racial Propositions: Ballot Initiatives and the Making of Postwar California* (Berkeley: University of California Press, 2010), 55–56.

60. Rotella, "Sun Village."

61. Simmons, "Feeling Burned in Sun Village."

62. Records of the National Association of Colored Women's Clubs, 1895–1992, Part 1: Minutes of National Conventions, Publications, and President's Office Correspondence, https://congressional.proquest.com/histvault?q=001554–021–0156&accountid=14552.

63. Records of the National Association of Colored Women's Clubs, 1895–1992, Part 1: Minutes of National Conventions, Publications, and President's Office Correspondence https://congressional.proquest.com/histvault?q=001554–021–0156&accountid=14552.

64. "County Buys Land Near Sun Village," *Valley Times* (North Hollywood, CA), March 7, 1958.

65. Dorn and Robinson were classmates in high school in Pasadena.

66. "Honor 'Jackie' Robinson in Naming Park," *Valley Times* (North Hollywood, CA), January 11, 1960.

67. Jackie Robinson, *I Never Had It Made* (New York: Harper Collins, 1995 [1972]).

68. The community's struggle to overturn the policy, led by local NAACP activists Ruby McKnight Williams and Dr. Edna Griffin, took nearly forty years. For more, see Lynn M. Hudson, *West of Jim Crow: The Fight Against California's Color Line* (Champaign: University of Illinois Press, 2020), 208–42.

69. "Blasts County 'Deadwood' in Budget," *Valley News* (Van Nuys, CA), June 11, 1961; "County Board to Consider Corporate Levy Protests," *Valley Times Today* (North Hollywood, CA), July 30, 1962; "City Slates 'Jackie Day," *Valley Times* (North Hollywood, CA), May 26, 1965.

70. "Jackie Robinson Park Summer Schedule Set," *Antelope Valley (CA) Press*, June 26, 1966.

71. Minutes of Board of Directors Meetings with Executive Officers' Reports. (1956). Papers of the NAACP, Part 01: Supplement, 1956–1960.

72. "Obituary of Lois Emma Patton."

73. "Obituary of Lois Emma Patton."

74. *South Antelope Valley (CA) Press*, October 31, 1957.

75. Simmons served as the NAACP Field Secretary for the Southern California Region during this period. In later years, she became the NAACP's National Education Director, led civil rights opposition to the appointment of William H. Rehnquist to the Supreme Court, helped pass federal recognition of the Martin Luther King, Jr., Holiday, and campaigned for the passage of sanctions legislation targeting the apartheid government of South Africa.

76. *South Antelope Valley (CA) Press*, February 25, 1962.

77. "California Publications Related to the President's Committee on Migratory Labor," in *Papers of the President's Committee on Migratory Labor, Part 1: Correspondence with States, 1955–1963; Publications by State, 1957–1962*, 1933. https://www.proquest.com /archival-materials/california-publications-related-presidents/docview/3014022934/se-2.

78. "Althea T. L. Simmons, Field Secretary Reports, 1963–1964," in *NAACP Papers, Part 25: Branch Department Files, 1941–1965; General Department File, A-W*, 1963, https:// www.proquest.com/archival-materials/althea-t-l-simmons-field-secretary-reports-1963 /docview/2623634000/se-2.

79. "Officers' Reports and Fiftieth Annual Convention of California State Federation of Labor Held at Santa Barbara," in *State Labor Proceedings: AFL, CIO, and AFL-CIO Conventions, 1885–1974; AFL (CA)*, 1952, https://www.proquest.com/archival-materials/officers-re ports-fiftieth-annual-convention/docview/3048060472/se-2.

80. "Officers' Reports and Fiftieth Annual Convention of California State Federation of Labor Held at Santa Barbara."

81. "Officers' Reports and Fifty-Fifth Annual Convention of California State Federation of Labor Held at Oakland, "in *State Labor Proceedings: AFL, CIO, and AFL-CIO Conventions, 1885–1974; CIO (CA)*, 1957, https://www.proquest.com/archival-materials /officers-reports-fifty-fifth-annual-convention/docview/3048079229/se-2.

82. "Herbert Hill Speaking Engagements," in *NAACP Papers, Part 13: NAACP and Labor; General Office File*, 1963, https://www.proquest.com/archival-materials/herbert-hill -speaking-engagements/docview/2623446230/se-2.

83. *South Antelope Valley (CA) Press*, September 27, 1963.

84. "Althea T. L. Simmons, Field Secretary Reports, 1963–1964."

85. "Althea T. L. Simmons, Field Secretary Reports, 1963–1964."

86. "Branch Department Monthly Reports to the Board of Directors, 1963," in *NAACP Papers, Part 25: Branch Department Files, 1941–1965; General Department File, A-W,* 1963, https://proxy.cc.uic.edu/login?url=https://www.proquest.com/archival-materials/branch-department-monthly-reports-board-directors/docview/2623633590/se-2.

2. REDEEMING THE RIGHT TO DISCRIMINATE

1. Daniel Levitas, *The Terrorist Next Door: The Militia Movement and the Radical Right* (New York: St. Martin's Press, 2004), 24.

2. Levitas, *The Terrorist Next Door.*

3. The Klan used "pure Americanism" in its public flyers, songs, and campaigns. See, for example "Membership in the Ku Klux Klan," Digital Public Library of America, https://dp.la/item/fa1fc80731d276ebda242dcea4a83dc5; Jerzy Sobieraj, "'Pure Americanism': The Ku Klux Klan, Nativism, and the Moral Crusade in the Jazz Age," *Polish Journal for American Studies* 3 (2009): 107–115; Hiram Wesley Evans, "The Klan's Fight for Americanism," *The North American Review* 223, no. 830 (March-May 1926): 33–63.

4. Ocen, "The New Racially Restrictive Covenant."

5. Ana Laura Bochicchio, "Justification by Race: Wesley Swift's White Supremacy and Antisemitic Theological Views in His Christian Identity Sermons," *Journal of Hate Studies* 17, no. 1 (2021): 35–51.

6. For a thorough tracing of British-Israelism from its origins into the American far right, as well as an account of Swift's political influence, see John Ganz, *When the Clock Broke: Con-Men, Conspiracists, and How America Cracked up in the Early 1990s* (New York: Farrar, Strauss, and Giroux, 2024), 294–98.

7. Michael Barkun, *Religion and the Racist Right: The Origins of the Christian Identity Movement* (Chapel Hill: University of North Carolina Press, 1997), 11. See also Dianne Dentice, "Hate Speech, Prejudice, and Biblical Interpretations," *Journal of Faith, Education, and Community* 3, no. 1 (2019): 3.

8. Swift was not alone in bringing Klan activity to Los Angeles's peripheries; the Klan was fighting a defensive struggle against Black integration in several of Los Angeles's peripheral areas. As Black residents moved out of the city for better work and housing opportunities (including following World War II patterns of industrial development), the Klan met them with violence. Lynn Hudson documents the likely Klan involvement in the arson death of O'Day Short, an engineer who moved to Fontana to work in the new Kaiser steel mill (*West of Jim Crow,* 172–73). Swift's focus on Los Angeles' peripheries was of a piece with these developments.

9. "Pastor's Aide is Accused in Hate Incident," *California Eagle* (Los Angeles, California), September 27, 1962.

10. Alvin P. Meyer, "Helen Gahagan Douglas and The Campaigns For Congress," an oral history conducted 1978 by Ingrid Winther Scobie, in Helen Gahagan Douglas Oral History Project, Volume I, Regional Oral History Office, The Bancroft Library, University of California, Berkeley, 1981, https://digitalassets.lib.berkeley.edu/rohoia/ucb/text/helengahaganproo1dougrich.pdf.

11. Colleen M. Oconnor, "'Pink Right Down to Her Underwear,'" *Los Angeles Times*, April 9, 1990, https://www.latimes.com/archives/la-xpm-1990–04–09-me-664-story.html.

12. "Charges Fly as Dr. Swift Set for Talk," *The Peninsula Times Tribune* (Palo Alto, California), January 22, 1951. For a more thorough account of the incident, see David Austin Walsh, *Taking America Back: The Conservative Movement and the Far Right* (New Haven: Yale University Press, 2024). See also Christopher C. Gorham, *The Confidante: The Untold Story of the Woman Who Helped Win WWII and Shape Modern America* (New York: Citadel Press, 2023).

13. "Senators to Hold Closed Session on Warren Post," *Hanford Morning Journal* (Hanford, California), February 19, 1954.

14. "Pre 1956 News Note," *Ventura County Star* (Ventura, California), March 2, 1954.

15. Levitas, *The Terrorist Next Door*, 36–37.

16. "Follow L.A. Lead, Utahns Urged by Anti-Red Aid," *Salt Lake Tribune* (Salt Lake City, UT), October 19, 1950. Swift also visited Oklahoma in 1958, speaking to Citizens Councils.

17. Swift was a talented manipulator and self-promoter. For example, he once organized a speaking engagement through a masonic lodge by convincing them that the FBI had recommended him as a speaker. He walked into FBI offices to meet with Assistant Director A. H. Belmont, and then portrayed Belmont's taciturn reaction as secretly supportive. By 1958 he had purchased three new cars. He explained it by claiming to have been written into Henry Ford's will. Numerous FBI records in his file suggest that the bureau spent significant time investigating his claim that he had prophesied JFK's death. According to FBI files, the bureau believed he was being provided with classified intelligence from a member of the Army, and sought to interview him to expose the source. The bureau believed that Swift also had knowledge of bombings in the South, but its memos advised against interrogating him on this matter as he would be unlikely to cooperate.

18. Victor Perry, "California Hate Peddler Whipped in Primary Election," *The National Jewish Post* (Marion County, Indianapolis), June 11, 1954

19. The event was so popular that attendees asked for a tape of Tenney's remarks, perhaps the germ of Swift's idea of taping and distributing his sermons.

20. Bill Becker, "Rightist Mailings Stir Coast Clash; Merchant Threatens Suit on Anti-Semitism Charges," *The New York Times*, February 9, 1964, https://www.nytimes.com/1964/02/09/archives/rightist-mailings-stir-coast-clash-merchant-threatens-suit-on.html.

21. KLAC Transcript, "The California Klan: Hotbed of Hatred," July 15, 1965.

22. Federal Bureau of Investigation, "Freedom of Information and Privacy Acts Release of Subject: Christian Defense League." File Number: 62–105253, Section 1.

23. David Mark Chalmers, *Backfire: How the Ku Klux Klan Helped the Civil Rights Movement* (Lanham, MD: Rowman & Littlefield, 2005), 53–54.

24. David Neiwert, "The Radical Right's Terrorist Faction Has Long Followed an 'Anti-Communist' Blueprint from the 1960s," *Daily Kos*, February 2, 2020, https://www.dailykos.com/stories/2020/2/2/1914915/-The-radical-right-s-terrorist-faction-has-long-followed-an-anti-Communist-blueprint-from-the-1960s.

25. "Dynamite Theft Suspect Eludes Police Search," *Los Angeles Times*, February 27, 1965.

26. "Ex Idaho Neo-Nazi Arrested," *The Spokesman-Review* (Spokane, Washington), February 16, 2005, https://www.spokesman.com/stories/2005/feb/16/ex-idaho-neo-nazi-arrested.

27. Alon Milwicki, "Baptizing Nazism: An Analysis of the Religious Roots of American Neo-Nazism" (PhD diss., American University, 2019), 179–80.

28. "States Rights Party Stirring in California," *Los Angeles Times*, April 13, 1965.

29. Martin Dobrow, "Beaten by the Klan in 1963, a Black Man Just Spoke to the White Pastor Who Helped Rescue Him," *The Washington Post*, February 23, 2022. https://www.washingtonpost.com/history/2022/02/12/st-augustine-klan-rally.

30. "J. B. Stoner, 81, Fervent Racist and Benchmark for Extremism, Dies," *New York Times*, April 29, 2005, https://www.nytimes.com/2005/04/29/us/j-b-stoner-81-fervent-racist-and-benchmark-for-extremism-dies.html.

31. Chalmers, *Backfire*, 175.

32. The process is more broadly documented in HoSang, *Racial Propositions*, as well as Gene Slater, *Freedom to Discriminate: How Realtors Conspired to Segregate Housing and Divide America* (Berkeley: Heyday Books, 2021).

33. "CREA Head Announces Crusade for the New 'Forgotten Man,'" *Antelope Valley (CA) Press*, May, 1963.

34. "Open Housing Issue," *San Bernardino County (CA) Sun*, March 11, 1968.

35. "Letters to the Editor," *Los Gatos Times-Saratoga (CA) Observer*, April 27, 1964.

36. "Unitarians to Hear NAACP Guest Speaker," *South Antelope Valley Press (CA)*, June, 1964.

37. "No on Prop 14 Essay Contest Extension Made," *South Antelope Valley Press (CA)*, September 13, 1964.

38. HoSang, *Racial Propositions*, 83.

39. Tyler T. Reny and Benjamin J. Newman, "Protecting the Right to Discriminate: The Second Great Migration and Racial Threat in the American West, " *The American Political Science Review* 112, no. 4 (2018): 1104–10. See replication files for the Palmdale vote. https://dataverse.harvard.edu/file.xhtml?persistentId=doi:10.7910/DVN/UAQZRO/1FHKS9&version=1.0. Lancaster, having not been incorporated, does not have data available.

40. "CREA Head Blasts CG Statement," *Antelope Valley (CA) Press*, July 18, 1965.

41. "CREA Files Petition on Proposition 14," *Antelope Valley (CA) Press*, August 28, 1966.

42. "CREA Endorses Initiative to Repeal Rumford Act," *Antelope Valley (CA) Press*, July 24, 1966.

43. "CREA Asks Lynch to Urge Review of '14,'" *Antelope Valley (CA) Press*, September 18, 1966.

44. Charles McC. Mathias and Marion Morris, "Fair Housing Legislation: Not an Easy Row To Hoe," *Cityscape* 4, no. 3 (1999): 21–33.

45. "Rodgers Asks Help from Realtors," *Antelope Valley (CA) Press*, September 18, 1966.

46. Daisy Gibson, "Sun Village Housing Proposals Discussed," *South Antelope Valley (CA) Press*, November 19, 1964.

47. "New Street Lighting Set for Village," *Antelope Valley (CA) Press*, January 3, 1965.

48. Sebastian Rotella, "Sun Village: Black Enclave Withers Amid Antelope Bloom," *Los Angeles Times*, August 27, 1989, https://www.latimes.com/archives/la-xpm-1989-08-27-me-1851-story.html.

49. Prior scholarship suggests that Totem Pole Ranch was originally the Serrano village Maviayek. At the time of its use for powwows, it was owned by the Los Angeles County

Sheriff's Department and used to stable its horses. That usage heavily disturbed the site. Between 1982 and 1986, Roger Robinson and students at Antelope Valley College excavated the area. The items they unearthed and brought back to AVC were essentially abandoned for several decades until Darcy Lynn Wiewall and students attempted to catalog and analyze them; see "Up From The Dust: Orphaned Collections and Innovative Undergraduate Research," *Proceedings of the Society for California Archaeology* 33 (2019). The area was later donated to the Antelope Valley Search and Rescue Team for use as a meeting place, training facility, and shooting range; see William P. Warford, "LASD Reserve Capt. Les White was AV Hero," *Antelope Valley (CA) Press*, March 26, 2021, https://web.archive.org /web/20241128020336/https://www.avpress.com/news/lasd-reserve-capt-les-white-was-av -hero/article_7edddc7e-8dd7-11eb-a888-6780639d035b.html.

50. For more on its organizing, see, for example, "Indian News Via California," *Navajo Times*, October 12, 1967, and "Indian News Via California," *Navajo Times*, November 28, 1968.

51. See National Council on Indian Opportunity, *Public Forum Before the Committee on Urban Indians in Los Angeles, California* (1968), https://www.google.com/books/edition /Public_Forum_Before_the_Committee_on_Urb/5dhGLeApDoIC.

52. "NAACP Unit Holds Officer Installation," *Antelope Valley (CA) Press*, February 9, 1967.

53. "Dignity of Man, Topic at CREA Convention," *Antelope Valley (CA) Press*, October 1, 1967.

54. "Reinecke Explains Stand on New Civil Rights Bill," *Antelope Valley (CA) Press*, April 18, 1968.

55. "Education, Taxes, Crime Headline CREA Convention," *Antelope Valley (CA) Press*, October 6, 1968.

56. "Dr. Wesley Swift, Noted Conservative Leader, Dies," *Antelope Valley (CA) Press*, October 11, 1970.

57. "Picture of Angela Davis Stirs College Controversy," *Antelope Valley (CA) Press*, October 11, 1970.

58. "Richard Butler," Southern Poverty Law Center, accessed August 17, 2022, https:// www.splcenter.org/fighting-hate/extremist-files/individual/richard-butler.

59. Milwicki, "Baptizing Nazism."

60. "Edwards Base Jobs Discussed," *Los Angeles Sentinel*, April 7, 1977, sec. C11.

61. Elaine Lewinnek, "Social Studies Controversies in 1960s Los Angeles: Land of the Free, Public Memory, and the Rise of the New Right," *Pacific Historical Review* 84, no. 1 (2015): 48–84.

62. Lisa McGirr, *Suburban Warriors: The Origins of the New American Right* (Princeton, NJ: Princeton University Press, 2001).

63. Larry Tomlinson, "Right Wing Mounts Campaign against State History Textbook in California," *American Teacher* 52, no. 8 (April 1968): 9.

64. "Social Change and Upheaval Comes to AVC: The Kepley Era, 1967–1975," Campus History, Antelope Valley College, accessed September 1, 2022, https://www.avc.edu /aboutavc/campushistory/TheKepleyEra#_edn26.

65. "NAACP Takes Confederate Flag Mascot Fight to Lancaster School," *Los Angeles Sentinel*, May 11, 1995, sec. A4.

66. Chris McCormick, "Op-Ed: My California High School Had a Confederate Mascot," *Los Angeles Times*, August 24, 2017, https://www.latimes.com/opinion/op-ed/la-oe-mccormick-antelope-valley-confederate-20170824-story.html.

67. Julie Drake, "No More Quartz Hill High Rebels: School Makes it Official; Mascot Will Be Changed," *Antelope Valley (CA) Press*, June 20, 2020, https://www.avpress.com/news/no-more-quartz-hill-high-rebels/article_a641b440-b298–11ea-a951-d7c2352fd5b6.html.

68. "Record Settlement in Housing Bias Case," *Los Angeles Sentinel*, December 19, 1991, sec. A13.

69. William Finnegan, *Cold New World: Growing Up in Harder Country* (New York: Random House, 1998), 272.

70. Finnegan, *Cold New World*, 272.

71. Finnegan, *Cold New World*, 273.

72. Davis, *City of Quartz*, 6.

73. Ocen, "The New Racially Restrictive Covenant."

74. Finnegan, *Cold New World*.

75. Kathleen Belew, *Bring the War Home: The White Power Movement and Paramilitary America* (Cambridge, MA: Harvard University Press, 2018), 194–95.

76. Evelyn Larrubia, "Lancaster Slaying Victim Had Feared a Racial Attack," *Los Angeles Times*, November 2, 1997.

77. "Hate Crimes Against Blacks Up 50 Percent," *Los Angeles Sentinel*, May 1, 1997, sec.A1.

78. Josh Meyer, "Flyers Spread Message of Hate in the Valley," *Los Angeles Times*, January 2, 1994, sec. VYA1.

79. See Frank Zappa and Peter Occhiogrosso, *The Real Frank Zappa Book* (New York: Poseidon Press, 1989).

80. For more on the broader lineage of anti-racist skinheads, see Robin Maria Valeri and Kevin Borgeson, *Skinhead History, Identity, and Culture* (London: Routledge, 2017), and Robert T. Wood, "The Indigenous, Nonracist Origins of the American Skinhead Subculture," *Youth & Society* 31, no. 2 (1999): 131–51.

81. Josh Johnson, "Events of 1993 Cost Valley its Last Vestige of Serenity," *Los Angeles Times*, December 31, 1993, sec. VYA1.

82. Steven Bender, *Greasers and Gringos: Latinos, Law, and the American Imagination* (New York: New York University Press, 2003), 73. For more on this moment's place in national anti-immigration politics, see Daniel Denvir, *All-American Nativism: How the Bipartisan War on Immigrants Explains Politics as We Know It* (New York: Verso, 2020).

83. The establishment of Latinos for Social Justice in the 1990s marked a departure from findings in an earlier study of Mexican American life in the valley conducted by graduate urban planning student Saul Solache (who also co-painted the Chicano Mural at UCLA). In 1971, Solache surveyed residents of the Antelope Valley with Spanish surnames, seeking to understand patterns of community formation. Solache's results suggested that Mexican Americans in the valley were integrating into the larger white community rather than establishing a unique identity and social and cultural institutions. Solache conducted the study anticipating that the valley would grow significantly in coming decades, and speculated that this growth might engender the very organizing that Latinos for Social Justice came to represent. For more, see Saul Solache, "The Impact of Urban Development in the

Antelope Valley on Its Mexican-American Residents" (MA thesis, University of California, Los Angeles—Urban planning, 1971).

84. Sharon Moeser, "Latinos Weighing Boycott Over Racist Poem: Protest: Statewide Group May Oppose Home Purchases in the Antelope Valley District of Assemblyman Who Distributed the Verses," *Los Angeles Times*, June 4, 1993.

85. "Campaign Calendar," *Los Angeles Times*, August 4, 1994, 32.

86. The church had recently re-ordained televangelist Jim Bakker after he had been accused of infidelity and illegal misuse of funds at his PTL ministries in the Carolinas.

87. David Colker, "Anti-Gay Video Highlights Church's Agenda," *Los Angeles Times*, February 22, 1993.

88. "Sometimes Just Say No: State Senator Accepts Invitation to Speak to Alleged Supremacists," *Los Angeles Times*, August 26, 1994, sec. VYB14.

89. Kurt Streeter, "2 Men Arrested in Racial Attack at Lancaster Store," *Los Angeles Times*, March 25, 1999.

90. Greg Sandoval, "U.S. Widens Role in Probe of Hate Crimes in Antelope Valley," *Los Angeles Times*, February 16, 1997.

91. Biography, Frank C. Roberts, accessed September 2, 2022, https://web.archive.org /web/20170201140421/https://www.fcroberts.com/bio.

92. Darrell Satzman, "New Program Targets Gang Crime in Antelope Valley," *Los Angeles Times*, July 14, 1998, https://www.latimes.com/archives/la-xpm-1998-jul-14-me-3633 -story.html.

93. Caitlin Liu, "Reports of 3 Racist Incidents Are Probed in Antelope Valley," *Los Angeles Times*, September 11, 2000.

94. Sean Kennedy, "50 Years Of Deputy Gangs: Identifying Root Causes And Effects To Advocate For Meaningful Reform in The Los Angeles County Sheriff's Department" (Los Angeles: Loyola Marymount Center for Juvenile Law and Policy, 2020), https://lmu.app .box.com/s/uci2ir4mkpudtvvfp7z8iu4kv1gre1dj. See also Cerise Castle, "What We Don't Know," *Knock LA*, April 7, 2021, https://knock-la.com/lasd-gangs-pirates-rattlesnakes -buffalo-soldiers.

95. Werner Troesken and Randall Walsh. "Collective Action, White Flight, and the Origins of Racial Zoning Laws," *Journal of Law, Economics, and Organization* 35, no. 2 (2019): 289–318.

96. G. Slater, *Freedom to Discriminate*.

97. Alexander Sahn, "Racial Diversity and Exclusionary Zoning: Evidence from the Great Migration," *Journal of Politics* (forthcoming).

98. Jeannine Bell, *Hate Thy Neighbor: Move-In Violence and the Persistence of Racial Segregation in American Housing* (New York: New York University Press, 2013).

99. The original data referenced by Bell in *Hate Thy Neighbor* is in Jack Levin and Jack McDevitt, "Police Response," in *Hate Crimes* (Boston: Springer, 1993), 159–78. While I use the term "hate crime" in order to maintain consistency with the original study's terminology, I also note critiques of the term and its limited, and sometimes counterproductive role in understanding violence.

100. Bell, *Hate Thy Neighbor*, 68.

101. For more on the case and its context, see Norrinda Brown, "Section 8 is the New N-Word: Policing Integration in the Age of Black Mobility," *Washington University Journal of Law and Policy* 51, no. 1 (2016): 61–93.

102. Warren J. Samuels, "The Economy as a System of Power and Its Legal Bases: The Legal Economics of Robert Lee Hale," *University of Miami Law Review* 27, no. 3–4 (1972): 261–371.

103. K-Sue Park, "The History Wars and Property Law: Conquest and Slavery as Foundational to the Field," *Yale Law Journal* 131, no. 4 (February 2022): 1062.

104. See, for example, Luc Boltanski and Eve Chiapello, *The New Spirit of Capitalism* (New York: Verso, 2007); Henry Jenkins, Sam Ford, and Joshua Green, *Spreadable Media: Creating Value and Meaning in a Networked Culture* (New York: New York University Press, 2013); Gary Yeritsian, "Participation from Above and Below: Brand Community and the Contestation of Cultural Participation," *Journal of Consumer Culture* 21, no. 2 (2021): 278–95; and Erik Olin Wright, *Envisioning Real Utopias* (New York: Verso, 2020).

105. Matthew Desmond and Nicol Valdez, "Unpolicing the Urban Poor: Consequences of Third-Party Policing for Inner-City Women," *American Sociological Review* 78, no. 1 (2013): 117–41.

106. James Garofalo and Maureen McLeod, "The Structure and Operations of Neighborhood Watch Programs in the United States," *Crime & Delinquency* 35, no. 3 (1989): 326–44.

107. This is a subset of a larger trend in punishment named "governing through crime." See Jonathan Simon, *Governing Through Crime: How the War on Crime Transformed American Democracy and Created a Culture of Fear* (New York: Oxford University Press, 2007).

108. Sebastian Rotella, "1st Week Success of Gang Hot Line Amazes Operators," *Los Angeles Times*, February 3, 1990.

109. Phil Sneiderman, "School Board's Pricer Gains Power, Critics," *Los Angeles Times*, December 25, 1994, https://www.latimes.com/archives/la-xpm-1994–12–25-mn-12979-story .html.

110. John Chandler, "2 Cities Target Decaying Neighborhoods," *Los Angeles Times*, October 8, 1992.

111. The Partners Against Crime program continues to operate today. See https://web .archive.org/web/20191029173545/https://cityofpalmdale.org/249/Partners-Against-Crime -PAC.

112. Chandler, "2 Cities Target Decaying Neighborhoods."

113. Ronald Reagan, "Remarks on Signing the Anti-Drug Abuse Act of 1988," speech, Washington, DC, November 18, 1988, Ronald Reagan Presidential Library and Museum, https://www.reaganlibrary.gov/archives/speech/remarks-signing-anti-drug-abuse-act -1988.

114. Tanya Jones, "Clinton Gets Tough on Criminals in Public Housing: One-Strike-And-You're-Out Issued to Fight Drugs," *Baltimore Sun*, March 28, 1996, https://www .baltimoresun.com/news/bs-xpm-1996–03–29-1996089072-story.html; US Library of Congress, Congressional Research Service, *No-Fault Eviction of Public Housing Tenants for Illegal Drug Use: A Legal Analysis of Department of Housing and Urban Development v. Rucker, Name Redacted*, RS21199 (2002), https://www.everycrsreport.com/files/20020415 _RS21199_d6a607f036f9ea74a314bf3d355ffcd0a1434bf3.pdf; Human Rights Watch, "Federal 'One-Strike' Legislation," in *No Second Chance: People with Criminal Records Denied Access to Public Housing* (New York: Human Rights Watch, 2004), https://www.hrw.org/reports /2004/usa1104/5.htm. The section epigraph is from President Bill Clinton, "Remarks by

the President at One Strike Symposium," The White House, Office of the Press Secretary, March 28, 1996, available online at: https://web.archive.org/web/20170216155629/https://clinton6.nara.gov/1996/03/1996-03-28-president-remarks-at-one-strike-crime-symposium.html.

115. Alexis Karteron, "When Stop and Frisk Comes Home: Policing Public and Patrolled Housing," *Case Western Reserve Law Review* 69, no. 3 (2019): 669–729.

116. Kathryn Ramsey, "One-Strike 2.0: How Local Governments Are Distorting a Flawed Federal Eviction Law," *UCLA Law Review* 65, no. 5 (2018): 1146–99.

117. Liam Dillon, Ben Poston, and Julia Barajas, "Black and Latino Renters Face Eviction, Exclusion Amid Police Crackdowns in California," *Los Angeles Times*, November 19, 2020, https://www.latimes.com/homeless-housing/story/2020–11–19/california-housing-policies-hurt-black-latino-renters.

118. The rule does not distinguish between properties with just one tenant or large apartment buildings with hundreds.

119. HOPE Fair Housing Center v. City of Peoria, No. 1:17-cv-1360 (C.D. Ill.). N.B. The author served as an expert witness in this case.

120. Somai v. City of Bedford. 2019. No. 1:19-cv-373:526 (N.D. OH)

121. Peoria Police Department, *Armadillos: Starting a Trend* (Peoria, IL: Peoria Police Department, 2011), 7–8, https://popcenter.asu.edu/sites/default/files/library/awards/goldstein/2011/11–07.pdf.

122. Dillon, Poston, and Barajas, "Black and Latino Renters."

123. Jones et. al. v. City of Faribault, Minnesota, No. 0:18-cv-01643 (D.C. MN 2018).

124. Deborah N. Archer, "The New Housing Segregation: The Jim Crow Effects of Crime-Free Housing Ordinances," *Michigan Law Review* 118, no. 2 (November 2019): 173–232.

125. Godsil, "Race Nuisance," 505.

3. APARTHEID'S AFTERLIVES

The epigraph is from Dennis Anderson, "Economy in Aerospace Valley Soars," *Times-Advocate* (Escondido, CA), October 25, 1989.

1. Judith Cummings, "California City Outgrows its 'Boom or Bust' Cycles; The Talk of Palmdale," *New York Times*, February 9, 1982, sec. A14, https://www.nytimes.com/1982/02/09/us/california-city-outgrows-its-boom-or-bust-cycles-the-talk-of-palmdale.html.

2. George Skelton, "Reagan Aides Rejoice, Believe Victory Certain," *The Los Angeles Times*, October 23, 1984, page 1.

3. Dennis Anderson, "Economy in Aerospace Valley Soars," *Times-Advocate* (Escondido, CA), October 25, 1989.

4. Anderson, "Economy in Aerospace Valley Soars."

5. This chapter uses Saidiya Hartman's notion of the afterlives of slavery to show how policing extending prior regimes of unfreedom in the valley. See *Lose Your Mother: A Journey along the Atlantic Slave Route* (New York: Farrar, Straus and Giroux, 2007).

6. For an account of the shifting social and political history of this logic, see David A. Freund, *Colored Property: State Policy and White Racial Politics in Suburban America* (Chicago: University of Chicago Press, 2010). Despite how the articulated logic of race and

property value has changed, however, the association between the two has grown stronger; see Junia Howell and Elizabeth Korver-Glenn, "The Increasing Effect of Neighborhood Racial Composition on Housing Values, 1980–2015," *Social Problems* 68, no. 4 (2021): 1051–71.

7. Harris, "Whiteness as Property."

8. As Harris points out, this marker of property has waned somewhat in importance, as the law has recognized non-transferrable things—a college diploma or credential—as nevertheless having the status of property.

9. Claire Herbert and Jay Orne, "No Lawless Place: Foregrounding Property in Sociology," *Socius* 7 (2021): 1.

10. Nicholas Blomley, "The Territory of Property," *Progress in Human Geography* 40, no. 5 (2016): 593.

11. Harris, "Whiteness as Property."

12. Carol Rose, *Property and Persuasion: Essays on the History, Theory and Rhetoric of Ownership* (Boulder, CO: Westview Press, 1994).

13. Nicholas Blomley, "Law, Property, and the Geography of Violence: The Frontier, the Survey, and the Grid," *Annals of the Association of American Geographers* 93, no. 1 (2003): 121–41.

14. Adolph Reed Jr. cautions us not to interpret the wages of whiteness as entirely psychological—noting that the mechanisms Du Bois identified as breaking interracial class solidarity were rooted in public policy. It is therefore a union of public policy and social forces that merits our attention. In the contemporary case of policing, I attend to this caution by noting both the public policy that structures participation in policing as well as its more social rewards. For Reed's critique, see "Du Bois and the Wages of Whiteness: What He Meant, What He Didn't, and Besides, It Shouldn't Matter for Our Politics Anyway," *Nonsite.Org*, June 29, 2017, https://nonsite.org/du-bois-and-the-wages-of-whiteness.

15. Nikhil Pal Singh, "The Whiteness of Police," *American Quarterly* 66, no. 4 (2014): 1097.

16. Nikhil Pal Singh. "On Race, Violence, and So-Called Primitive Accumulation," *Social Text* 34, no. 3 (2016): 27–50.

17. Du Bois, *Darkwater*, 90.

18. Grace Kyungwon Hong, The Ruptures of American Capital: Women of Color Feminism and the Culture of Immigrant Labor (Minneapolis: University of Minnesota Press, 2006), 6; Craig Willse. *The Value of Homelessness: Managing Surplus Life in the United States* (Minneapolis: University of Minnesota Press, 2006), 106.

19. Ananya Roy, "Paradigms of Propertied Citizenship: Transnational Techniques of Analysis," *Urban Affairs Review* 38, no. 4 (2003): 463–91.

20. Willse. *The Value of Homelessness*, 106.

21. For more on police as race-making, see Micol Seigel, *Violence Work: State Power and the Limits of Police* (Durham: Duke University Press, 2018); and Robin D. G. Kelley, "Insecure: Policing Under Racial Capitalism," *Spectre Journal* 1, no. 2 (2020): 12–38.

22. Rinaldo Walcott, *On Property: Policing, Prisons, and the Call for Abolition* (Windsor, Ontario: Biblioasis, 2021).

23. Doug Willis, "Two California Cities that Could, and Couldn't, in Aerospace Industry," *North County Times* (Oceanside, CA), December 29, 1999.

24. Sonia Nazario, "Class Struggle Unfolds in Antelope Valley Tracts," *Los Angeles Times*, June 24, 1996.

25. Gilmore, *Golden Gulag*.

26. County of Los Angeles Sheriff Civilian Oversight Commission, "Mira Loma Women's Detention Center Project Update," May 15, 2018, https://coc.lacounty.gov/LinkClick .aspx?fileticket=hJeTWcPA-V0%3D&portalid=35.

27. "California State Prison, Los Angeles County (LAC)," LAC Institution Statistics, California Department of Corrections and Rehabilitation, archived August 8, 2009, https://web.archive.org/web/20090808115142/http://www.cdcr.ca.gov/Visitors/Facilities /LAC-Institution_Stats.html.

28. Nazario, "Class Struggle Unfolds in Antelope Valley Tracts."

29. Nazario, "Class Struggle Unfolds in Antelope Valley Tracts."

30. Octavia Butler, *Parable of the Sower* (New York: Grand Central Publishing, 2023).

31. Darrell Satzman, "New Program Targets Gang Crime in Antelope Valley," *Los Angeles Times*, July 14, 1998.

32. Nazario, "Class Struggle Unfolds in Antelope Valley Tracts."

33. Vesla M. Weaver, "Frontlash: Race and the Development of Punitive Crime Policy," *Studies in American Political Development* 21, no. 2 (November 2007): 230–65.

34. Camilla A. Hawthorne and Jovan Scott Lewis, "Black Geographies: Material Praxis of Black Life and Study," in *The Black Geographic: Praxis, Resistance, Futurity*, ed. Camilla A. Hawthorne and Jovan Scott Lewis (Durham, Duke University Press, 2023).

35. Sometimes having a car was the problem—it signaled you were financially well off enough to work and pay full rent. Other times not having a car was the problem—it signaled that you were too poor or too lazy to work and be a productive member of society.

36. For more on racialized emotions and their role in the production of race and racism, see Eduardo Bonilla-Silva, "Feeling Race: Theorizing the Racial Economy of Emotions," *American Sociological Review* 84, no. 1 (2019): 1–25. Specifically, Michael's enthusiasm for participating in and speaking about anti-Blackness recalls Du Bois's notions of the enjoyments of anti-Blackness. For more, see chapter 3 of Ella Myers, *The Gratifications of Whiteness: W. E. B Du Bois and the Enduring Rewards of Anti-Blackness* (New York: Oxford University Press, 2022).

37. Julie Drake, "Parris Seeks Fifth Term as Mayor," *Antelope Valley (CA) Press*, April 12, 2020, https://www.avpress.com/news/parris-seeks-fifth-term-as-mayor/article_72bf00aa -7c6a-11ea-9228-3bd6baab6e3e.html.

38. Sherri Okamoto, "R. Rex Parris: Overcoming Adversity, He Became a Mega-Star Trial Lawyer, Accomplished Mayor," *Metropolitan News-Enterprise* (Los Angeles, CA), January 11, 2019, http://www.metnews.com/articles/2019/POYperriso11119.htm.

39. For more on Mitchell and Newburgh, see for example Jennifer Mittelstadt, *From Welfare to Workfare: The Unintended Consequences of Liberal Reform, 1945–1965* (Chapel Hill: University of North Carolina Press, 2005).

40. Okamoto, "R. Rex Parris."

41. Sharon Moser, "'Buckwheat' Remark Spurs Suit Over Yearbook," *Los Angeles Times*, April 13, 1994.

42. Associated Press, "Suit: Michelin teaches cops to cite drivers for accidents," *The Lompoc Record*, October 4, 2000.

43. Jessica Garrison and Ted Rohrlich, "A Not-So-Welcome Mat," *Los Angeles Times*. June 17, 2007.

44. Ann M. Simmons, "Dogs a Target in the War on Gangs," *Los Angeles Times*, January 26, 2009.

45. John Rogers, "The Mayor Who Would Rather Be King," *Record Searchlight* (Redding, CA), July 18, 2010.

46. City of Lancaster, "LANCAS 13 Gang Bust," September 4, 2009, https://www.youtube.com/watch?v=b4CvlalhGPM.

47. Bob Wilson, "AV Reaches Turning Point in War on Crime," *Antelope Valley Press*, February 2, 2009.

48. 2010 Goldstein Award Submissions, https://popcenter.asu.edu/content/2010-goldstein-award-submissions-year; Award documents: https://popcenter.asu.edu/sites/default/files/library/awards/goldstein/2010/10–02.pdf.

49. These views reflected the period's malicious national discourse on Section 8, emblematized by Hanna Rosin's 2008 feature story in *The Atlantic* casting the program as a cause of suburban crime. The article was subsequently disproved in Ingrid Gould Ellen, Michael C. Lens, and Katherine O'Regan, "American Murder Mystery Revisited: Do Housing Voucher Households Cause Crime?" *Housing Policy Debate* 22, no.4 (2012): 551–72.

50. This shift didn't spell an end to vicious anti-gang rhetoric, however. In 2004, Lancaster gang investigators began a program of reading inmate Christmas and birthday cards to attempt to determine gang affiliations and residences; see Richard Fausset, "Sending Greetings from All the Gang," *Los Angeles Times*, April 5, 2004, https://www.latimes.com/archives/la-xpm-2004-apr-05-me-cards5-story.html. In 2012, Parris sent a campaign mailer accusing a rival, Jonathon Ervin, of being a "gang candidate"; see KCAL News, "Lancaster Mayor Circulates Flier," March 25, 2014, https://www.youtube.com/watch?v=7hfPDuV6M00.

51. Mark Neocleous, *A Critical Theory of Police Power* (New York: Verso Books, 2021), 115.

52. Lancaster City Council Meeting, September 28, 2010.

53. Lancaster Section 8 Commission Meeting, March 24, 2009.

54. Bob Wilson, "City to Ready Responses for Section 8 Idea," *Antelope Valley (CA) Press*, October 12, 2009.

55. "Rental Housing Business License (LANCAP)," Business Licensing, City of Lancaster, CA, https://www.cityoflancasterca.org/our-city/departments-services/finance/business-licensing/rental-housing-business-license-lancap.

56. Staff Report, "Presentation on Results of the Feasibility of Developing a Multi-Jurisdiction Housing Authority to Administer the Housing Choice Voucher Program" City of Lancaster. March 24, 2009.

57. The Community Action League et al. v. City of Lancaster and City of Palmdale, No. 2:2011cv04817 (C.D. Cal. June 7, 2011).

58. Bob Wilson, "No Section 8 Cut for Truancy—Yet," *AV Press*, February 3, 2011.

59. Bob Wilson, "Lancaster Scrutinizes Section 8 Data," *AV Press*, April 25, 2011.

60. Housing Authorities: Housing Certificates, California Senate Bill 660 (2011–2012) http://www.leginfo.ca.gov/pub/11-12/bill/sen/sb_0651-0700/sb_660_bill_20110425_amended_sen_v98.html.

61. I cannot prove beyond a doubt that the poster really was Brody.

62. Staff Report, "Presentation on Results of the Feasibility of Developing a Multi-Jurisdiction Housing Authority to Administer the Housing Choice Voucher Program," City of Lancaster. March 24, 2009.

63. Blomley, "Law, Property, and the Geography of Violence."

64. The Community Action League et al. v. City of Lancaster and City of Palmdale, No. 2:2011cv04817 (C.D. Cal. June 7, 2011).

65. "Good Neighbor Guide," City of Lancaster (CA), 2009.

66. Jonathan Rieder, *Canarsie: The Jews and Italians of Brooklyn Against Liberalism* (Cambridge, MA: Harvard University Press, 1985), 171.

67. "The Corporeality of Checkpoints under Settler Colonization," speech given by Professor David Shorter at Palestine Awareness Week, April 26, 2013, copy in author's possession.

68. Cristina Beltrán, *Cruelty as Citizenship: How Migrant Suffering Sustains White Democracy* (Minneapolis: University of Minnesota Press, 2020).

4. UNMAKING HOME

1. Rory Kramer and Brianna Remster, "The Slow Violence of Contemporary Policing," *Annual Review of Criminology* 5, no. 1 (2022): 43–66.

2. Kidada E. Williams, *I Saw Death Coming: A History of Terror and Survival in the War Against Reconstruction* (New York: Bloomsbury Publishing, 2023).

3. Saidiya Hartman, *Wayward Lives, Beautiful Experiments: Intimate Histories of Riotous Black Girls, Troublesome Women, and Queer Radicals* (New York: W.W. Norton & Company, 2019).

4. Hartman, *Wayward Lives, Beautiful Experiments.*

5. Hartman, *Wayward Lives, Beautiful Experiments.*

6. Richard A. Chikota, "Pre-Dawn Welfare Inspections and the Right of Privacy"; Charles A. Reich, "Midnight Welfare Searches and the Social Security Act," *Yale Law Journal* 72, no. 7 (June 1963): 1347–61.

7. Abramovitz, *Regulating the Lives of Women*; Roberts, "Welfare and the Problem of Black Citizenship."

8. Friedrichs, *The Pruitt-Igoe Myth.*

9. Freedman, "Sylvester Smith, Unlikely Heroine."

10. Karteron, "When Stop and Frisk Comes Home."

11. LaShawn Harris, "Beyond the Shooting: Eleanor Gray Bumpurs, Identity Erasure, and Family Activism against Police Violence," *Souls* 20, no.1 (2018): 86–109.

12. William E. Schmidt, "Chicago's Housing Raids Challenged," *The New York Times*, December 17, 1988.

13. Beth Richie, *Arrested Justice: Black Women, Violence, and America's Prison Nation* (New York: New York University Press, 2012), 8–11.

14. Theresa Auch Shutz, "ACLU Sues East Chicago Housing Authority," *The Chicago Tribune*, May 13, 2019.

15. Emma Whitford, "NYC Agency Uses Brooklyn Gang Raid To Encourage Evictions Of Entire Families From Public Housing," *The Appeal*, January 31, 2018.

16. Hernández, *City of Inmates*, 174.

17. Marques Vestal, Jr., "Property Conflict in the Promised Land: A History of Black Home Struggles in Los Angeles, 1920–1950" (PhD diss., University of California, Los Angeles, 2020).

18. For more, see Treva B. Lindsey, *America, Goddam: Violence, Black Women, and the Struggle for Justice* (Berkeley: University of California Press, 2022); and Heather

Montes-Ireland, "'She's Been Doing Everything Right': Mothers of Color and Economic Violence," *Women, Gender, and Families of Color* 10, no. 1 (2022): 41–70.

19. Samuel Momodou, "Operation Hammer (1987–1990)," *Black Past*, March 8, 2022, https://www.blackpast.org/african-american-history/operation-hammer-1987-1990. For more on the effects of these raids on tenants, see David Helps, "Broken Homes of the Drug War," *Protean Magazine*, February 25, 2022.

20. "Early Morning Wake-Up Call for Gangs Members in the Antelope Valley," *LAPD Online*, https://www.lapdonline.org/newsroom/early-morning-wake-up-call-for-gangs-members-in-the-antelope-valley, accessed July 23, 2023.

21. Susila Gurusami, "Motherwork Under the State: The Maternal Labor of Formerly Incarcerated Black Women," *Social Problems* 66, no. 1 (2019): 128–43.

22. Terra Graziani, Joel Montano, Ananya Roy, and Pamela Stephens, "Property, Personhood, and Police: The Making of Race and Space through Nuisance Law," *Antipode* 54, no. 2 (October 2021).

23. "Man Cleared for Killing Neighbor's Burglars," *ABC News*, June 30, 2008, https://abcnews.go.com/TheLaw/story?id=5278638&page=1.

24. The rules come from the federal government's Department of Housing and Urban Development, but local housing authorities have latitude in how they interpret and implement them.

25. "Counting toothbrushes" has a long history in the punitive regulation of women on welfare. See, for example, Michele Estrin Gilman, "Privacy is a Luxury not for the Poor," in *The Poverty Law Canon: Exploring the Major Cases*, ed. Marie A. Failinger and Ezra Rosser (Ann Arbor: University of Michigan Press, 2016), 153–69.

26. Dorothy Roberts, *Shattered Bonds: The Color of Child Welfare* (New York: Basic Books, 2009).

27. Gurusami, "Motherwork Under the State."

28. Damien M. Sojoyner, "Another Life is Possible: Black Fugitivity and Enclosed Places," *Cultural Anthropology* 32, no. 4 (2017): 514–36. As Sojoyner notes, practices of fugitivity are not just about non-compliance with a system, but may also inform radical action. The social movement against policing documented in the next chapter may be read as following from or contextualized by tenants' refusal to be evicted—as such a practice bought time and created conditions under which organizing might be fruitful.

29. Peggy Cooper Davis, *Neglected Stories: The Constitution and Family Values* (New York: Hill and Wang, 1998).

30. Davis, *Neglected Stories*, 39.

31. Davis, *Neglected Stories*, 117.

32. Gilmore, "Abolition Geography and the Problem of Innocence."

33. bell hooks, *Yearning: Race, Gender, and Cultural Politics* (Boston: South End Press, 1990), 77.

34. Hartman, *Wayward Lives, Beautiful Experiments*, 249.

35. Cayce C. Hughes, "A House but Not a Home: How Surveillance in Subsidized Housing Exacerbates Poverty and Reinforces Marginalization," *Social Forces*, 100 no.1: (September 2021): 293–315.

36. Terra Graziani, Joel Montano, Ananya Roy, and Pamela Stephens, "Policing Tenancy: The Struggle for Housing and Land in Los Angeles," *Urban Geography* (January 2024): 1–20; Kate Weisbrud, "The Carceral Home," *Boston University Law Review* 103,

no. 7 (2023): 1879–1928; Anna Reosti, Rahim Kurwa, and Robin Bartram, "Rental Housing and the Continuum of Carcerality," *Theoretical Criminology* 28(4): 534–553

37. To probe this argument further, consider Khiara Bridges's study of Medicaid, in which she illustrates how the state surveils and accesses information about the intimate private lives of poor people, including their home lives, particularly as part of the process of enrolling participants. See *The Poverty of Privacy Rights* (Redwood City: Stanford University Press, 2017). Bridges argues that because poor people must utilize these services to provide certain standards of care to their children or risk being deemed an unfit parent and losing them, they have no choice but to become subjected to this scrutiny (*The Poverty of Privacy Rights*). Thus, Bridges argues that it is not that poor people's privacy rights are being violated, but rather that the poor do not have a right to privacy. The parallels to the testimonies of tenants in this chapter are manifest. Voucher tenants often have no alternative to using a voucher and therefore have no choice but to be exposed to piercing scrutiny of their homes and lives. In the same vein as Bridges's argument, they may have housing but not home.

38. hooks, *Yearning*, 85.

5. THE SECOND SUN

The epigraph is from "Activists Respond to DOJ Settlement," OurWeekly, July 31, 2015. https://ourweekly.com/news/2015/07/31/activists-respond-doj-settlement/.

1. Du Bois, *Darkwater*, 40.

2. Robert N. Proctor and Londa Schiebinger, eds., *Agnotology: The Making and Unmaking of Ignorance* (Stanford: Stanford University Press, 2008).

3. This chapter draws from Christopher Galeano's foundational work chronicling TCAL's campaign in "An Im-Perfect Storm: The Access to Justice Gap in the Antelope Valley" (unpublished manuscript, copy in author's possession).

4. Garrison and Rohrlich, "A Not-So-Welcome Mat."

5. Kathryn A. Sabbeth, "(Under) Enforcement of Poor Tenants' Rights," *Georgetown Journal on Poverty Law and Policy* 27, no. 1 (2019): 97–146.

6. For an overview, see Tonya L. Brito, Kathryn A. Sabbeth, Jessica K. Steinberg, and Lauren Sudeall, "Racial Capitalism in the Civil Courts," *Columbia Law Review* 122, no. 5 (2022): 1243–86. For a case study, see Isaiah Fleming-Klink, Brian J. McCabe, and Eva Rosen, "Navigating an Overburdened Courtroom: How Inconsistent Rules, Shadow Procedures, and Social Capital Disadvantage Tenants in Eviction Court," *City & Community* 22, no. 3 (2023): 220–45.

7. See Poverty and Race Research Action Council, National Housing Law Project, "Expanding Federal Support for Tenant Organizing in Federally Assisted Housing and the Housing Choice Voucher Program," Policy Brief, February 15, 2022, https://www.prrac .org/expanding-federal-support-for-tenant-organizing-in-federally-assisted-housing -and-the-housing-choice-voucher-program-february-2022.

8. Here I invoke Aziz Huq's term, rights without remedies, to connote the disconnect between legal rights and the actual realization of them. Huq's critique sits in other areas of the law, like criminal justice, but as evidence from the case of housing shows, it applies here as well. For more, see Aziz Z. Huq, *The Collapse of Constitutional Remedies* (New York: Oxford University Press, 2021).

9. "Section 8 Recipients in the AV Speak Out," *Antelope Valley Times*. September 2, 2011.

10. M. Dilworth, "DOJ Attorneys, Investigators Hear from AV Residents," *Antelope Valley Times*, December 14, 2011.

11. Gautam Bhan, *In the Public's Interest: Evictions, Citizenship, and Inequality in Contemporary Delhi* (Athens: University of Georgia Press, 2016).

12. For more on these themes, see Elizabeth F. Cohen, *The Political Value of Time: Citizenship, Duration, and Democratic Justice* (New York: Cambridge University Press, 2018); and Yuvraj Joshi, "Racial Time," *The University of Chicago Law Review* 90, no. 6 (2023): 1625–83.

13. Meeting Transcript, LA County Board of Supervisors, June 21, 2011, https://lacounty.granicus.com/DocumentViewer.php?file=lacounty_a4ef01d5605049bb07ebd3e26 4727a56.pdf.

14. The Community Action League et al. v. City of Lancaster and City of Palmdale, No. 2:2011cv04817, (C.D. Cal. June 7, 2011).

15. "Lancaster Mayor 'Extremely Disappointed' in Palmdale's Settlement of Section 8 Lawsuit," *The Antelope Valley Times*, February 3, 2012, https://theavtimes.com/2012/02/03/lancaster-mayor-extremely-disappointed-in-palmdales-settlement-of-section-8-lawsuit.

16. K. Enrique, "Lancaster Alleges 'Housing Discrimination' in Ongoing Section 8 Conflict," *The Antelope Valley Times*, March 14, 2012, https://theavtimes.com/2012/03/14/lancaster-alleges-housing-discrimination-in-ongoing-section-8-conflict/. The article links to the complaint, accessible here: https://www.theavtimes.com/wp-content/uploads/2012/03/Housing-Discrimination-Complaint.pdf.

17. US Department of Justice Civil Rights Division, "Re: Investigation of Los Angeles County Sheriffs Department Stations in Antelope Valley," June 28, 2013, https://clearinghouse.net/doc/74776.

18. The report examined the common claim that disproportionate stops are a product of disproportionate criminal activity by minority groups, and found the claim to be baseless. "The low contraband seizure rate for African Americans indicates that, overall, LASD deputies in the Antelope Valley appear to have a less accurate threshold of suspicion for searching African Americans, and that the greater frequency of searches of African Americans cannot be explained by a greater likelihood that they are carrying contraband (such as illicit drugs or weapons)."

19. Kaaryn Gustafson, "Degradation Ceremonies and the Criminalization of Low-Income Women," *UC Irvine Law Review* 3, no. 2 (2013): 297–358; Nicole Gonzalez Van Cleve, "Due Process & the Theater of Racial Degradation: The Evolving Notion of Pretrial Punishment in the Criminal Courts," *Daedalus* 151, no. 1 (2022): 135–52.

20. One example is as follows: "[T]wo Palmdale deputies stopped a car for a broken license plate light and detained all three passengers without apparent justification. All three people were asked to exit the car, and two of them—the driver and a Latino male—were detained in the backseat of a patrol car while the deputies checked their identification. According to the complaint, one of the deputies sarcastically commented he was surprised that the Latino male had valid identification. The investigation demonstrated that the deputy failed to document any "compelling justification" for the backseat detention, despite policy 194 Notes requiring an explanation if two or more deputies are present. In fact, the deputy failed to document that the backseat detention had even occurred at all. The civilian complainant

agreed to resolve the complaint with the deputy through informal dispute resolution, so LASD never formally determined whether the deputy's conduct was outside of policy."

21. In addition it is worth noting the degree to which LASD apparently hid these practices from its own records. As the report stated, "Of the 157 files provided by LASD, less than one-half included information demonstrating any reason for deputy presence. . . . Moreover, only one-quarter of the files that indicate the number of deputies present describe circumstances that would justify the number of deputies who responded."

22. For example, in 2007, LASD arrived at a voucher holder's residence to serve an arrest warrant for driving without a license and to assist with a HACoLA compliance check. The deputy also suspected the voucher holder of stealing property from her former landlord. The deputy participated in the compliance check, but did not disclose to the voucher holder the fact that a criminal investigation was also underway regarding the stolen property. During the compliance check, the deputy noted the presence of an item similar to the reported stolen property and photographed it. As a result of information obtained during this improper search, the deputy later obtained a search warrant to recover the property.

23. Litigation: United States v. County of Los Angeles, No. 2:15-cv-03174 (C.D. Cal. Apr 28, 2015); Settlement: Settlement Agreement, United States v. County of Los Angeles (Antelope Valley) (C.D. Cal.), https://www.justice.gov/crt/case/united-states-v-county -los-angeles-antelope-valley-cd-cal.

24. For more on the successes and continued importance of these legal tools, see Alaizah Koorji, "Defending Consent Decrees in the Wake of Horne v. Flores," *Harvard Law Review* Blog. November 13, 2024, https://harvardlawreview.org/blog/2024/11/defending-consent -decrees-in-the-wake-of-horne-v-flores.

25. Reviewing consent decrees in Seattle and New York, Finn Mayock documents clear patterns of police noncompliance that go unchallenged by federal monitors and the Department of Justice; see "Unending Reform: Police Resistance to Consent Decrees and Federal Monitors," *Journal of Law and Policy* 31, no. 1 (2022): 213–45.

26. Theresa Rocha Beardall, "Legal Reality or Legal Mirage? Examining the Relationship between Police Violence, Legal Consciousness, and the Promise Of Civil Legal Justice," *Punishment and Society* (2024), https://doi-org.proxy.cc.uic.edu/10.1177/14624745241237702.

27. See, for example, Tony Cheng, *The Policing Machine: Enforcement, Endorsements, and the Illusion of Public Input* (Chicago: University of Chicago Press, 2024) and Theresa Rocha Beardall, "Police Legitimacy Regimes and the Suppression of Citizen Oversight in Response to Police Violence," *Criminology* 6, no. 4 (2022): 740–65.

28. Cindy Chang, "Tensions Ease in the High Desert," *Los Angeles Times*, June 22, 2015.

29. This strategy was common. Sheriff's deputies had also given local residents opposed to the voucher program their cell phone numbers (such as Jim, whom we met in chapter 3).

30. The deputy later told the *Times* that "he pursued the men to prove to a reporter and photographer that they would run away. He had no legal reason to stop them, he said, and would not have treated them like suspects had he spoken with them."

31. Todd Franke, Jorja Leap, and Stephanie Benson, "The Antelope Valley Community Survey: Year 1," October 2018, http://www.antelopevalleysettlementmonitoring.info /content/documents/surveys/AV%20Community%20Survey%20Year%20One%20-%20 Final%20Report%202018.pdf.

32. Similarly, "Approximately 21% of Section 8 recipients and 31% of formerly detained responded that the Sheriff's Department in the AV have 'come to their home when they did not request them,' compared with only 14% of the general population."

33. "AV Focus Group Final Report 2018," Monitoring of the Antelope Valley Settlement Agreement, http://www.antelopevalleysettlementmonitoring.info/content/documents/surveys/AV%20Focus%20Group%20Final%20Report%202018.pdf.

34. Leila Miller, "Sheriff's Department Reform in Antelope Valley Has Lagged for Years, Court Monitors Say," *Los Angeles Times*, February 25, 2021, https://www.latimes.com/california/story/2021-02-25/la-me-antelope-valley-settlement-agreement-progress.

35. It may also have come from historical experience in Los Angeles, as the LAPD managed to adopt some reforms while resisting fundamental transformation during its 2000s-era consent decree.

36. Miller, "Sheriff's Department Reform in Antelope Valley Has Lagged for Years."

37. Todd Franke, Robert Blagg, and Melanie Sonsteng-Person, "The Antelope Valley Community Survey: Year 2" September 2020. http://www.antelopevalleysettlementmonitoring.info/content/documents/surveys/AV%20Community%20Survey%20Year%20Two%20-%20Final%20Report%202020.pdf.

38. These details are found in the full report dataset, available at https://public.tableau.com/app/profile/robert.blagg/viz/AntelopeValleyWorkbook_NormalColor_200701_THPicks_RDBrevperToddfeedback200720_THrevisedcompareby/RespondentOverview.

39. Miller, "Sheriff's Department Reform in Antelope Valley Has Lagged for Years."

40. Chelsea Helena et. al., "Not Just Stops: Mapping Racially Biased Policing in the Antelope Valley," October 2021, https://nlsla.org/wp-content/uploads/2021/10/Mapping-Racially-Biased-Policing-in-the-AV_compressed.pdf.

41. Miller, "Sheriff's Department Reform in Antelope Valley Has Lagged for Years."

42. Vivian Ho, "'The Confederacy of California': Life in the Valley Where Robert Fuller Was Found Hanged," *The Guardian*, June 27, 2020, https://www.theguardian.com/us-news/2020/jun/27/california-racism-policing-robert-fuller-antelope-valley.

43. "Antelope Valley Monitoring Team 14th Semi-Annual Report," http://antelopevalleysettlementmonitoring.info/content/documents/reports/14%20Semi-Annual%20Report,%20June%202022.pdf.

44. Keri Blakinger, "Deputy Who Killed Mother in Front of Child Also Body-Slammed School Janitor, Lawsuit Says," *Los Angeles Times*, April 5, 2024, https://www.latimes.com/california/story/2024-04-05/deputy-who-killed-mother-in-front-of-her-child-body-slammed-school-janitor-suit-says; Sam Levin, "Police Killed Niani Finlayson Seconds after Responding to her 911 Call, Video Shows," *The Guardian*, December 29, 2023, https://www.theguardian.com/us-news/2023/dec/29/la-police-fatally-shot-niani-finlayson-body-camera; Christina Carrega, "This Mom Is the 2nd Black Person Seeking Help That One Deputy Has Killed in 3 Years," *Capital B News*, January 5, 2024, https://capitalbnews.org/niani-finlayson-police-shooting/; "'He tried to kill me': Lawsuit Announced in LASD Use of Force Incident outside Lancaster Winco," *Fox 11 News*, July 31, 2023, https://www.foxla.com/news/lawsuit-lasd-use-of-force-incident-video-caught-on-camera-lancaster-winco; and Sam Levin, "LA Sheriff's Office under Scrutiny after Deputy Punches Mother Holding Baby," *The Guardian*, July 13, 2023, https://www.theguardian.com/us-news/2023/jul/13/la-sheriff-office-deputy-punches-mother-baby. Shelton was fired in March 2024; see Christina Gonzalez, "LA Deputy Relieved of Duties Following Fatal Shooting in Lancaster," *Fox 11 News*, July 18, 2024, https://www.foxla.com/news/la-deputy-fired-following-fatal-shooting-lancaster.

45. Cindy Chang, "In Antelope Valley, Relations between Minorities and Sheriff's Department Are Improving," *Los Angeles Times*, June 21, 2015.

46. *Jones et. al. v. City of Faribault, Minnesota*, No. 0:18-cv-01643 (D.C. MN 2018).

47. *HOPE Fair Housing Center v. City of Peoria*, No. 1:17-cv-1360 (C.D. Ill.). N.B. The author served as an expert witness in this case.

48. Mike Nemeth, "Newsom Signs Legislation on 'Crime Free Housing' Policies," California Apartment Association, October 10, 2023, https://caanet.org/newsom-signs-legislation-on-crime-free-housing-policies.

49. "Dear Colleague Letter," U.S. Department of Justice Civil Rights Division, August 15, 2024, https://www.justice.gov/d9/2024-08/doj_crime-free_and_nuisance_letter.pdf.

50. Jauregui v. City of Palmdale, 226 Cal.App.4th 781 (Cal. Ct. App. 2014), https://casetext.com/case/jauregui-v-city-of-palmdale.

CONCLUSION

1. Aldous Huxley and Paul Kagan, "A Double Look at Utopia: The Llano del Rio Colony," *California Historical Quarterly* 51, no. 2 (1972): 117–54; Davis, *City of Quartz*; and Laura Nelson, "Thinking in Ruins: On the Llano del Rio Experiment," *Los Angeles Review of Books*, August 2023, https://lareviewofbooks.org/article/thinking-in-ruins-on-the-llano-del-rio-experiment.

2. Otis M. Wiles, "Huge Granite Pile in Lonely Waste will be Angeleno's Home." *The Los Angeles Times*, February 22, 1925.

3. Raj Chetty, Nathaniel Hendren, and Lawrence F. Katz, "The Effects of Exposure to Better Neighborhoods on Children," *The American Economic Review* 106, no. 4 (2016): 855–902.

4. Jens Ludwig, "Urban Transformation," University of Chicago, July 27, 2015, https://youtu.be/UrTyaXJfwjo?si=JxwdkPDSoEoyUSZp.

5. These dynamics have both exclusionary and internally repressive dynamics across lines of race and class subordination. For scholarship illustrating this, see Stefano Bloch, "Aversive Racism and Community-Instigated Policing: The Spatial Politics of Nextdoor," *Environment and Planning C, Politics and Space* 40, no. 1 (2022): 260–78; and Armando Lara-Millán and Melissa Guzman-Garcia, "Digital Platforms and the Maintenance of the Urban Order," *Social Problems* (December 2023), https://doi.org/10.1093/socpro/spad053.

6. These trends can also be contextualized among broader efforts to delegate policing to non-police state actors such as teachers, doctors, and social workers, who may be induced to report on their students, patients, and clients to law enforcement.

7. Jon D. Michaels and David L. Noll, "Vigilante Federalism" *Cornell Law Review* 108, no. 5 (2023): 1187–1264.

8. Aziz Huq, "The Private Suppression of Constitutional Rights," *Texas Law Review* 101, no. 6 (2023): 1259–1339.

9. For more on this, see Hilary Malson, "Tearing Down and Building Up': A History, Theory and Practice of Abolitionist Housing Justice in the US," in *Handbook on Planning and Power*, ed. Michael Gunder, Kristina Grange, and Tanja Winkler (Cheltenham, UK: Edward Elgar Publishing, 2023), 211–27.

10. For an overview of these processes, see Reosti, Kurwa, and Bartram, "Rental Housing and the Continuum of Carcerality."

11. Larisa G. Bowman, "Eviction Abolition," *Loyola University Chicago Law Journal* 55, no.3 (Spring 2024): 541–620.

12. John O. Calmore, "Spatial Equality and the Kerner Commission Report: A Back-to-the-Future Essay," *North Carolina Law Review* 71, no. 5 (June 1993): 1487–1518.

13. I situate this call within Norrinda Brown's argument for urban decolonization; see "Urban Decolonization," *Michigan Journal of Race and Law* 21, no. 1 (2018): 75–109.

14. Undersigned Professors to the Regional Council of the Southern California Association of Governments, "Re: Regional Housing Needs Assessment (RHNA) Allocation Methodology," Open Letter, August 31, 2019, https://docs.google.com/document/d/1NeXLD5IOK2kgE9Gpm-t-eVxvheDSTc_ZOHeUdUrdDXM/edit.

15. Steve Lopez, "Column: Karen Bass Wants to End Homelessness. Are Know-how and Connections Enough?," *Los Angeles Times*, May 7, 2022, https://www.latimes.com/california/story/2022–05–07/lopez-column-karen-bass-homelessness.

16. City of Lancaster, "Lancaster Declares State of Emergency Against 'Plan for a Mass Movement of Homeless Individuals to the Antelope Valley'," *The Antelope Valley Times* (press release), December 16, 2022, https://theavtimes.com/2022/12/16/lancaster-declares-state-of-emergency-against-plan-for-a-mass-movement-of-homeless-individuals-to-the-antelope-valley.

17. City News Service, "Palmdale City Council Looks to Fend Off 'Homeless Village' in Area," *The Antelope Valley Times*, January 12, 2023, https://theavtimes.com/2023/01/12/palmdale-city-council-looks-to-fend-off-homeless-village-in-area.

18. Kevin Smith, "Palmdale 10th in US for Biggest Increase in High-Income Households," *Los Angeles Daily News*, February 9, 2024, https://www.dailynews.com/2024/02/09/palmdale-10th-in-us-for-biggest-increase-in-high-income-households.

19. Allison Gatlin, "Palmdale, Santa Monica Talk Housing," *Antelope Valley Press*, February 17, 2023, https://www.avpress.com/news/palmdale-santa-monica-talk-housing/article_41407140-ae75–11ed-92f0–73dad0356de7.html.

20. Gatlin, "Palmdale, Santa Monica Talk Housing."

21. American Friends Service Committee, "Companies Profiting from the Gaza Genocide," https://afsc.org/gaza-genocide-companies, updated June 6, 2024.

22. Alexandro Ochoa, "Querida Palmdale," *CouRaGeouS Cuentos: A Journal of Counternarratives* 3, no. 1 (2019): 38–40.

23. BYD, "BYD and the City of Lancaster Announce Lancaster Energy Module and Electric Bus Manufacturing Facilities," n.d., https://en.byd.com/news/byd-and-the-city-of-lancaster-announce-lancaster-energy-module-and-electric-bus-manufacturing-faciliti.

24. In 2022, the Antelope Valley Transit Authority became the first all-electric transit agency in North America. See James Royal, "AVTA Becomes First All-Electric Zero-Emission Transit Agency," March 16, 2022, https://www.avta.com/avta-becomes-first-all-electric-zero-emission-transit-agency.

25. See Constellation Energy's website about its Antelope Valley installation at https://www.constellationenergy.com/our-company/locations/location-sites/antelope-valley-solar-ranch-one.html.

26. Juan D. De Lara, *Inland Shift: Race, Space, and Capital in Southern California* (Oakland: University of California Press, 2018.

27. Kevin Smith, "Trader Joe's to Build Massive Distribution Center in Palmdale," *Los Angeles Daily News*, June 22, 2023, https://www.dailynews.com/2023/06/22/trader-joes-to-build-massive-distribution-center-in-palmdale; Mariana Duran, "Three Months Ago They Unionized. Now a Strike by Amazon Contract Drivers Is Heating Up," *Los Angeles*

Times, July 28, 2023, https://www.latimes.com/california/story/2023–07–28/a-strike-by
-amazon-contract-drivers-is-heating-up; and Anna M. Phillips, "How Hot Is It Inside
Southern California's Warehouses? Ask the Workers at Rite Aid," *Los Angeles Times*, October 12, 2021, https://www.latimes.com/environment/story/2021–10–12/heat-risk-rite-aid
-workers-southern-california-warehouse.

28. Kim Stringfellow, "Shifting Dust: Development and Demographics in Antelope
Valley," *The Mojave Project*, December 2017, https://mojaveproject.org/dispatches-item
/shifting-dust-development-and-demographics-in-antelope-valley; Melody Petersen, "As
Crews Chainsaw Joshua trees, Mojave Desert Community Protests Solar Energy Project," *Los Angeles Times*, September 6, 2024, https://www.latimes.com/environment/story
/2024–09–06/california-desert-town-protests-solar-energy-project; Dana Goodyear,
"Death Dust," *The New Yorker*, January 12, 2014, https://www.newyorker.com/magazine
/2014/01/20/death-dust; Chris Clarke, "Uh Oh: Valley Fever Outbreak Linked to Solar Development," *PBS SoCal*, May 1, 2023, https://www.pbssocal.org/redefine/uh-oh-valley-fever
-outbreak-linked-to-solar-development; and Sarah Favot, "L.A. County Supervisors to
Ban Large Wind Turbines in Unincorporated Areas," *LA Daily News*, July 14, 2015, https://
web.archive.org/web/20200717115304/https://www.dailynews.com/2015/07/14/la-county
-supervisors-to-ban-large-wind-turbines-in-unincorporated-areas.

29. Kevin Smith, "Amazon Drivers, Dispatchers Stage Walkout at Palmdale Warehouse," *OC Register*, June 15, 2023, https://www.ocregister.com/2023/06/15/amazon-drivers
-dispatchers-stage-walkout-at-palmdale-warehouse; and Teamsters, "Teamsters Win
Groundbreaking Joint Employer Decision Against Amazon," August 2024, https://teamster
.org/2024/08/teamsters-win-groundbreaking-joint-employer-decision-against-amazon.

30. Waunette Cullors, "Op-ed: Lancaster and Palmdale: Cancel the Contract with the
LA County Sheriff," *Antelope Valley Times*, March 16, 2021, https://theavtimes.com/2021
/03/16/op-ed-lancaster-and-palmdale-cancel-the-contract-with-the-la-county-sheriff.

31. "Cancel The Contract," Cancel the Contract Coalition, updated February 14, 2022,
https://cancelthecontract.com.

32. Emily Elena Dugdale and Irena Hwang, "In a California Desert, Sheriff's Deputies Settle Schoolyard Disputes. Black Teens Bear the Brunt," *ProPublica* and *KPCC/LAist*, September 29, 2021, https://www.propublica.org/article/in-a-california-desert-sheriffs-deputies
-settle-schoolyard-disputes-black-teens-bear-the-brunt.

33. Khaleda Rahman, "Officer Bodyslams Black Girl in School, Sparking Outrage,"
Newsweek, September 16, 2021, https://www.newsweek.com/officer-bodyslams-black-girl
-school-sparking-outrage-1629728.

34. Alex S. Vitale, "Cancel the Contract: Alternatives to School Policing," The Policing and Social Justice Project, 2024, https://static1.squarespace.com/static/5de981188
ae1bf14a94410f5/t/674df63f6bc4e37ca84ea3de/1733162560273/CTCReport3.0.pdf.

35. Katherine McKittrick, "On Plantations, Prisons, and a Black Sense of Place," *Social
& Cultural Geography* 12, no. 8 (2011): 960

36. Sebastian Rotella, "Sun Village: Black Enclave Withers Amid Antelope Bloom," *Los
Angeles Times*, August 27, 1989, VY-A6.

37. From the 2020 decennial census: 37,032 of 173,516 residents reported being Black
or African American alone in Lancaster, and 23,080 of 169,450 residents reported being
Black or African American alone in Palmdale. These numbers likely undercount the

total Black population as they do not include people reporting two or more races, and do not include people outside the valley's two primary cities.

38. Whitney Richards-Calathes suggests employment in the valley's prison industry drove some Black movement during this period. See "Inheritances of Injustice/Transference of Freedom: An Intimate Project on Black Women's Intergenerational Relationships and the Consequences of the Punishment System" (PhD diss., City University of New York, 2019).

39. Danielle M. Purifoy and Louise Seamster, "Creative Extraction: Black Towns in White Space," *EPD: Society and Space* 39, no. 1 (2021): 47–66.

40. Louise Seamster, "The White City: Race and Urban Politics," *Sociology Compass* 9, no. 12 (2015): 1049–65.

41. Simmons, "Feeling Burned in Sun Village."

42. Simmons, "Feeling Burned in Sun Village."

43. McDermott, "History: Prioleau Family Objects to Bruce's Beach Plaque Language."

44. In 2019, Darren Parker, a key activist in the campaign to end the policing of Black voucher tenants in the valley, passed away. His funeral services were held in Sun Village, at the Living Stone Cathedral where Bishop Henry Hearns preached for decades. See California Democratic Party African American Caucus, "Homegoing Services for the Hon. Darren W. Parker," Facebook, July 24, 2019, https://www.facebook.com/events/355157005176318.

45. For example, Tyrone Beason, "Their Stolen Land in Orange County Was Given Back. Now They're Ready to Heal," *Los Angeles Times*, December 10, 2023, https://www.latimes.com/politics/story/2023-12-10/orange-county-returned-stolen-land-to-indigenous-californians-now-healing-begins; and Tyrone Beason, "California Has a History of Racist Land Seizures. Will Reparations Bills Bring Justice?," *Los Angeles Times*, June 19, 2024 https://www.latimes.com/environment/story/2024-06-19/a-california-bill-could-help-thousands-of-families-recover-losses-due-to-eminent-domain.

46. David Ponton, III, "Review: The Broken Heart of America: St. Louis and the Violent History of the United States," *Journal of American History* 109, no. 1 (2022): 128–29.

REFERENCES

Abramovitz, Mimi. *Regulating the Lives of Women: Social Welfare Policy from Colonial Times to the Present.* Boston: South End Press, 1996.

American Civil Liberties Union of Southern California. *Banished and Abandoned: Criminalization and Displacement of Unhoused People in Lancaster.* February 2021. https://www.aclusocal.org/en/publications/banished-and-abandoned-lancaster.

Andersen, Thom, dir. *Los Angeles Plays Itself.* New York: The Cinema Guild, 2014.

Archer, Deborah N. "The New Housing Segregation: The Jim Crow Effects of Crime-Free Housing Ordinances." *Michigan Law Review* 118, no. 2 (November 2019): 173–232.

Arena, John. *Driven from New Orleans: How Nonprofits Betray Public Housing and Promote Privatization.* Minneapolis: University of Minnesota Press, 2012.

Arias, Melanie Kayser Schmidt. "Experimental Citizens: The Experimental Housing Allowance Program and Housing Vouchers as American Social Policy in the 1970s and 1980s." PhD diss., University of California, Los Angeles, 2013.

Balto, Simon. *Occupied Territory: Policing Black Chicago from Red Summer to Black Power.* Chapel Hill: University of North Carolina Press, 2019.

Barkun, Michael. *Religion and the Racist Right: The Origins of the Christian Identity Movement.* Chapel Hill: University of North Carolina Press, 1997.

Beardall, Theresa Rocha. "Legal Reality or Legal Mirage? Examining the Relationship between Police Violence, Legal Consciousness, and the Promise Of Civil Legal Justice." *Punishment and Society* (2024). https://doi-org.proxy.cc.uic.edu/10.1177/14624745241237702.

———. "Police Legitimacy Regimes and the Suppression of Citizen Oversight in Response to Police Violence." *Criminology* 6, no. 4 (2022): 740–65.

Beasley, Delilah L. *The Negro Trailblazers of California.* Los Angeles: n.p., 1919.

Beckett, Katherine, and Steve Herbert. *Banished: The New Social Control in America.* New York: Oxford University Press, 2009.

Belew, Kathleen. *Bring the War Home: The White Power Movement and Paramilitary America.* Cambridge, MA: Harvard University Press, 2018.

Bell, Derrick A. "Brown v. Board of Education and the Interest-Convergence Dilemma." *Harvard Law Review* 93, no. 3 (1980): 518–33.

Bell, Jeannine. *Hate Thy Neighbor: Move-In Violence and the Persistence of Racial Segregation in American Housing.* New York: New York University Press, 2013.

Bell, Monica C. "Anti-Segregation Policing." *New York University Law Review* 95, no. 3 (2020): 650–765.

Beltrán, Cristina. *Cruelty as Citizenship: How Migrant Suffering Sustains White Democracy.* Minneapolis: University of Minnesota Press, 2020.

Bender, Steven. *Greasers and Gringos: Latinos, Law, and the American Imagination.* New York: New York University Press, 2003.

Bennett, Larry, Janet L. Smith, and Patricia A. Wright. *Where are Poor People to Live? Transforming Public Housing Communities.* Armonk, NY: M. E. Sharpe, 2006.

Berman, Elizabeth Popp. *Thinking Like an Economist: How Efficiency Replaced Equality in US Public Policy.* Princeton: Princeton University Press, 2022.

Bhan, Gautam. *In the Public's Interest: Evictions, Citizenship, and Inequality in Contemporary Delhi.* Athens: University of Georgia Press, 2016.

Blauner, Robert. *Racial Oppression in America.* New York: Harper and Row, 1972.

Bloch, Stefano. "Aversive Racism and Community-Instigated Policing: The Spatial Politics of Nextdoor." *Environment and Planning. C, Politics and Space* 40, no. 1 (2022): 260–78.

Blomley, Nicholas. "Law, Property, and the Geography of Violence: The Frontier, the Survey, and the Grid." *Annals of the Association of American Geographers* 93, no. 1 (2003): 121–41.

———. "The Territory of Property." *Progress in Human Geography* 40, no. 5 (2016): 593–609.

Bochicchio, Ana Laura. "Justification by Race: Wesley Swift's White Supremacy and Anti-Semitic Theological Views in His Christian Identity Sermons." *Journal of Hate Studies* 17, no. 1 (2021): 35–51.

Boltanski, Luc, and Eve Chiapello. *The New Spirit of Capitalism.* New York: Verso, 2007.

Bonds, Anne. "Race and Ethnicity I: Property, Race, and the Carceral State." *Progress in Human Geography* 43, no. 3 (2019): 574–83.

Bonilla-Silva, Eduardo. "Feeling Race: Theorizing the Racial Economy of Emotions." *American Sociological Review* 84, no. 1 (2019): 1–25.

Bowman, Larisa G. "Eviction Abolition." *Loyola University Chicago Law Journal* 55, no. 3 (Spring 2024): 541–620.

Brenner, Neil. "Theses on Urbanization." *Public Culture* 25, no. 1 (January 2013): 85–114.

Bridges, Khiara. *The Poverty of Privacy Rights.* Redwood City: Stanford University Press, 2017.

Brito, Tonya L., Kathryn A. Sabbeth, Jessica K. Steinberg, and Lauren Sudeall. "Racial Capitalism in the Civil Courts." *Columbia Law Review* 122, no. 5 (2022): 1243–86.

Brown Norrinda. "Section 8 is the New N-Word: Policing Integration in the Age of Black Mobility." *Washington University Journal of Law and Policy* 51, no. 1 (2016): 61–93.

Brown, Norrinda. "Urban Decolonization." *Michigan Journal of Race and Law* 21, no. 1 (2018): 75–109.

Browne, Simone. *Dark Matters: On the Surveillance of Blackness.* Durham: Duke University Press, 2015.

Butler, Octavia. *Parable of the Sower.* New York: Grand Central Publishing, 2023.

Calmore, John O., "Spatial Equality and the Kerner Commission Report: A Back-to-the-Future Essay." *North Carolina Law Review* 71, no. 5 (June 1993): 1487–1518.

Campbell, Marne L. *Making Black Los Angeles: Class, Gender, and Community, 1850–1917.* Chapel Hill: University of North Carolina Press, 2016.

Chalmers, David Mark. *Backfire: How the Ku Klux Klan Helped the Civil Rights Movement.* Lanham, MD: Rowman & Littlefield, 2005.

Cheng, Tony. *The Policing Machine: Enforcement, Endorsements, and the Illusion of Public Input.* Chicago: University of Chicago Press, 2024.

Chetty, Raj, Nathaniel Hendren, and Lawrence F. Katz. "The Effects of Exposure to Better Neighborhoods on Children." *The American Economic Review* 106, no. 4 (2016): 855–902.

Chikota, Richard A. 1966. "Pre-Dawn Welfare Inspections and the Right of Privacy." *Journal of Urban Law* 44, no. 1: 119–35.

Cisneros, Henry G., and Lora Engdahl, eds. *From Despair to Hope: Hope VI and the New Promise of Public Housing in America's Cities.* Washington, DC: Brookings Institution Press, 2009.

Clampet-Lundquist, Susan, and Douglas Massey. "Neighborhood Effects on Economic Self-Sufficiency: A Reconsideration of the Moving to Opportunity Experiment." *The American Journal of Sociology* 114, no. 1 (2008): 107–43.

Cohen, Elizabeth F. *The Political Value of Time: Citizenship, Duration, and Democratic Justice.* New York: Cambridge University Press, 2018.

Committee on Governmental Affairs. Recommendations of the Commission on Wartime Internment and Relocation of Citizens: Hearings before the Subcommittee on Civil Service, Post Office, and General Services of the Committee on Governmental Affairs, United States Senate, Ninety-Eighth Congress, Second Session, on S. 2116 . . . August 16, 1984, Los Angeles, CA, August 29, 1984, Anchorage, AK. Second Session sess., 1986.

Dantzler, Prentiss A. "The Urban Process under Racial Capitalism: Race, Anti-Blackness, and Capital Accumulation." *Journal of Race, Ethnicity and the City* 2, no. 2 (2021): 113–34.

Dantzler, Prentiss, Elizabeth Korver-Glenn, and Junia Howell. "Introduction: What Does Racial Capitalism Have to Do with Cities and Communities?" *City & Community* 21, no. 3 (2022): 163–72.

Davis, Mike. *City of Quartz: Excavating the Future in Los Angeles.* New ed. New York: Verso, 2006.

Davis, Peggy Cooper. *Neglected Stories: The Constitution and Family Values.* New York: Hill and Wang, 1998.

De Lara, Juan D. *Inland Shift: Race, Space, and Capital in Southern California.* Oakland: University of California Press, 2018.

de Souza Briggs, Xavier, Susan J. Popkin, and John Goering. *Moving to Opportunity: The Story of an American Experiment to Fight Ghetto Poverty.* New York: Oxford University Press, 2010.

Deener, Andrew. *Venice: A Contested Bohemia in Los Angeles.* Chicago: University of Chicago Press, 2012.

Delbanco, Andrew. *The War before the War: Fugitive Slaves and the Struggle for America's Soul from the Revolution to the Civil War.* New York: Penguin Press, 2019.

Dentice, Dianne. "Hate Speech, Prejudice, and Biblical Interpretations." *Journal of Faith, Education, and Community* 3, no. 1 (2019).

Denvir, Daniel. *All-American Nativism: How the Bipartisan War on Immigrants Explains Politics as We Know It*. New York: Verso, 2020.

Derenoncourt, Ellora. "Can You Move to Opportunity? Evidence from the Great Migration." *American Economic Review* 112, no. 2 (February 2022): 369–408.

Desmond, Matthew, and Nicol Valdez. "Unpolicing the Urban Poor: Consequences of Third-Party Policing for Inner-City Women." *American Sociological Review* 78, no. 1 (2013): 117–41.

Du Bois, W. E. B. *Black Reconstruction in America: An Essay Toward a History of the Part which Black Folk Played in the Attempt to Reconstruct Democracy in America, 1860–1880*. New York: The Free Press, 1998 [1935].

———. *Darkwater: Voices from within the Veil*. New York: Harcourt, Brace and Howe, 1920.

Ellen, Ingrid Gould, Michael C. Lens, and Katherine O'Regan. "American Murder Mystery Revisited: Do Housing Voucher Households Cause Crime?" *Housing Policy Debate* 22, no. 4 (2012): 551–72.

Ellen, Ingrid Gould, Katherine O'Regan, and Sarah Strochak. *Using HUD Administrative Data to Estimate Success Rates and Search Durations for New Voucher Recipients*. U.S. Department of Housing and Urban Development, Office of Policy Development and Research, December 2021. https://www.huduser.gov/portal/portal/sites/default/files/pdf/Voucher-Success_Rates.pdf.

Evans, Hiram Wesley. "The Klan's Fight for Americanism." *The North American Review* 223, no. 830 (March–May, 1926): 33–63.

Feldman, Roberta M., and Susan Stall. *The Dignity of Resistance: Women Residents' Activism in Chicago Public Housing*. Cambridge: Cambridge University Press, 2004.

Finnegan, William. *Cold New World: Growing Up in Harder Country*. New York: Random House, 1998.

Flamming, Douglas. *Bound for Freedom: Black Los Angeles in Jim Crow America*. Berkeley: University of California Press, 2005.

Fleming-Klink, Isaiah, Brian J. McCabe, and Eva Rosen. "Navigating an Overburdened Courtroom: How Inconsistent Rules, Shadow Procedures, and Social Capital Disadvantage Tenants in Eviction Court." *City & Community* 22, no. 3 (2023): 220–45.

Freedman, Henry. "Sylvester Smith, Unlikely Heroine: *King v. Smith* (1968)." In *The Poverty Law Canon: Exploring the Major Cases*, edited by Marie A. Failinger and Ezra Rosser, 51–71. Ann Arbor: University of Michigan Press, 2016.

Freund, David A. *Colored Property: State Policy and White Racial Politics in Suburban America*. Chicago: University of Chicago Press, 2010.

Freidrichs, Chad, dir. *The Pruitt-Igoe Myth: An Urban History*. Unicorn Stencil, 2011.

Ganz, John. *When the Clock Broke: Con-Men, Conspiracists, and How America Cracked up in the Early 1990s*. New York: Farrar, Strauss, and Giroux, 2024.

Garofalo, James, and Maureen McLeod. "The Structure and Operations of Neighborhood Watch Programs in the United States." *Crime & Delinquency* 35, no. 3 (1989): 326–44.

Geismer, Lily. *Left Behind: The Democrats' Failed Attempt to Solve Inequality*. New York: Public Affairs, 2022.

Gibbons, Andrea. *City of Segregation: One Hundred Years of Struggle for Housing in Los Angeles*. New York: Verso, 2018.

Gilman, Michele Estrin. "Privacy Is a Luxury Not for the Poor." In *The Poverty Law Canon: Exploring the Major Cases*, edited by Marie A. Failinger and Ezra Rosser, 153–69. Ann Arbor: University of Michigan Press, 2016.

Gilmore, Ruth Wilson. "Abolition Geography and the Problem of Innocence." In *Futures of Black Radicalism*, edited by Gaye Theresa Johnson and Alex Lubin, 225–40. New York: Verso, 2017.

———. *Golden Gulag: Prisons, Surplus, Crisis, and Opposition in Globalizing California*. Berkeley: University of California Press, 2007.

Go, Julian. "Three Tensions in the Theory of Racial Capitalism." *Sociological Theory* 39, no. 1 (2021): 38–47.

Godsil, Rachel D. "Race Nuisance: The Politics of Law in the Jim Crow Era." *Michigan Law Review* 105, no. 3 (2006): 505–57.

Goetz, Edward G. *New Deal Ruins: Race, Economic Justice, and Public Housing Policy*. Ithaca: Cornell University Press, 2013.

———. "The Audacity of HOPE VI: Discourse and the Dismantling of Public Housing." *Cities* 35 (December 2013): 342–48.

Gordon, Daanika. *Policing the Racial Divide: Urban Growth Politics and the Remaking of Segregation*. New York: New York University Press, 2022.

Gorham, Christopher C. *The Confidante: The Untold Story of the Woman Who Helped Win WWII and Shape Modern America*. New York: Citadel Press, 2023.

Grandin, Greg. *The End of the Myth: From the Frontier to the Border Wall in the Mind of America*. New York: Metropolitan Books, 2019.

Graziani, Terra, Joel Montano, Ananya Roy, and Pamela Stephens. "Property, Personhood, and Police: The Making of Race and Space through Nuisance Law." *Antipode* 54, no. 2 (2021): 439–61.

———. "Policing Tenancy: The Struggle for Housing and Land in Los Angeles." *Urban Geography* (January 2024): 1–20.

Greenstein, Paul, Lionel Rolfe, and Nigey Lennon. *Bread and Hyacinths: The Rise and Fall of Utopian Los Angeles*. Los Angeles: California Classic Books, 1992.

Gurusami, Susila. "Motherwork Under the State: The Maternal Labor of Formerly Incarcerated Black Women." *Social Problems* 66, no. 1 (2019): 128–43.

Gustafson, Kaaryn. 2013. "Degradation Ceremonies and the Criminalization of Low-Income Women." *UC Irvine Law Review* 3, no. 2 (2013): 297–358.

Haley, Sarah. *No Mercy Here: Gender, Punishment, and the Making of Jim Crow Modernity*. Chapel Hill: University of North Carolina Press, 2016.

Harris, Cheryl I. "Whiteness as Property." *Harvard Law Review* 106, no. 8 (1993): 1707–91.

Harris, LaShawn. "Beyond the Shooting: Eleanor Gray Bumpurs, Identity Erasure, and Family Activism against Police Violence." *Souls* 20, no. 1 (2018): 86–109.

Hartman, Saidiya. *Lose Your Mother: A Journey along the Atlantic Slave Route*. New York: Farrar, Straus and Giroux, 2007.

———. *Wayward Lives, Beautiful Experiments: Intimate Histories of Riotous Black Girls, Troublesome Women, and Queer Radicals*. New York: W.W. Norton, 2019.

Harvey, David. *Spaces of Capital: Towards a Critical Geography*. New York: Routledge, 2001.

Hawthorne, Camilla A., and Jovan Scott Lewis, eds. *The Black Geographic: Praxis, Resistance, Futurity*. Durham: Duke University Press, 2023.

Herbert, Claire, and Jay Orne. "No Lawless Place: Foregrounding Property in Sociology." *Socius* 7 (2021): 1–12.

Hernandez, Kelly Lytle. *City of Inmates: Conquest, Rebellion, and the Rise of Human Caging in Los Angeles, 1771–1965*. Chapel Hill: The University of North Carolina Press, 2017.

Hoffman, Abraham. "Angeles Crest: The Creation of a Forest Highway System in the San Gabriel Mountains." *Southern California Quarterly* 50, no. 3 (1968): 309–45.

Hong, Grace Kyungwon. *The Ruptures of American Capital: Women of Color Feminism and the Culture of Immigrant Labor.* Minneapolis: University of Minnesota Press, 2006.

hooks, bell. *Yearning: Race, Gender, and Cultural Politics.* Boston: South End Press, 1990.

HoSang, Daniel Martinez. *Racial Propositions: Ballot Initiatives and the Making of Postwar California.* Berkeley: University of California Press, 2010.

Howell, Junia, and Elizabeth Korver-Glenn. "The Increasing Effect of Neighborhood Racial Composition on Housing Values, 1980–2015." *Social Problems* 68, no. 4 (2021): 1051–71.

Howell, Junia, Ellen Whitehead, and Elizabeth Korver-Glenn. "Still Separate and Unequal: Persistent Racial Segregation and Inequality in Subsidized Housing." *Socius* 9 (2023): 1–16.

Hudson, Lynn M. *West of Jim Crow: The Fight Against California's Color Line.* Champaign: University of Illinois Press, 2020.

Hughes, Cayce C. "A House but Not a Home: How Surveillance in Subsidized Housing Exacerbates Poverty and Reinforces Marginalization." *Social Forces* 100, no. 1 (September 2021): 293–315.

Hugill, David. *Settler Colonial City: Racism and Inequality in Postwar Minneapolis.* Minneapolis: University of Minnesota Press, 2021.

Huq, Aziz Z. *The Collapse of Constitutional Remedies.* New York: Oxford University Press, 2021.

———. "The Private Suppression of Constitutional Rights." *Texas Law Review* 101, no. 6 (2023): 1259–1339.

Huxley, Aldous, and Paul Kagan. "A Double Look at Utopia: The Llano del Rio Colony." *California Historical Quarterly* 51, no. 2 (1972): 117–54.

Jefferson, Brian Jordan. "Cities, Crime, and Carcerality: Beyond the Ecological Perspective." *Journal of Planning Literature* 32, no. 2 (2017): 103–16.

Jenkins, Henry, Sam Ford, and Joshua Green. *Spreadable Media: Creating Value and Meaning in a Networked Culture.* New York: New York University Press, 2013.

Johnson, Walter. *The Broken Heart of America: St. Louis and the Violent History of the United States.* New York: Basic Books, 2020.

Joshi, Yuvraj. "Racial Time." *The University of Chicago Law Review* 90, no. 6 (2023): 1625–83.

Karp, Michael. "The St. Louis Rent Strike of 1969: Transforming Black Activism and American Low-Income Housing." *Journal of Urban History* 40, no. 4 (2014): 648–70.

Karteron, Alexis. "When Stop and Frisk Comes Home: Policing Public and Patrolled Housing." *Case Western Reserve Law Review* 69, no. 3 (Spring 2019): 669–729.

Katz, Lawrence F., Jeffrey R. Kling, and Jeffrey B. Liebman. "Moving to Opportunity in Boston: Early Results of a Randomized Mobility Experiment." *The Quarterly Journal of Economics* 116, no. 2 (2001): 607–54.

Kelley, Robin D. G. "Insecure: Policing Under Racial Capitalism." *Spectre Journal* 1, no. 2 (Fall 2020): 12–38.

Kennedy, Sean. "Deputy Gangs: 50 Years of Identifying Root Causes and Effects to Advocate for Meaningful Reform in the Los Angeles County Sheriff's Department." Los Angeles: The Center for Juvenile Law and Policy at Loyola Marymount University, 2021.

Kerner Commission. *Report of the National Advisory Commission on Civil Disorders.* Washington, DC: US Government Printing Office, 1968.

Kessler, Lauren. *The Happy Bottom Riding Club: The Life and Times of Pancho Barnes.* New York: Random House, 2000.

Kling, Jeffrey R., Jeffrey B. Liebman, and Lawrence F. Katz. "Experimental Analysis of Neighborhood Effects." *Econometrica* 75, no. 1 (2007): 83–119.

Kramer, Rory, and Brianna Remster. "The Slow Violence of Contemporary Policing." *Annual Review of Criminology* 5, no. 1 (January 2022): 43–66.

Kurashige, Scott. *The Shifting Grounds of Race: Black and Japanese Americans in the Making of Multiethnic Los Angeles.* Princeton: Princeton University Press, 2008.

Ladner, Joyce. *Tomorrow's Tomorrow: The Black Woman.* Garden City: Doubleday 1971.

Lara-Millán, Armando, and Melissa Guzman-Garcia. "Digital Platforms and the Maintenance of the Urban Order." *Social Problems* (December 2023): https://doi.org/10.1093/socpro/spado53.

Leavitt, Jacqueline. "Women Under Fire: Public Housing Activism in Los Angeles." *Frontiers: A Journal of Women Studies* 13, no. 2 (1993): 109–130.

Lefebvre, Henri. *The Production of Space.* Translated by Donald Nicholson-Smith. Oxford: Blackwell, 1991.

Legassick, Martin, and David Hemson. *Foreign Investment and the Reproduction of Racial Capitalism in South Africa.* London: Anti-Apartheid Movement, 1976.

Leventhal, Tama, and Jeanne Brooks-Gunn. "Moving to Opportunity: An Experimental Study of Neighborhood Effects on Mental Health." *American Journal of Public Health* 93, no. 9 (2003): 1576–82.

Levin, Jack, and Jack McDevitt. *Hate Crimes: The Rising Tide of Bigotry and Bloodshed.* New York: Plenum Press, 1993.

Levitas, Daniel. *The Terrorist Next Door: The Militia Movement and the Radical Right.* New York: St. Martin's Press, 2004.

Lewinnek, Elaine. "Social Studies Controversies in 1960s Los Angeles: Land of the Free, Public Memory, and the Rise of the New Right." *Pacific Historical Review* 84, no. 1 (2015): 48–84.

Lindsey, Treva B. *America, Goddam: Violence, Black Women, and the Struggle for Justice.* Berkeley: University of California Press, 2022.

Loewen, James W. *Sundown Towns: A Hidden Dimension of American Racism.* New York: New Press, 2005.

Lotchin, Roger W. *Fortress California, 1910–1962: From Warfare to Welfare.* New York: Oxford University Press, 1992.

MacLean, Nancy. *Democracy in Chains: The Deep History of the Radical Right's Stealth Plan for America.* New York: Penguin, 2017.

Malson, Hilary. "'Tearing Down and Building Up': A History, Theory and Practice of Abolitionist Housing Justice in the US." In *Handbook on Planning and Power*, edited by Michael Gunder, Kristina Grange, and Tanja Winkler, 211–27. Cheltenham, UK: Edward Elgar Publishing, 2023.

Masur, Kate. *Until Justice Be Done: America's First Civil Rights Movement, from the Revolution to Reconstruction.* New York: W.W. Norton, 2021.

Mathias, Charles McC., and Marion Morris. "Fair Housing Legislation: Not an Easy Row to Hoe." *Cityscape* 4, no. 3 (1999): 21–33.

Mayock, Finn. "Unending Reform: Police Resistance to Consent Decrees and Federal Monitors." *Journal of Law and Policy* 31, no. 1 (2022): 213–45.

McGirr, Lisa. *Suburban Warriors: The Origins of the New American Right.* Princeton: Princeton University Press, 2001.

McKittrick, Katherine. *Demonic Grounds: Black Women and the Cartographies of Struggle*. Minneapolis: University of Minnesota Press, 2006.

———. "On Plantations, Prisons, and a Black Sense of Place." *Social & Cultural Geography* 12, no. 8 (2011): 947–63.

Metzger, Molly W. "The Reconcentration of Poverty: Patterns of Housing Voucher Use, 2000 to 2008." *Housing Policy Debate* 24, no. 3 (2014): 544–67.

Michaels, Jon D., and David L. Noll. 2023. "Vigilante Federalism." *Cornell Law Review* 108, no. 5 (2023): 1187–1264.

Milwicki, Alon. "Baptizing Nazism: An Analysis of the Religious Roots of American Neo-Nazism." PhD diss., American University, 2019.

Mittelstadt, Jennifer. *From Welfare to Workfare: The Unintended Consequences of Liberal Reform, 1945–1965*. Chapel Hill: University of North Carolina Press, 2005.

Montes-Ireland, Heather. "'She's Been Doing Everything Right': Mothers of Color and Economic Violence." *Women, Gender, and Families of Color* 10, no. 1 (2022): 41–70.

Morris, Aldon D. *The Scholar Denied: W. E. B. Du Bois and the Birth of Modern Sociology*. Oakland: University of California Press, 2017.

Mueller, Jennifer C. "''Imagine an Ignorance that Fights Back": Honoring Charles Mills, Our Inheritance and Charge." *Sociology of Race and Ethnicity* 8, no. 4 (2022): 443–50.

Myers, Ella. *The Gratifications of Whiteness: W. E. B. Du Bois and the Enduring Rewards of Anti-Blackness*. New York: Oxford University Press: 2022.

Nelson, Laura. "Thinking in Ruins: On the Llano del Rio Experiment." *Los Angeles Review of Books*, August 2023, https://lareviewofbooks.org/article/thinking-in-ruins-on-the-llano-del-rio-experiment.

Neocleous, Mark. *A Critical Theory of Police Power*. New York: Verso Books, 2021.

Ocen, Priscilla. 2012. "The New Racially Restrictive Covenant: Race, Welfare, and the Policing of Black Women in Subsidized Housing." *UCLA Law Review* 59, no. 6: 1540–82.

Ochoa, Alexandro. "Querida Palmdale." *CouRaGeouS Cuentos: A Journal of Counternarratives* 3, no. 1 (2019): 38–40.

Orlebeke, Charles J. "The Evolution of Low-Income Housing Policy, 1949 to 1999." *Housing Policy Debate* 11, no. 2 (2000): 489–520.

Park, K-Sue. "The History Wars and Property Law: Conquest and Slavery as Foundational to the Field." *The Yale Law Journal* 131, no. 4 (2022): 1062–1153.

Park, Robert, and Ernest Burgess, eds. *The City*. Chicago: University of Chicago Press, 1925.

Parson, Don. *Making a Better World: Public Housing, the Red Scare, and the Direction of Modern Los Angeles*. Minneapolis: University of Minnesota Press, 2005.

Petersen, Camille. "Capitalizing on Heritage: St. Augustine, Florida, and the Landscape of American Racial Ideology." *City & Community* 21, no. 3 (2022): 193–213.

PolicyLink and USC Program for Environmental and Regional Equity. *An Equity Profile of the Los Angeles Region*. 2017. https://dornsife.usc.edu/eri/publications/equity-profile-los-angeles-region.

Polikoff, Alexander. *Waiting for Gautreaux: A Story of Segregation, Housing, and the Black Ghetto*. Chicago: Northwestern University Press, 2007.

Pollakowski, Henry O., Daniel H. Weinberg, Fredrik Andersson, John C. Haltiwanger, Giordano Palloni, and Mark J. Kutzbach. "Childhood Housing and Adult Outcomes: A Between-Siblings Analysis of Housing Vouchers and Public Housing." *American Economic Journal: Economic Policy* 14, no. 3 (2022): 235–72.

Popkin, Susan J., Victoria E. Gwiasda, Lynn M. Olson, Dennis P. Rosenbaum, and Larry Buron. *The Hidden War: Crime and the Tragedy of Public Housing in Chicago*. New Brunswick: Rutgers University Press, 2000.

Ponton, David, III. "Review: The Broken Heart of America: St. Louis and the Violent History of the United States." *Journal of American History* 109, no. 1 (2022): 128–29.

Poverty and Race Research Action Council and National Housing Law Project. "Expanding Federal Support for Tenant Organizing in Federally Assisted Housing and the Housing Choice Voucher Program." February 15, 2022. https://www.prrac.org/expanding-federal-support-for-tenant-organizing-in-federally-assisted-housing-and-the-housing-choice-voucher-program-february-2022.

Proctor, Robert N. and Londa Schiebinger, eds. *Agnotology: The Making and Unmaking of Ignorance*. Stanford: Stanford University Press, 2008.

Purifoy, Danielle M. "Black Towns and (Legal) Marronage." *Annals of the American Association of Geographers* 113, no. 7 (2023): 1599–1614.

Purifoy, Danielle M., and Louise Seamster. "Creative Extraction: Black Towns in White Space." *EPD: Society and Space* 39, no. 1 (2021): 47–66.

Rainwater, Lee. *Behind Ghetto Walls: Black Families in a Federal Slum*. Chicago: Aldine, 1970.

Ramsey, Kathryn. "One-Strike 2.0: How Local Governments Are Distorting a Flawed Federal Eviction Law." *UCLA Law Review* 65, no. 5 (2018): 1146–99.

Reich, Charles A. "Midnight Welfare Searches and the Social Security Act." *Yale Law Journal* 72, no. 7 (June 1963): 1347–61.

Reny, Tyler T., and Benjamin J. Newman. "Protecting the Right to Discriminate: The Second Great Migration and Racial Threat in the American West." *The American Political Science Review* 112, no. 4 (November 2018): 1104–10.

Reosti, Anna, Rahim Kurwa, and Robin Bartram. "Rental Housing and the Continuum of Carcerality." *Theoretical Criminology* 28, no. 4 (2024): 534–553.

Richards-Calathes, Whitney. "Inheritances of Injustice/Transference of Freedom: An Intimate Project on Black Women's Intergenerational Relationships and the Consequences of the Punishment System." PhD diss., City University of New York, 2019.

Richie, Beth. *Arrested Justice: Black Women, Violence, and America's Prison Nation*. New York: New York University Press, 2012.

Rieder, Jonathan. *Canarsie: The Jews and Italians of Brooklyn Against Liberalism*. Cambridge: Harvard University Press, 1985.

Roberts, Dorothy. *Shattered Bonds: The Color of Child Welfare*. New York: Basic Books, 2009.

———. 1996. "Welfare and the Problem of Black Citizenship." *The Yale Law Journal* 105, no. 6 (1996): 1563–1602.

Robinson, Cedric J. *Black Marxism: The Making of the Black Radical Tradition*. 3rd ed. Chapel Hill: University of North Carolina Press, 2020.

Robinson, Jackie. *I Never had it Made*. New York: Harper Collins, 1995 [1972].

Robinson, Paul. "Race, Space, and the Evolution of Black Los Angeles." In *Black Los Angeles: American Dreams and Racial Realities*, edited by Darnell Hunt and Ana-Christina Ramon, 21–59. New York: New York University Press, 2010.

Rodriguez, Akira Drake. *Diverging Space for Deviants: The Politics of Atlanta's Public Housing*. Athens: University of Georgia Press, 2021.

Rongerude, Jane, and Mônica Haddad. "Cores and Peripheries: Spatial Analysis of Housing Choice Voucher Distribution in the San Francisco Bay Area Region, 2000–2010." *Housing Policy Debate* 26, no. 3 (2016): 417–36.

Rose, Carol. *Property and Persuasion: Essays on the History, Theory and Rhetoric of Ownership*. Boulder, CO: Westview Press, 1994.

Rosen, Eva. *The Voucher Promise: "Section 8" and the Fate of an American Neighborhood*. Princeton: Princeton University Press, 2020.

Rosenthal, Tracy, and Leonardo Vichlis, *Abolish Rent: How Tenants Can End the Housing Crisis*. Chicago: Haymarket Books, 2024.

Roy, Ananya. "Paradigms of Propertied Citizenship: Transnational Techniques of Analysis." *Urban Affairs Review* 38, no. 4 (2003): 463–91.

———. "Racial Banishment." In *Keywords in Radical Geography: Antipode at 50*, edited by Antipode Editorial Collective, 227–30. Hoboken, NJ: Wiley, 2019.

Sabbeth, Kathryn A. "(Under) Enforcement of Poor Tenants' Rights." *Georgetown Journal on Poverty Law and Policy* 27, no. 1 (2019): 97–146.

Sampson, Robert J. "Moving to Inequality: Neighborhood Effects and Experiments Meet Social Structure." *American Journal of Sociology* 114, no. 1 (2008): 189–231.

Samuels, Warren J. "The Economy as a System of Power and Its Legal Bases: The Legal Economics of Robert Lee Hale." *University of Miami Law Review* 27, no. 3–4 (1972): 261–371.

Schafran, Alex. *The Road to Resegregation: Northern California and the Failure of Politics*. Berkeley: University of California Press, 2018.

Schwartz, Alex F. *Housing Policy in the United States*. 3rd ed. New York: Routledge, 2014.

Seamster, Louise. "The White City: Race and Urban Politics." *Sociology Compass* 9, no. 12 (2015): 1049–65.

Seigel, Micol. *Violence Work: State Power and the Limits of Police*. Durham: Duke University Press, 2018.

Sides, Josh. *L.A. City Limits: African American Los Angeles from the Great Depression to the Present*. Berkeley: University of California Press, 2006.

Simon, Jonathan. *Governing Through Crime: How the War on Crime Transformed American Democracy and Created a Culture of Fear*. New York: Oxford University Press, 2007.

Singh, Nikhil Pal. "On Race, Violence, and So-Called Primitive Accumulation." *Social Text* 34, no. 3 (2016): 27–50.

———. "The Whiteness of Police." *American Quarterly* 66, no. 4 (2014): 1091–99.

Slater, Gene. *Freedom to Discriminate: How Realtors Conspired to Segregate Housing and Divide America*. Berkeley: Heyday, 2021.

Slater, Tom. *Shaking up the City: Ignorance, Inequality, and the Urban Question*. Oakland: University of California Press, 2021.

Slocum, Karla. *Black Towns, Black Futures: The Enduring Allure of a Black Place in the American West*. Chapel Hill: University of North Carolina Press, 2019.

Smith, Neil. "Gentrification and Uneven Development." *Economic Geography* 58, no. 2 (1982): 139–55.

Smith, Russell M., and Leora Waldner. "Why Majority-Minority Cities Form: Non-White Municipal Incorporation in the United States, 1990–2010." *Urban Geography* 39, no. 1 (2018): 149–66.

Sobieraj, Jerzy. "'Pure Americanism': The Ku Klux Klan, Nativism, and the Moral Crusade in the Jazz Age." *Polish Journal for American Studies* 3 (2009): 107–15.

Sojoyner, Damien M. "Another Life is Possible: Black Fugitivity and Enclosed Places." *Cultural Anthropology* 32, no. 4 (2017): 514–36.

Solache, Saul. "The Impact of Urban Development in the Antelope Valley on Its Mexican-American Residents." MA thesis, University of California, Los Angeles, 1971.

Sweeney, Shauna J. "Gendering Racial Capitalism and the Black Heretical Tradition." In *Histories of Racial Capitalism*, edited by Justin Leroy and Destin Jenkins, 53–84. New York: Columbia University Press, 2021.

Taylor, Keeanga-Yamahtta. *Race for Profit: How Banks and the Real Estate Industry Undermined Black Homeownership.* Chapel Hill: University of North Carolina Press, 2019.

Taylor, Quintard. "Slaves and Free Men: Blacks in the Oregon Country, 1840–1860." *Oregon Historical Quarterly* 83, no. 2 (1982): 153–70.

Tighe, J. Rosie, Megan E. Hatch, and Joseph Mead. "Source of Income Discrimination and Fair Housing Policy." *Journal of Planning Literature* 32, no. 1 (2017): 3–15.

Troesken, Werner, and Randall Walsh. "Collective Action, White Flight, and the Origins of Racial Zoning Laws." *Journal of Law, Economics, and Organization* 35, no. 2 (2019): 289–318.

Valeri, Robin Maria, and Kevin Borgeson. *Skinhead History, Identity, and Culture.* London: Routledge, 2017.

Van Cleve, Nicole Gonzalez. "Due Process & the Theater of Racial Degradation: The Evolving Notion of Pretrial Punishment in the Criminal Courts." *Daedalus* 151, no. 1 (2022): 135–52.

Vargas, Robert. "Four Ways Race and Capitalism Can Advance Urban Sociology." *City & Community* 21, no. 3 (2022): 256–62.

Vestal, Marques Augusta Jr. "Property Conflict in the Promised Land: A History of Black Home Struggles in Los Angeles, 1920–1950." PhD diss., University of California, Los Angeles, 2020.

Wacquant, Loïc. *The Invention of the "Underclass": A Study in the Politics of Knowledge.* Newark: Polity, 2022.

Walcott, Rinaldo. *On Property: Policing, Prisons, and the Call for Abolition.* Windsor, Ontario: Biblioasis, 2021.

Walsh, David Austin. *Taking America Back: The Conservative Movement and the Far Right.* New Haven: Yale University Press, 2024.

Weaver, Vesla M. "Frontlash: Race and the Development of Punitive Crime Policy." *Studies in American Political Development* 21, no. 2 (2007): 230–65.

Wells-Barnett, Ida B. *The East St. Louis Massacre: The Greatest Outrage of the Century.* Chicago: The Negro Fellowship Herald Press, 1917.

Weisbrud, Kate. "The Carceral Home." *Boston University Law Review* 103, no. 7 (2023): 1879–1928.

Wiewall, Darcy Lynn. "Up from the Dust: Orphaned Collections and Innovative Undergraduate Research." *Proceedings of the Society for California Archaeology* 33 (2019): 14–18.

Williams, Kidada E. *I Saw Death Coming: A History of Terror and Survival in the War Against Reconstruction.* New York: Bloomsbury Publishing, 2023.

Williams, Rhonda Y. *The Politics of Public Housing: Black Women's Struggles Against Urban Inequality.* New York: Oxford University Press, 2004.

Willse, Craig. *The Value of Homelessness: Managing Surplus Life in the United States*. Minneapolis: University of Minnesota Press, 2006.

Wilson, William J. *The Truly Disadvantaged: The Inner City, the Underclass, and Public Policy*. Chicago: University of Chicago Press, 1987.

Winnick, Louis. "The Triumph of Housing Allowance Programs: How a Fundamental Policy Conflict Was Resolved." *Cityscape* 1, no. 3 (1995): 95–121.

Wolfe, Patrick. "Settler Colonialism and the Elimination of the Native." *Journal of Genocide Research* 8, no. 4 (2006): 387–409.

Wolfe, Tom. *The Right Stuff*. New York: Farrar, Straus and Giroux, 1978.

Wood, Robert T. "The Indigenous, Nonracist Origins of the American Skinhead Subculture." *Youth & Society* 31, no. 2 (1999): 131–51.

Wright, Erik Olin. *Envisioning Real Utopias*. New York: Verso, 2020.

Yeritsian, Gary. "Participation from Above and Below: Brand Community and the Contestation of Cultural Participation." *Journal of Consumer Culture* 21, no. 2 (2021): 278–95.

Zappa, Frank, and Peter Occhiogrosso. *The Real Frank Zappa Book*. New York: Poseidon Press, 1989.

AB-1418 (2023), 138
abandonment, 4, 7, 108
abolition, 18, 150–51
academia, 11, 17, 139–40
activism, 26; anti-war, 15, 58, 60; Cancel the
    Contract, 155–56, 159; civil rights, 27, 58,
    155; community, 124; legal, 123–24; against
    segregation, 26–27; student, 15, 60–61.
    See also Community Action League, The;
    National Association for the Advancement
    of Colored People; organizing
aerospace industry, 7–8, 18, 22, 43; decline of, 8,
    62, 75, 79–80, 85; desegregation of, 44; and
    housing, 30–31, 84, 152. *See also* military
    investment
Afroman, 2
agnotology, xiii, 123
Aid to Families with Dependent Children
    program (AFDC), 13–14, 108, 141
alienation, 64, 113
Alien Land Law (1913), xi
Amazon, 154
America First Party, 50–51. *See also* Smith,
    Gerald L. K.
American Jewish Congress, 28
American Nazi Party, 60. *See also* Nazism
Americans for Democratic Action, 28
American Veterans Association, 28
Anderson, Thom, 8
Angeles Forest Highway, 29, 176n31

Antelope Valley, CA: as aerospace valley, xiii, 7, 18,
    31; agriculture in, xi, 29, 43; Black migration
    to, 18, 22–23, 30, 157; Black residents of, x–xi,
    8, 17, 19, 198n37; class in, 90–91;
    de-development, 7, 63; economic decline, 8,
    14, 61–63, 78–81; economy, 7, 29, 43–44, 48,
    154; as foreclosure hub, 80, 83; history of,
    ix–xiv, 6–8, 165; Indigenous peoples in, ix–x,
    56, 147, 167n2, 181n49; Japanese migration
    to, xi–xii, xiv, 29; as land of opportunity, 34;
    Latino residents of, 15, 65, 134, 183n83; and
    Los Angeles, 1–2, 4, 29, 62, 81, 83, 152–53,
    156–57, 169n10; population growth, 34, 62–63,
    75; public housing in, 152; as safety valve, 4,
    6–7, 8, 17, 154; segregation in, 7, 164; as spatial
    fix, 8, 18, 22, 30, 83, 152; voucher tenants in,
    8–9, 83–84, 89, 96; 29; whiteness of, 14–15;
    white supremacy in, 15, 33, 61, 63–64, 67
Antelope Valley American Indian League
    (AVAIL), xiv, 56
Antelope Valley Church of God in Christ
    (Sun Village, CA), 36
Antelope Valley College, 58, 60–61, 181n49
Antelope Valley Indian Museum State Historic
    Park, ix, 167n2
Antelope Valley Press, 5, 123
anti-Blackness, xiii, 15, 64, 65, 159, 188n36;
    and policing, 20, 67, 103; and residential
    segregation, 22–23, 61; and voucher status, 5,
    87. *See also* racism

anti-communism, 49, 51
Anti-Communist League, 51
anti-discrimination law, 54–55
Anti-Drug Abuse Act (1988), 71
anti-fraud rule, 111
anti-immigrant sentiment, 64, 65–66, 87
Antioch, CA, 8, 144
anti-racism, 15, 64–65
antisemitism, 49, 51, 64
anti-war activism, 15, 58, 60
Antonovich, Mike, 94, 130, 131, 143–44
Arbery, Ahmaud, 61, 165
arson, 26, 52, 68, 179n8
Aryan Nation, 52, 59, 66. *See also* Nazism
atomization, 110–12, 124
autonomy, 107, 121
AV Latino Education, 127

background checks, 71–72
banishment, 120, 153; racial, 8
Barajas, Julia, 72
Bass, Charlotta, 26, 50
Bass, Karen, 153
Beardall, Teresa Rocha, 139
Belew, Kathleen, 63
Bell, Derrick, 11
Bell, Jeannine, 68
Beltrán, Cristina, 103
Bethel A.M.E. Church (Sun Village, CA), 19, 24, 26, 40
Bettencourt, Laura, 153
Bhan, Gautam, 128
Black Los Angeles, 19, 23–24, 29, 84
Black mobility, 4, 6, 10, 12–14, 15
Black motorists, 34–35
Blackness, 13, 107–8
Black Panthers, 60–61
Black placemaking, 3, 24
"Black towns," 22–23, 168n17. *See also* Sun Village, CA
Black women, 48, 87; as evictable, 111; policing of, 15, 106–8
Blasi, Gary, 94, 125–27, 128, 131, 143, 163
Blomley, Nicholas, 77, 96
Bluford, Guion, Jr., 33
Bonds, Anne, 12
Bowers, Sam, 53
Bowman, Larissa, 151
Boyle Heights, Los Angeles, 27
Brann, Joseph, 141
Brenner, Neil, 169n10
Brody, Gary, 4–5, 95, 189n61
broken-windows policing, 20

Brown, Norrinda, 5, 136
Brown, Simone, 13
Brown v. Board of Education (1954), 9
Bruce's Beach, CA, 19, 22, 24, 26, 158
Buchanan, Pat, 66
Buchanan v. Warley (1917), 68
Buffalo Soldiers, 24
bullying, 116–17. *See also* harassment
Burgess, Ernest, 9–10, 16, 18, 149
Butler, Octavia, 82
Butler, Richard Grint, 49, 52, 58–59, 165
BYD, 154

California CIO Council, 28
California City, CA, 7
California Eagle, The, 26, 50
California High Speed Rail Line, 154
California Rangers, 51
California Real Estate Association (CREA), 34, 35, 48, 53–55, 57–58
California State Federation of Labor, 28, 43–44
California State University, Northridge, 39, 141
California Un-American Activities Committee, 51. *See also* Red Scare
California Voting Rights Act (CVRA), 145
Calmore, John O., 151
Campbell v. City of Berwyn (1993), 68
Cancel the Contract, 155–56, 159
capitalism, 15–16, 55, 174n3. *See also* racial capitalism
carcerality, 12–13, 17, 19, 143, 149; in housing, 109, 122
caregiving, 14, 119–20, 126, 128, 192n37
Carroll, Jessie, 36–38
castle doctrine, 110
censorship, 60, 150
Chicago, IL, 9, 12, 108
Chicago School, 9–10, 149. *See also* urban sociology
Child Protective Services, 95, 128
Christian Defense League, 51–52, 59
Christian Knights of the Invisible Empire (CKIE), 52, 53. *See also* Ku Klux Klan
Christian Nationalism, 47, 49; British-Isrealism, 49; Christian Identity Movement, 19, 47, 49, 51, 66; Christian Nationalist Crusade, 51
Church of Jesus Christ-Christian (Lancaster, CA), 49, 52
Citizen (app), 110, 150. *See also* surveillance
citizenship: and policing, 74, 76, 79, 103, 150; and property, 76, 79, 121; and race, 15, 76–77
Civil Aeronautics Authority, 30
Civilian Conservation Corps, 29, 176n27

Civilian Production Administration, 30
civil rights, 8–10, 21, 43, 48, 55–57, 125–26;
    activism, 27, 58, 155; in housing, 10; as injury,
    85–86; legislation, 57; opposition to, 52–53;
    organizing, 8, 19, 23, 36
Civil Rights Act (1964), 157
Civil Rights Bill (1966), 55, 57
Civil Rights Movement, 41, 52
Civil War, xi
Clinton, Bill, 71
code enforcement, 70, 92–93, 97, 101–2, 128, 151
"Coffee with a Cop," 140
Cold War, 7–8, 62, 75, 79
Community Action League, The (TCAL),
    20–21, 123–28, 142–44, 155, 159; community
    meetings, 126–28, 133; creation of, 124. See
    also *TCAL v. Cities*
*Community Action League et al. v. City of
    Lancaster and City of Palmdale, The.* See
    TCAL v. Cities
commuting, 1–2, 8, 33–34, 75, 117, 120, 152
complaints, 4–6, 14, 72–73, 95–97, 100–102, 114;
    as grounds for eviction, 6, 13, 19–20, 78, 100;
    hotlines for, 5, 13, 111
compliance checks, 4–5, 104–5, 108, 115, 117,
    130–31, 135; police at, 105, 124, 128–29, 135
Confederate symbols, 61, 104, 156, 159
Congress on Racial Equity (CORE), 59, 61
consent decrees, 138, 141–42, 165, 194n25, 195n35
core, 7; and periphery, 19–20, 22, 164
Coronado, Miguel, 139
covenants. *See* restrictive covenants
COVID-19, 151, 159, 165
"creative extraction," 157
crime, 57–58, 150; legislation, 1–2; policy, 69; and
    Section 8, 90, 189n49; as segregation, 48, 49,
    93–94. *See also* war on crime
crime-free ordinances, 13, 70, 71–72, 90, 95, 111,
    165; and eviction, 5–6, 21, 69, 72; invalidating,
    138; nullifying, 151; as unconstitutional, 144
criminal justice, 124, 192n8
cross-burnings, 26, 47, 64, 68, 104
Cullors, Waunette, 155
Culver, Jesse, 36

Dantzler, Prentiss, 7, 16
Davis, Angela, 58, 60
Davis, Jaquinn, 110, 116–18, 119
Davis, Mike, xii, 14, 62, 147
Davis, Peggy Cooper, 121
Defense Plant Corporation, 30
defensible space, 109–10
degradation ceremonies, 133–34

deindustrialization, 7, 10
delegation, 68, 196n6
democracy, 30, 68, 102, 138
Department of Children and Family
    Services, 112
Department of Housing and Urban
    Development (HUD), 10, 12, 21, 144,
    149–50
Department of Justice Civil Rights Division
    (DOJ), 123, 126–27, 133–36
Department of Public Social Services
    (DPSS), 117
"deputy gangs," 67. *See also* Los Angeles County
    Sheriff's Department
Derfler, Raquel, 156
desegregation, 22, 33–34, 41, 44–46; in housing,
    45, 49; of public pools, 19, 27, 37. *See also*
    integration
Dillon, Liam, 72
discrimination, 11–12, 19, 97; against Black
    renters, 61; in education, 59–61; in
    employment, 33, 41–45, 59; institutional,
    48; institutionalized, 46; as property
    right, 54–55; against voucher tenants, 12,
    130–31, 140
disinvestment, 10, 149
disposal, 55, 78, 101–2
dispossession, xii, 6, 8, 79, 97, 108
Dobson, James C., 66
Dorn, Warren M., 37, 177n65
Douglas, Helen Gahagan, 51
doxxing, 5, 95
drug-free rules, 111, 116, 118
drugs, 63, 70–71, 85, 88, 116, 124, 126, 193n18
Du Bois, W. E. B., 15, 16–18, 77–79, 98, 123,
    173n71, 187n14
due process, 54, 144–45
Dwight, Ed, 31–33, 154

East Los Angeles, CA, 28
East St. Louis, IL, 16–17, 173n71
ecological model of the city, 9–10, 16–17
education, 149; discrimination in, 59–61;
    segregation in, 9, 36, 41–43, 48
Edwards, Howard Arden, ix–x, xiv
Edwards, R. E., 35, 41
Edwards Air Force Base, 30–35, 58, 59, 85
Ekimoto, Kiyoko, xi–xii
Ekimoto, Yoshio, xi–xii, xiv
eminent domain, 26, 27
employment, 11, 33–34, 95, 107, 134;
    discrimination in, 33, 41–45, 59; and
    incarceration, 80, 199n38

eviction, 4, 48, 100, 111, 119–20, 150–51, 165–66; and crime-free ordinances, 5–6, 21, 69, 72; fear of, 93, 112, 118; and nuisance ordinances, 5–6, 13, 21, 69, 72, 97, 151; one-strike, 20, 71, 144, 151

exclusion, 76, 77, 78, 102, 153

exclusionary zoning, 68

Experimental Housing Allowance Program (EHAP), 10

Facebook, 5, 95, 150

fair housing, 8–11, 48, 55–58, 136; opposition to, 19, 55–56; organizing, 4, 8, 124

Fair Housing Act (1968), 45–46, 47, 48, 57, 63, 69, 96; and policing, 134, 136, 144, 165

Falloon v. Schilling (1882), 13

false reports, 112–13

family, 20–21, 70, 107, 111–12, 116–22; nuclear, 14; regulation of, 18; separation, 13–14, 20

fear, 81–82, 118, 120, 151

Federal Housing Administration (FHA), 30, 31

federal housing funds, 7, 23, 27, 30

Federal Public Housing Authority, 28

Ferguson, MO, 143

Finlayson, Niani, 142

Finnegan, William, 62, 63, 64

First Missionary Baptist Church (Sun Village, CA), 35, 41

Floyd, George, 61, 165

Ford, Henry, 58

foreclosure, 14, 62, 80, 83

Fourteenth Amendment, 121

Fourth Amendment, 71, 108, 136, 144

Franke, Todd, 139–40, 141

fraud, 132; hotlines for, 5–6, 95–96, 111, 138, 143; voucher, 4–5, 115–16, 117, 136; welfare, 130

Free Angela Davis movement, 58, 60

freedom, 7, 109, 121; and home, 121; and property rights, 79

Fugitive Slave Act (1850), 13

Fuller, Robert, 141, 165

Gale, William Potter, 49, 50, 53, 58

gangs, 63, 67, 69–70, 76, 82, 90, 130, 189n50

Gautreaux v. HUD (1966), 9–10, 12

Gaza, 154

gentrification, 8, 9

"ghettos," 10, 70, 170n22

Gibson, Daisy, 33–34, 39, 56

Gibson, Oscar, 33–34

Gilbert, Keith, 52

Gilmore, Ruth Wilson, 7, 121

globalization, 8

Goetz, Edward, 10–11

Goldberg v. Kelley (1970), 145

governance, 68, 141; of public housing, 63, 71; urban, 106–9

Grandin, Greg, 7

Graves, Charles, x–xi, xiii, 13, 156, 174n4

Great Depression, xiv, 29, 147

Great Migration, 13, 27

Grubbs, Melvin Ray, xiii, 15, 33–34

Gurusami, Susila, 109, 120

HACoLA. *See* Housing Authority of the County of Los Angeles

Haley, Sarah, 18

Hancock, Hunter, 34

harassment, 3, 45, 59, 68, 89, 103, 130–31, 164; by landlords, 120–21; by neighbors, 5, 150–51; by police, 94, 108, 113, 117, 124–25, 134–36, 139

Harriman, Job, xii

Harris, Cheryl I., 15, 20, 77

Hart, Charles, 136

Hartman, Saidiya, 107, 111, 121–22

Harvey, David, 6

hate crimes, 63–64, 66–67, 68, 184n99

Hawthorne, Camilla A., 86

Hearns, Henry, 32, 33, 35, 58, 90, 129, 159

Herbert, Claire, 76

Hernández, Kelly Lytle, 108

heteronormativity, 114–15

hierarchies, x, 48–49; racial, 17, 59, 61, 70, 76; social, 15, 46, 85, 109, 164

highways, 1, 29, 33, 44, 176n31. *See also* commuting

Hill, Betty, 27, 37, 175n16

Hill, Herbert, 44

home, 14, 18, 19, 21, 119; and freedom, 121; "homeplace," 121–22; as indefensible space, 110–11; as mere shelter, 20, 110, 120; and personhood, 107; as platform for violence, 109–10; policing of, 122; as refuge, 114, 120; safety of, 112

homelessness, 21, 95, 119, 130, 151, 153

homeowners' associations, 26

Home Ownership Loan Corporation (HOLC), 34

home raids, 14, 105–10, 112, 120, 126, 144, 145; jump, 107–8, 111, 121–22; midnight, 14, 20, 108; no-knock, 109; as public policy, 107

homophobia, 66

Hong, Grace, 79

hooks, bell, 19, 121–22

HoSang, Daniel Martinez, 35
housing: abolitionist, 151; civil rights in, 10; construction, 7, 27–29, 30, 56, 75, 80, 82, 152; costs, 1, 88; crisis, 23, 152–53; de-policing, 144, 151; shortage, 27, 152; unfree, 109; as universal right, 21, 151
Housing Act of 1937, 27, 28, 31, 175n19
Housing Authority of the County of Los Angeles (HACoLA), 4–6, 27–28, 91–96, 125, 163; Fraud Hotline, 95–96; partnership with Antelope Valley cities, 5–6, 76, 91–92, 94–96
Housing Choice Voucher program, 2–3, 8–9, 47, 73–74, 83. See also Section 8; vouchers
housing justice, 4, 18, 21, 29, 148, 150–51
Housing Opportunities for People Everywhere (HOPE VI), 10–11
Housing Opportunity Extension Act (1996), 71
housing policy, 148; federal, 4, 9–10, 10–11, 27, 149
HUD. See Department of Housing and Urban Development
HUD v. Rucker (2001), 71
Hunter, Bernyse, 36
Huq, Aziz, 150
Huxley, Aldous, 147

incarceration, 13, 21, 67, 80, 87, 119, 150–51, 199n38
indefensible spaces, 19–20, 110–11
Indigenous peoples, ix–x, 56, 147, 167n2, 181n49
inspections, 94. See also compliance checks
integration, 42–43; opposition to, 26, 48, 62, 88, 95, 102–3; and property values, 76. See also desegregation
interest convergence theory, 11
internal colonialism, 17
intimidation, 5, 101, 103, 126–27, 134, 136. See also harassment; surveillance

Jackie Robinson Park, 33, 36–38, 56, 158
Japanese internment, xii, xiv
Jauregui v. City of Palmdale (2014), 145
Jewish Labor Committee, 44
Jim Crow, 13, 67–68, 73
John Birch Society, 52, 60
Johnson, Jacob, 142
Johnson, Lyndon B., 57
jump raids, 107–8, 111, 121–22

Karteron, Alexis, 71
Kennedy, John F., 31, 180n17
Kenny, Robert, 49–50
Keppel Union School, 36, 39, 43, 45

Kerner Commission on Civil Unrest, 10
Kido, Saburo, xiv
King, Martin Luther, Jr., 52–53, 57, 117, 178n75
King, Rodney, 65
King v. Smith (1968), 14, 108, 145
Knight, William J. (Pete), 65–66, 87
Korematsu v. United States (1944), xiv
Ku Klux Klan (KKK), 26, 47, 49, 52–53, 64–66, 117, 165, 179n3, 179n8. See also racism; white supremacy
Kurashige, Scott, 168

labor, 7, 16, 27–29, 43–45, 88, 120; convict, 29; organizing, 43–44, 154
Ladner, Joyce, 14
Lake Los Angeles, CA, 7
Lancaster, CA, 5–7, 19–20, 153; economic decline, 79–80; foreclosures, 83; history, xi–xiv; housing construction, 82, 152; housing projects, 30; partnership with HACoLA, 5–6, 76, 91–92, 94–96; population growth, 62, 75, 157; segregation, 7, 18, 22, 33, 35, 41; settlement with TCAL, 132–33; voucher tenants, 6, 89, 97, 111; white supremacy in, 49, 51–52, 59, 66–67
Lancaster Homes, 30, 176n34
landlords, 8, 12, 18, 68, 71–72, 83–84, 165
Lanham Act (1940), 28
LAPD. See Los Angeles Police Department
LASD. See Los Angeles County Sheriff's Department
Latinos for Social Justice, 65–66, 69, 159, 183n83
law enforcement, 4, 62, 77. See also police
Leap, Jorja, 139–40
Leap and Associates, 139–40, 141
Ledford, Jim, 129
Lee, Peg, 33, 34, 36, 158–59
Lewis, Jovan Scott, 86
Lhamon, Catherine, 126
Lindsey, George, 26
litigation, 9, 21, 26, 123, 125–28, 130–31, 145. See also specific cases
Littlerock, CA, 40, 41, 43, 55–56, 157–58
Living Stone Cathedral of Worship (Sun Village, CA), 36
Llano del Rio, CA, xii–xiv, 147–48
Loa, Richard, 65–66
"locational seesaw," 7
Locke, Amir, 109
Lockheed Martin, 30–31, 39, 42, 44, 58, 154. See also aerospace industry
Long, Huey, 50

Los Angeles, CA: and Antelope Valley, 1–2, 4, 29, 62, 81, 83, 152–53, 156–57, 169n10; Black residents in, 2; as core, 7, 23–24; development of, 1–2, 29; gentrification in, 8, 9; growth of, 27; housing crisis in, 28; public housing in, 164; recession, 8; segregation in, 18–19, 22–23, 26–27, 120; as urban racial capitalism, 17; voucher tenants in, 8
Los Angeles Building Trades Council, 28
Los Angeles County Board of Supervisors, 5, 129–31, 137, 143–44
Los Angeles County Development Authority, 169n4. *See also* Housing Authority of the County of Los Angeles
Los Angeles County Sheriff's Department (LASD), 5, 63, 69, 82, 123, 133–42, 193n18, 193n20, 194n21, 194n22; complaints against, 133–34; DOJ investigation, 133–36; partnership with Antelope Valley cities, 67, 76, 94, 126–28, 131, 155–56; public opinion of, 139–41
Los Angeles Police Department (LAPD), 108–9, 195n35
Los Angeles Sentinel, 34
Ludwig, Jens, 149–50
Lynch, Conrad "Connie," 52–53

Make America Better program, 57–58
Malson, Hilary, 150
Manhattan Beach, CA, 24, 26, 158
"man in the house rules," 20, 108, 114
Mapp v. Ohio (1961), 151
Marquez, Sherry, 129
McCarthyism, 51. *See also* Red Scare
McGowan, Maurice, 40–41
McKittrick, Katherine, x, 8, 156
McWilliams, Carey, xiv
Merriam, Frank, 27
Mexican-American Political Association of California, 65
Michaels, Jon, 150
midnight raids, 14, 20, 108
military investment, 23, 29–31, 48, 154; decline of, 75, 79–80. *See also* aerospace industry
Miller, Loren, xiv
Mills, Charles, xiii
Mira Loma Detention Center, 80
Mitchell, Joseph, 88
Mitchell, Pharaoh, 123, 124, 126–28, 130, 140, 143, 159–60
mobility, 11, 16, 17, 148–49, 151; Black, 4, 6, 10, 12–14, 15; in the city, 9–10; of poor people, 10, 12–13, 18; as solution to inequality, 10

mobility theory, 149. *See also* Moving to Opportunity Demonstration Project; neighborhood effects
Mont, Max, 44
Morris, Aldon, 18
mortgage banking, 82–83
move-in violence, 68
Moving to Opportunity Demonstration Project (MTO), 11, 148–49
Moynihan, Daniel, 14
Muhammad, David, 140
Muroc Field, 30, 31. *See also* Edwards Air Force Base
Murrell, Emmett, 125, 138, 143, 145–46

National Aeronautics and Space Administration (NASA), 31–33
National Association for the Advancement of Colored People (NAACP), xiv, 27, 28, 53, 59, 61, 64, 85; Antelope Valley, 59, 61, 156, 159; Freedom Fund, 40–41, 53; Los Angeles, 26–27; South Antelope Valley (SAV-NAACP), 22, 38–41, 42–46, 53; Sun Village, 19, 48, 55
National Association of Real Estate Boards (NAREB), 56
National Commission on Severely Distressed Public Housing, 10
National Negro Congress, 28
National States Rights Party, 52–53
Nazi Low Riders, 63, 64, 66–67
Nazism, 15, 19, 47, 58–60, 63–64. *See also* white supremacy
neighborhood effects, 11, 149
Neighborhood Legal Services, 125–26, 130, 141
neighborhood watch, 68–69, 97, 100–101. *See also* participatory policing; surveillance
Nelson, Laura, 147
Neocleous, Mark, 90
New Deal, 8, 11
New Llano, LA, xiv
Newman, Oscar, 109–10
New York Tenement Act (1901), 107–8
Nextdoor (app), 110, 150
Nixon, Richard M., 10, 51
no-knock raids, 109
Noll, David, 150
"non-reformist reforms," 143
normalcy, 139–40
North American Aviation, 35. *See also* aerospace industry
Northrup Grumman, 31, 154. *See also* aerospace industry

nuisance ordinances, 70, 71–73, 89, 101, 113, 138, 165; and eviction, 5–6, 13, 21, 69, 72, 97, 151; as unconstitutional, 144
nuisance properties, 72, 109

Ocen, Priscilla, 6, 47–48, 62–63
Ochikubo v. Bonesteel (1944), xiv
Ochoa, Alexandro, 154
Oliver, Grace Wilcox, ix
one-strike eviction, 20, 71, 144, 151
Operation Gangwatch, 69–70
Operation Hammer, 109
Operation High Desert Storm, 70
ordinances, 5–6, 68. *See also* crime-free ordinances; nuisance ordinances
organizing, 19; anti-policing, 4, 191n28; civil rights, 8, 19, 23, 36; fair housing, 4, 8, 124; labor, 43–44; tenant, 9, 151. *See also* activism; Community Action League, The; National Association for the Advancement of Colored People
Orne, Jay, 76
Oviatt, James, 52
Owens, Robert, 37
ownership, xi, 78–79. *See also* property

Painted Rocks, 147
Palmdale, CA, 2, 4–5, 7, 153; economic decline, 79–80; electoral politics, 70, 145; foreclosures, 83; housing construction, 30, 80, 82, 152; military investment, 30; partnership with HACoLA, 5–6, 76, 91–92, 94; population growth, 31, 75, 80, 157; segregation, 22, 33, 34–35, 41; settlement with TCAL, 132–33; voucher tenants, 6, 111
Palomares, Maria, 125–26, 128
Park, K-Sue, 68
Park, Robert, 9–10, 16, 18, 149
Parker, Darren, 127, 130, 139, 165, 199n44
Parris, Raymond "Rex," Jr., 19–20, 88–94, 133, 145, 153, 165; against gangs, 90; legal career, 1, 88–89; against Section 8, 19, 90–94, 98, 130, 132
participation, 68–69, 78
participatory policing, 19–20, 59, 73, 76, 94; as empowering, 6, 62–63, 73, 95, 98–99; as re-segregation, 62–63, 68–69; and whiteness, 15, 17, 48, 73, 77–78
Partners in Crime program, 70
Patton, Lois Emma Prioleau, 19, 22, 23, 24, 39–40, 44–45
Patton, Patrick N., 41, 44–45

Perez, Ronda, 153
Perez, Thomas E., 126–27, 133
periphery, 6, 8–9, 17–19, 23; and core, 19–20, 22, 164; as safety valve, 4; as spatial fix, 17
personhood, 103; and home, 107; and policing, 79, 150; and race, 79. *See also* citizenship
Polaris Flight Academy, 30
police: brutality, 46; at compliance checks, 105, 124, 128–29, 135; harassment, 94, 108, 113, 117, 124–25, 134–36, 139; killings, 61, 108–9, 141–42, 165; legitimacy, 69, 77; reform, 124, 141–43, 155–56, 195n35; violence, 65, 134, 142, 156; and white supremacists, 50. *See also* Los Angeles County Sheriff's Department; Los Angeles Police Department
policing, 46, 149–50; and anti-Blackness, 20, 67, 103; and Black mobility, 4, 6, 13–14, 15; broken-windows, 20; and citizenship, 74, 76, 79, 103, 150; collective, 150; definition of, 3–4; and personhood, 79, 150; and power, 73–74, 96, 100–103, 143, 144, 150; as property, 15, 20, 48–49, 74, 76, 78–79, 96, 98–99, 143; and property rights, 19; and race, 78, 79; as re-segregation, 74; in schools, 69–70, 156; and segregation, 6, 12–14, 48; and social status, 15, 20, 74, 78, 93, 98–99, 103, 107, 150, 187n14; as subjectivity, 73; as violation of Fair Housing Act, 144; of voucher tenants, 3, 13, 78, 93–95, 130, 143; and whiteness, 77–78. *See also* participatory policing
policy violence, 48
Polikoff, Alexander, 9
Ponton, David, 159
Posse Comitatus, 49, 53
Poston, Ben, 72
poverty, 16, 79, 108, 144–45, 153, 192n37; and mobility, 10
power, 5, 46, 68–69, 114, 164; and policing, 73–74, 96, 100–103, 143, 144, 150
pretextual investigations, 111, 114. *See also* compliance checks
Pricer, Billy, 69–70, 82
Prince Edward County, VA, 9
Prioleau, Ethel, 19, 22, 24, 26–27, 37, 39, 158, 174n5
Prioleau, George Washington, 19, 22, 24, 26, 39, 154, 158, 175n5
prisons, 7, 29, 149. *See also* incarceration
privacy, 21, 107, 113–14, 120, 145, 192n37
Progressive Citizens of America, 28
Project Mercury, 31

property, 54–55, 187n8; as active, 77, 96; and citizenship, 76, 79, 121; definition of, 55; as human right, 54–55; insecurity of, 90–91; ownership of, 19, 79; policing as, 15, 20, 48–49, 74, 76, 78–79, 96, 98–99, 143; and race, 77; as relational, 76–77; and social status, 77–78; traditional view, 76–77; and violence, 77; and whiteness, 48, 57; whiteness as, 77–78

property damage, 109. *See also* vandalism

Property Owner's Bill of Rights, 54

property rights, 54–57, 73, 78–79; discrimination as, 54–55; and freedom, 79; as human rights, 57; and policing, 19; and whiteness, 19, 48, 54–55

property values, 15, 26, 35, 72, 88, 90–91; and integration, 76; symbolic, 48; and voucher tenants, 76, 78, 96

public housing, 10; as carceral, 149; construction of, 27–29; criminalization of, 71; demolition of, 10–11, 12; as encouraging crime, 110; expansion of, 21; federal funding for, 10, 23, 28; opposition to, 11, 27, 28, 176n25; segregation in, 9, 28; as socialist, 28; state funding for, 28, 53; voucherization of, 4, 8–9, 150

Public Works Administration, 27

"pure Americanism," 26, 47, 53, 179n3. *See also* Ku Klux Klan

Purifoy, Danielle, 157, 168n17

race: and citizenship, 15, 76–77; as nuisance, 13, 73; and personhood, 79; and policing, 78, 79; and property, 77. *See also* Blackness; whiteness

race mixing, 48

Racial and Identity Profiling Act (2015), 141

racial backlash, 84–85

"racial banishment," 8

racial capitalism, xiii, 15–18, 19, 173n71, 174n3

racial difference, 18, 79

racial exclusivity, 77, 88

racial hierarchies, 17, 59, 61, 70, 76

racial steering, 35, 41, 132

racism, 15–16, 164; and capitalism, 55, 174n3; and solidarity, 17; and space, 86. *See also* anti-Blackness; white supremacy

Rainwater, Lee, 10

Ramona Gardens, 27

Rankin, John, 51

Rawlinson, Marion, 56

Raytheon, 82. *See also* military investment

Reagan, Ronald, 10, 56–57, 60, 71, 75

real estate associations, 26, 28, 68. *See also* California Real Estate Association

real estate speculation, 92

realtors, 35, 41, 54–56

Reconstruction, 77, 121

redlining, 34

Red Scare, 28, 30, 51

Red Summer, 16

Reider, Jonathan, 102–3

Reinecke, Ed, 57

Rental Housing Business License ordinance, 92

rent supplements. *See* vouchers

reparations, xiv, 137, 159

resistance, 4, 22, 120, 122, 128, 159

restrictive covenants, 13, 17, 23, 34, 41, 47–48, 62–63, 68, 177n53; new, 6, 48, 63; as segregation tool, 26; as unenforceable, 47, 151

Richie, Beth, 108

right to discriminate, 54–55, 73

Ring doorbell, 150. *See also* surveillance

Rios, Eric, 142

Roberts, Cordia Anita, xi, 156

Roberts, Frank, 67

Robertson, Pat, 66

Robinson, Jackie, 19, 37

Rogers, Don, 66

Roosevelt, Franklin Delano, 27

Rosamond, CA, xi

Rose, Carol, 77

Rosenberg, Anna, 51

Rosenthal, Tracy, 4

Ross, Michelle, 2–6, 14, 119, 150, 163

Roy, Ananya, 8, 79

Rubin, Robert, 145

Ruby Ridge, 59

Rumford Fair Housing Act (1963), 23, 45, 54–57; attacks on, 55–57

safety, 14, 107, 112, 140

Salas, George, 69

SAV-NAACP. *See* South Antelope Valley NAACP

scarcity, 22–23, 120, 174n3

school segregation, 9, 36, 41–43, 48

school vouchers, 9

Seamster, Louise, 157

Section 8, 2–3, 47–48, 83–84, 86–87; and crime, 90, 189n49; protests against, 115; as slur, 5; "war on," 91–94, 97. *See also* Housing Choice Voucher program

Section 8 Commission (Lancaster, CA), 92–93, 96, 124

"Section 8 tenants," 76. *See also*
   voucher tenants
securitization, 82. *See also* policing
security, 90–91, 122
segregation, 10, 13, 77; crime as, 48, 49, 93–94;
   economic, 44; in education, 9, 36, 41–43, 48;
   enforcement of, 34–35; and housing market,
   88; legislated, 68; and policing, 12–14, 48; in
   public housing, 9, 28; residential, 19, 23, 42,
   45, 48, 67–68, 163; and scarcity, 22–23, 120,
   174n3; of swimming pools, 26–27; violence
   of, 13, 26, 68, 103
Sessions, Jeff, 141
settler colonialism, x, 17
shantytowns, 27
Shapiro v. Thompson (1969), 145
Shea, Richard Peter, 147
Shea's Castle, 147–48
Shelley v. Kraemer (1948), 34, 68, 151
Shelton, Ty, 141, 142
Shorter, David, 103
Simmons, Althea T. L., 40, 43, 44, 45, 178n75
Simmons, Ann, 34, 35
Singh, Nikhil Pal, 78
skinheads, 63–65, 104
Skinheads Against Racial Prejudice
   (S.H.A.R.P.s), 15, 64–65
Smith, Gerald L. K., 49, 50–52, 58
Smith, Neil, 7
Smith, V. Jesse, 93–94, 95, 124, 128, 131, 132,
   136–38, 143, 145
social hierarchies, 15, 46, 85, 109, 164
socialism, xii, 28, 147, 148
social status, 57, 150; and policing, 15, 20, 74, 78,
   93, 98–99, 103, 107, 150, 187n14; and property,
   77–78
solidarity, 17, 77, 79, 177n53, 187n14
South Antelope Valley NAACP (SAV-NAACP),
   22, 38–41, 44–46, 53, 156
South Antelope Valley Press, 34, 40–41
South Central Los Angeles, 8, 23, 28, 108–9
Southern California Association of
   Governments (SCAG), 152–53
Southern Pacific Railroad, xi
"spatial equality," 151–52
spatial fix, 6–7, 12, 153; Antelope Valley as, 8, 18,
   22, 30, 83, 152; periphery as, 17
Springs of Life Church (Lancaster, CA), 66, 69
stalking, 5. *See also* surveillance
state violence, 69
Stoner, J. B., 53
sundown towns, 13, 172n55

Sun Village, CA, xiii, 7–8, 15, 17, 18–19, 85–86,
   93–94, 157, 177n53; churches, 35–36; community
   building, 41; community institutions, 35, 158;
   creation, 22–23, 33–34; erasure of, 157–58; as
   escape, 34; growth, 34, 56; history, 165; housing
   construction, 56; infrastructure, 34; Jackie
   Robinson Park, 33, 36–38, 56, 158; and Los
   Angeles, 41; parks, 36–37; as periphery, 23–24;
   population decline, 157
Sun Village NAACP, 19, 48, 55
Sun Village Women's Club, 36–38, 40–41,
   41, 46
surveillance, 3, 19–21, 87, 99–101, 109, 122, 131,
   192n37; by inspectors, 94, 112–13, 164; by
   neighbors, 6, 14, 48, 62, 69–70, 78, 99, 116, 164
Sweeney, Shauna, 18
Swift, Wesley A., 19, 47–53, 58–59, 165,
   179n8, 180n17

Talley, G. L., 36
Taylor, Breonna, 61, 109, 165
Taylor, Linda Thompson, 61
TCAL. *See* Community Action League, The
TCAL v. Cities (2011), 97, 110, 112, 119–20,
   130–33, 165
tenants: empowering, 11–12; organizing, 9, 151;
   protections for, 126, 151; retaliation against,
   163; rights of, 11–12, 21, 126, 144; testimonies
   from, 127–28, 164; "war on," 4. *See also*
   voucher tenants
tenement housing, 107–8
Tenney, Jack, 51–52, 180n19
Terry, Jesse L., 175n19
"third-party policing," 68
Thomas, Michael, 141–42
traffic stops, 133–34, 135, 193n20
truancy, 69, 93
Trump, Donald J., 140–41

unauthorized tenant rule, 105–6, 111, 114, 116,
   118–19, 145
unfreedom, 109, 186n5
unionization, 43–44, 154
United Community Action Network (UCAN),
   69–70
United States v. County of Los Angeles, 136
Urban League, 26, 61
urban renewal, 11–12
Urban Revitalization Demonstration Program, 10
urban sociology, 4, 9–10, 11, 16–18, 170n21
U.S. Air Force, 30–32, 58
U.S. Army, 24, 30, 31, 180n17

U.S. Commission on Civil Rights, 41
U.S. Supreme Court, 51, 71, 178n75

vagrancy, 29, 107. *See also* homelessness
Valle Verde, CA, 24, 34, 177n53
vandalism, xii, 5, 26, 68
Vargas, Robert, 17
Vasquez Rocks, 1
Vestal, Marques, 109
veterans, 28, 47, 176n25
Vichlis, Leonardo, 4
Vietnam War Moratorium, 60. *See also* anti-war activism
vigilantism, 13, 102, 107, 165; "vigilante federalism," 150
Villanueva, Alex, 141
violence, 1–2, 68, 103, 106, 108, 110; anti-Black, 16–17; move-in, 68; police, 65, 134, 142, 156; policy, 48; and property, 77; segregationist, 13, 26, 68, 103; state, 69; white supremacist, 16, 48–49, 59, 63–64, 66–67
vouchers, 9, 11; efficacy of, 12; exploitation by landlords, 84; fraud, 4–5, 115–16, 117, 136; negative views of, 85–86; opposition to, 5, 86–88, 115, 149; policy, 9–10; regulation, 114, 116; against segregation, 9; shortcomings of, 12; termination of, 4, 14, 108, 111, 112, 114, 117–18, 126, 134, 136, 138, 143
voucher tenants: in Antelope Valley, 8–9; as criminal, 5, 90, 130; discrimination against, 12, 130–31, 140; as "entitled," 86; experiences of, 99–100, 104–6, 110–21, 130; hostility toward, 86–88, 113; as "inferior," 99; policing of, 3, 13, 78, 93–95, 130, 143; privacy of, 113–14, 120, 145, 192n37; and property values, 76, 78, 96; punishing, 101, 135–36; rights of, 12, 144–45; as scapegoats, 89–90; terrorizing, 94–95, 128

Walcott, Rinaldo, 79
Walker, Milton, Jr., 63
war housing projects, 28–29
war on crime, 19, 69, 89–90, 111
war on drugs, 71

"war on Section 8," 91–94, 97
"war on tenants," 4
Warren, Earl, 51
Watergate, 57
welfare, 13–14, 76, 80–81, 118; fraud, 130; opposition to, 20, 65, 70, 87
welfare queens, 87
welfare-rights movement, 144–45
Westmont, Los Angeles, 164
White Aryan Resistance, 64. *See also* white supremacy
white consensus, 64–65
white flight, 73
White Knights of the Ku Klux Klan, 53. *See also* Ku Klux Klan
white nationalism, 58
whiteness, xiii, 17, 187n14; and participatory policing, 15, 17, 48, 73, 77–78; and policing, 77–78; and property, 48, 57; as property, 77–78; and property rights, 19, 48, 54–55
white power movement, 19, 49, 64–65
white separatism, 47, 49, 59
white supremacy, 16, 17, 19, 48–49, 51, 66; in Antelope Valley, 15, 33, 61, 63–64, 67; in Lancaster, 49, 51–52, 59, 66–67; violence of, 16, 48–49, 59, 63–64, 66–67
Williams, Jacqueline, 14
Williams, Kidada E., 107
Williams, Paul R., 175n19
Williams, Sheila, 110, 112–13, 119
Willse, Craig, 79
Wilson, William Julius, 10
Wirin, A.L., xiv
Wolfe, Tom, 31
Women's Political Study Club (Sun Village, CA), 27
Works Progress Administration, 30
World War II, xii, 7, 18, 23, 179n8

Yamamoto, Elmer, xiv
Yeager, Chuck, 31, 32–33
Young, Anjanette, 109

Zappa, Frank, 64

Founded in 1893,
UNIVERSITY OF CALIFORNIA PRESS
publishes bold, progressive books and journals
on topics in the arts, humanities, social sciences,
and natural sciences—with a focus on social
justice issues—that inspire thought and action
among readers worldwide.

The UC PRESS FOUNDATION
raises funds to uphold the press's vital role
as an independent, nonprofit publisher, and
receives philanthropic support from a wide
range of individuals and institutions—and from
committed readers like you. To learn more, visit
ucpress.edu/supportus.